THE SOCIALIST CAR

THE SOCIALIST CAR

Automobility in the Eastern Bloc

Lewis H. Siegelbaum, *editor*

CORNELL UNIVERSITY PRESS ITHACA AND LONDON

Copyright © 2011 by Cornell University

All rights reserved. Except for brief quotations in a review, this book, or parts thereof, must not be reproduced in any form without permission in writing from the publisher. For information, address Cornell University Press, Sage House, 512 East State Street, Ithaca, New York 14850.

First published 2011 by Cornell University Press
First printing, Cornell Paperbacks, 2011

Printed in the United States of America

Library of Congress Cataloging-in-Publication Data

The socialist car : automobility in the Eastern Bloc / Lewis H. Siegelbaum, editor.
   p. cm.
 Includes bibliographical references and index.
 ISBN 978-0-8014-4991-8 (cloth : alk. paper)
 ISBN 978-0-8014-7738-6 (pbk. : alk. paper)
1. Automobiles—Social aspects—Europe, Eastern—History—20th century. 2. Automobiles—Social aspects—Soviet Union—History. 3. Automobile industry and trade—Social aspects—Europe, Eastern—History—20th century. 4. Automobile industry and trade—Social aspects—Soviet Union—History. 5. Socialism and culture—Europe, Eastern—History—20th century. 6. Socialism and culture—Soviet Union—History. I. Siegelbaum, Lewis H.
 HE5662.9.A6S63 2011
 388.3'42094709045—dc23   2011018880

Cornell University Press strives to use environmentally responsible suppliers and materials to the fullest extent possible in the publishing of its books. Such materials include vegetable-based, low-VOC inks and acid-free papers that are recycled, totally chlorine-free, or partly composed of nonwood fibers. For further information, visit our website at www.cornellpress.cornell.edu.

Cloth printing   10 9 8 7 6 5 4 3 2 1

Paperback printing   10 9 8 7 6 5 4 3 2 1

CONTENTS

Acknowledgments   vii

Introduction   1
Lewis H. Siegelbaum

Part One: **Socialist Cars and Systems of Production, Distribution, and Consumption**

1. The Elusive People's Car: Imagined Automobility and Productive Practices along the "Czechoslovak Road to Socialism" (1945–1968)   17
   Valentina Fava
2. Cars as Favors in People's Poland   30
   Mariusz Jastrząb
3. Alternative Modernity? Everyday Practices of Elite Mobility in Communist Hungary, 1956–1980   47
   György Péteri

Part Two: **Mobility and Socialist Cities**

4. Planning for Mobility: Designing City Centers and New Towns in the USSR and the GDR in the 1960s   71
   Elke Beyer
5. Automobility in Yugoslavia between Urban Planner, Market, and Motorist: The Case of Belgrade, 1945–1972   92
   Brigitte Le Normand

6. On the Streets of a Truck-Building City: Naberezhnye Chelny
   in the Brezhnev Era   105
   Esther Meier

7. Understanding a Car in the Context of a System:
   Trabants, Marzahn, and East German Socialism   124
   Eli Rubin

Part Three: Socialist Car Cultures and Automobility

8. The Common Heritage of the Socialist Car Culture   143
   Luminita Gatejel

9. *Autobasteln:* Modifying, Maintaining, and Repairing Private
   Cars in the GDR, 1970–1990   157
   Kurt Möser

10. "Little Tsars of the Road": Soviet Truck Drivers
    and Automobility, 1920s–1980s   170
    Lewis H. Siegelbaum

11. Women and Cars in Soviet and Russian Society   186
    Corinna Kuhr-Korolev

Notes   205
Notes on Contributors   237
Index   239

ACKNOWLEDGMENTS

The Socialist Car was put into gear thanks to the willingness of the Berliner Kolleg für Vergleichende Geschichte Europas (BKVGE) at the Freie Universität Berlin and its managing director, Dr. Arnd Bauerkämper, to host the conference from which this book emanated. Luminita Gatejel, then a graduate student at BKVGE, deserves special acknowledgment and thanks for having served as local organizer. Corinna Kuhr-Korolev, another contributor, always responded promptly and with sound advice to all my e-mailed queries and expressions of anxiety, thereby becoming a closer friend. The other contributors are to be thanked for their cooperativeness at every stage of the writing and revision process. I also express my appreciation to Mark Aaron Keck-Szajbel, Leslie Page Moch, Gijs Mom, Nordica Nettleton, and Sergei Zhuravlev for their various contributions at the conference; to Mark Kornbluh and Walter Hawthorne, successive chairpersons of the Department of History at Michigan State University, who provided key support; to Tatiana Gushchina at the Lumiere Brothers Photogallery for granting permission to use the photograph on the book cover; and to Candace Akins and Jamie Fuller for agreeing to copyedit and doing such a splendid job. Finally, thanks again to John Ackerman for sticking with the Socialist Car.

THE SOCIALIST CAR

INTRODUCTION

Lewis H. Siegelbaum

In March 1992, less than a year after Communism fell in Albania, Henry Kamm of the *New York Times* traveled to Noj, a "dirt-poor village" north of the capital, Tirana. There he encountered "shattered buildings, piles of rubble," and other signs of the wave of vengeful destructiveness that had swept through the village months earlier. "They felt they were destroying Communism," a young shopkeeper told him. But some, it turned out, regretted their actions, in particular sacking the local clinic to empty it of the medicines that had been delivered just the day before. "Under the Communist Government," Kamm reported, "even people in remote zones could count on a car from the cooperative to take them to the clinic. Now, as one resident told him, "no cooperative, no car."

It is not clear from Kamm's report whether the villagers regretted more the loss of the clinic or their access to the car. For under the Communists there were no privately owned cars in Albania, and by the time Kamm arrived, the drivers of collective vehicles had taken them over and were using them "as they see fit." The daily bus that used to link Noj with Tirana now came only when the driver "felt like it." Yet only five years later, the *Times* reported that "free" Albania had become "one of the best customers for Europe's stolen cars." Tirana, where "big sedans jostle[d] each other on potholed and dusty roads" as they whizzed by donkeys pulling carts, allegedly had more Mercedes per capita than most other European cities. The residents of Noj and most of the rest of the country, however, probably did not share in the bounty. At twenty-three per thousand people, Albania's passenger car density was still Europe's lowest.[1]

Albania under the dictator Enver Hoxha represents an extreme case—as it did in many other ways—in the awkward fit between cars and Communism. Only Kim Il Sung's Democratic People's Republic of Korea matched its ban on private car ownership. Elsewhere in the socialist camp the situation was more complicated and, because of its many ambiguities, more fascinating too.[2] The principal objective of this book—the outgrowth if a workshop held in June 2008 at the Berlin School for Comparative European History (BKVGE)—is to explore the interface between the motor car and the state socialist countries of Eastern Europe, including the USSR. We posit a dynamic tension between these two artifacts of human invention—the car and socialism—each of which in its own way promised liberation from age-old constraints. This tension inhered in the Socialist Car.

The Socialist Car and Consumption

In this book "socialism" has two meanings. One is the project to transform society from its bourgeois past to its Communist future, a project embarked upon and guided by a supposedly far-sighted political party and its apparatus acting on behalf of all nonantagonistic social groups. The other refers to those actually existing societies under such tutelage, societies confronting problems unforeseen in their ambiguity, complexity, and even contradictoriness. The procedures for the production, distribution, and consumption of goods and services comprised a significant zone of interaction between the project and the actuality of socialism, between its ideals defined in terms of an enlightened awareness of the collective interest and the reality of shortages, competing priorities, external pressures, privilege, venality, and desires for imagined comforts, bourgeois or otherwise.

Within this zone, the Socialist Car occupied an extremely important place. The Socialist Car was more than the metal, glass, upholstery, and plastic from which the Ladas, Dacias, Trabants, and other still extant and erstwhile models were fabricated; it also absorbed East Europeans' longings and compromises, their hopes and disappointments. The Socialist Car thus can be situated at the point of convergence between the state and the private sphere. It embodied aspirations for overcoming the gap in technology between the capitalist and socialist worlds, as well as for enhancing personal mobility, flexibility, and status in the latter. It brought those who possessed one a little closer to an imagined West even as its own limitations and those imposed on it frustrated the fulfillment of those imaginings. Because the Socialist Car competed for resources with other modes of transportation, and because it had to cope with certain ideologically driven notions questioning its appropriateness to the socialist project, it had to adapt even as it provoked adaptation. The question of the limits of those adaptations over time and from one country to another is a major focus of this book. If the particularities of state socialism can better inform us about the history of the automobile, then the Socialist Car can improve our understanding of state socialism in practice.

Our book interprets its subject broadly. Combining expertise in the history of technology and urban planning with social and cultural history, it reflects and at the same time seeks to advance recent scholarly interest in both the automobile and the consumer and material cultures of the socialist Second World countries. Commenting a decade ago on the material cultures of the former Eastern Bloc countries, the architectural historian Catherine Cooke asserted that "these materialized manifestations always seemed more revealing and enduring descriptors of their attributes and tensions than the ephemera of properly 'political' analysis."[3] Perhaps, but at the time she wrote those lines analyses of the material cultures and consumption practices in that part of the world were hardly abundant and certainly had not featured prominently in the theorization of either subject. Books on material culture and consumption, including an influential collection of articles edited by Arjun Appadurai, ranged far and wide across the globe and chronologically back to medieval Europe without touching down on the terrain of state socialism.[4] To some an oxymoron, socialist consumption remains underrepresented in this literature. It could be that the outsized role that the central administrative organs of the "command economies" played in predetermining social needs and substituting their decisions for market mechanisms obscured the extent to which consumption in the socialist world sometimes could assume unpredictable forms and often involved creative practices.[5] Whatever the cause of neglect, the present book's inquiry into the forms and practices that private car consumption assumed in the Eastern Bloc countries has much to offer students of consumer behavior, whether they understand consumption as a site of identity formation or view it as part of larger political struggles over the meaning of citizenship.[6]

Within Soviet and East European studies, consumption has been understood largely as an arena in which the state and its agents negotiated with hard-pressed though resourceful citizens. Among Soviet historians, rationing—the attempt to establish a "hierarchy of consumption" based on services rendered to the state—has received considerable attention, but so too has the proffering to privileged segments of society of "socialist luxuries" via "cultured trade" and the forging of a Big Deal with the new "Soviet middle class" after the Great Patriotic War.[7] The siphoning of scarce goods such as cars to underground markets, the mania for foreign-made goods, and the clever strategies for acquiring them so typical of Soviet consumers appear to have been no less common in Communist East Europe.[8] Aside from controlling the distribution of goods themselves, Communist authorities sought to shape desire through both "hard" and "soft" propaganda, that is, by denouncing Western "bourgeois" culture as wasteful and decadent and by instructing the masses in suitably modest tastes. But, as demonstrated by recent research on the *stiliagi* (the generic name for youth subcultures that flourished in the larger Soviet cities from the late 1940s onward) and analogous nonconformist groups elsewhere in the bloc, not everyone bought this line.[9]

More collective and violent challenges to the stringency of Communist wage and distribution practices erupted in the years after Stalin's death—most notably in East Germany in 1953, in Poland and Hungary in 1956, and in the Soviet Russian city of Novocherkassk in 1962—persuading authorities to shift more resources to consumer goods production and correspondingly revise the basis of their own political legitimacy. Tito's Yugoslavia—and perhaps the memory of Lenin's New Economic Policy of the 1920s—paved the way for the adoption of market socialist policies known in Kadarist Hungary as the New Economic Mechanism (or more colloquially, "goulash Communism") and in Walter Ulbricht's GDR as the Neues Ökonomisches System (NÖS). Although the USSR also shifted gears, a considerable gap opened up in the 1950s and '60s between the more authoritarian "austere consumerism" of Khrushchev and the "consumer socialism" of much of the rest of the bloc.[10] Not until the 1970s under Brezhnev did the Soviet Union begin to catch up to its satellites. Western social scientists conceptualized this reorientation toward "acquisitive socialism" in transactional terms as a "Little Deal" or more generally a "social contract."[11] Much of the literature on the "second," "gray," or "parallel" economies in the Eastern Bloc at least implicitly understood their existence and functions in similar terms.[12]

On the other side of the state-consumer divide, scholars have explored the relationships between consumption, material culture, and everyday life. Some of the best of these draw on personal experiences or participant observation. Svetlana Boym's innovative archeology of domestic space in Moscow and Leningrad, for example, turns the Soviet intelligentsia's well-known disdain for kitsch on its head by celebrating "domestic trash" as "the secret residue of privacy that shielded people from imposed and internalized communality."[13] Susan E. Reid has made a similar point about the way that residents of the high-rise apartment buildings erected in the Khrushchev era defied the Soviet state's attempts to control the newly distributed space: they "contradicted the modernist norms promoted by taste professionals" by filling their flats with "incoherent bricolage" and engaging in handiwork and repair that also filled a privatizing need.[14] How such goods (and services) were obtained is the focus of Alena Ledeneva's sociological investigation of *blat*, or informal exchange in the late Soviet and post-Soviet decades, and Ina Merkel's ethnology of consumer culture in the GDR.[15]

Scholarship with respect to consumption regimes and responses to them in the Eastern Bloc is still unevenly developed, with the German Democratic Republic (GDR) probably best represented and the Balkan region least so, at least in English.[16] Moreover, though binaries of "the state and the people" and "oppression and resistance" continue to structure some work on the subject, one can discern an alternative approach. This posits the power of the state working through the modes of everyday life to intersect with the articulation of individual desires and needs. Official discourses are therefore understood as having been appropriated and reproduced in heterodox fashion such as to make real existing socialism coconstructed.[17] Still other emphases—including how catering to consumer desires sacrificed "systemic identity" and the peculiarities of leisure and luxury in the bloc—are evident in two new collections.[18] No pretense toward unanimity of approach is made in the present book, though contributors have benefited from sharing each other's frameworks.

With the exception of the Trabant, whose plastic body many regard as a symbol of the GDR's misplaced aspirations for modernity, the literature on consumption has had almost nothing to say about one of the most sought-after articles of consumption, the passenger car.[19] But if we can speak of a distinct socialist form of consumption, then no material object is more exemplary of that distinctiveness than the private car, beginning with how one went about obtaining it and extending through what was required to keep it in working order. Both in Poland and in Hungary—as Mariusz Jastrzab and György Péteri demonstrate here—coupons, waybills, and other techniques intended to maintain control over car ownership and use proved insufficient to accommodate well-placed individuals' desires for automobility. "Behind-the-scenes distribution" and "sneaking privatization" were the perhaps inevitable result. Our book thus expands upon discussions of socialist consumption by interrogating the role of cars in the evolution of state socialist law, ethics, and a great deal else.[20]

Entangled Modernities

The near absence of the car in studies of consumption and material culture in the Eastern Bloc countries is paralleled by the slim representation of the bloc in the burgeoning scholarship on cars and car cultures. "The historiography of automobilism is so far mostly a Western affair confined to the capitalist nations," Gijs Mom, one of the leading scholars in mobility studies, has noted. For Mom this historiography is dominated by a master narrative that begins with the automobile as the plaything of the well-to-do classes and proceeds to its increasing accessibility and "necessity." In this narrative, the United States is always in the forefront of innovation with Western Europe a distant second and the rest of the world (when mentioned at all) lagging farther behind.[21]

Of course, it would be foolish to deny the importance of techniques pioneered in the United States, techniques generally known as Taylorism and Fordism and including the assembly line, vertical integration of production, the interchangeability of workers, the standardization of parts, and the transformation of workers into the consumers of the products they make. Sloanism, the marketing techniques developed by Alfred P. Sloan during the Great Depression to keep General Motors afloat, would also spawn imitations worldwide. But two qualifying points need to be made here. First, no matter where techniques originated, their adoption elsewhere did not happen automatically or smoothly. In France, Taylorism had to contend with not only French auto workers but Fayolism (named after Henri Fayol), a more top-down approach to management that won fervent adherents at Renault and other French firms in the 1920s. In Germany, the debate about Fordism—its nature, appropriateness to German conditions, traditions, and workers—raged from 1924 until shortly before the Nazis came to power. Carmakers in particular resisted its application—probably at the expense of their profits—because of their insistence on the pursuit of quality work. Even within Ford's empire there were spectacular failures such as the vast Amazonian rubber plantation known as Fordlandia, as well as moderate successes. Elsewhere, including Soviet Russia, adaptations and emendations bore but scant resemblance to the original.[22]

Second, while American automakers undoubtedly led the way in technology, design, and marketing during the period when oil flowed cheaply, their supremacy did not go unchallenged. Certainly since the early 1970s the significant innovations such as just-in-time inventory, variable valve timing and lift, and hybrid cars have come from elsewhere in the world. Thus the master narrative might need revision. If, as Mom argues, it has seriously exaggerated American exceptionalism, that is not to say that the West should be homogenized any more than should the East. Rather than simply adding another quirky story to the master narrative, this book seeks to contribute to its disruption and replacement by a more complex understanding of the global dynamics of automobile production and reception. That understanding is derived from the notion, common in the above-mentioned literature on consumption and material culture, that what Eastern Bloc ideologues aspired to was an "alternative modernity," alternative to Western liberal democracy if not Western capitalist norms of development.[23]

Yet one of the themes threaded throughout our book is the multiplicity of ways that the West was implicated in the production and reception of the Socialist Car and hence of that alternative modernity. Michael David-Fox has theorized such a relationship as a transnational history of "entangled modernities." Instead of a comparative approach that would involve "joint analysis of national histories or elements thereof, transnational history," he writes, "focuses on features and aspects . . . that transcend internal or domestic phenomena and . . . explore specific links or connections with other countries and realms."[24] Several contributions to this book take this approach. Brigitte Le Normand, for example, discusses the first postwar master plan for Belgrade's renovation as inspired by Le Corbusier's 1935 model of the Radiant City and conforming to the principles of the Athens Charter, the urban planning manifesto of the international modernist movement written by the Swiss-born architect and published in 1943. Le Corbusier also made his presence felt in Marzahn, the enormous housing settlement in the far northeast of Berlin, which is the subject of Eli Rubin's chapter. Marzahn's planners intended it to be, like Le Corbusier's City of Tomorrow, not just a housing settlement but "a total concept . . . with every conceivable need of the citizens planned in advance." However, the planners claimed as their inspiration not Le Corbusier himself but rather Bauhaus leftovers and Soviet literature influenced by the master's work, an interesting example of the complexity of transnational circuits. Finally, as Esther Meier points out in her chapter on Naberezhnye Chelny, the quintessentially Brezhnevite city from the 1970s, the idea for its linear design harks back to a nineteenth-century Spanish architect.

Valentina Fava's chapter illustrates another kind of transnational entanglement in the case of automotive engineering and production in postwar Czechoslovakia. The engineers and management at Mladá Boleslav initially inclined the factory toward the American mass-production model, ironically to realize the dream of a "people's car for a people's democracy." But by the end of the 1940s, the American assembly line had met the Communist Party line, and within a few years, Skoda was applying—however reluctantly—methods of work organization and incentive schemes developed in the Soviet Union during its industrialization drive in the 1930s. The story does not end here, though. In a fascinating case study of how national politics and labor practices intertwined, Fava shows how Skoda's technical experts took advantage of the long de-Stalinization process of the 1950s and '60s to reintroduce the original postwar program, only to be frustrated with the limits of socialist planning even before the Prague Spring and the Soviet-led invasion of their country.

Western automotive technology in fact cast a long shadow over the Socialist Car. The display of cars from Britain, France, Italy, and the United States at national and thematic exhibitions in the USSR during the late 1950s and early 1960s raised disturbing questions among the public about the capacity of the Soviet government to provide life's comforts. Luminita Gatejel's account of a retired Soviet car mechanic's strenuous efforts to acquire a decrepit Chevrolet exemplified the fanaticism such vehicles could inspire. Foreign trucks also intruded on the consciousness—or subconscious—of drivers, as suggested by their appearance and reappearance in the different versions of a folk song discussed by Lewis Siegelbaum. At the same time, Western automotive companies provided an essential shortcut to the production of the Socialist Car and, as Jastrzab points out

Table I.1 Private car density in Eastern Bloc countries (cars per 1,000 people)

Country	1970	1975	1980	1985	1989
Bulgaria	19.2	22.7	55.6	114.9	137.0
Czechoslovakia	55.6	101.0	149.2	172.4	200.0
GDR	66.7	111.1	151.5	200.0	232.6
Hungary	18.5	55.6	83.3	135.1	163.9
Poland	15.9	31.3	66.7	100.0	126.6
Romania	6.4	6.5	10.8	n.a.	n.a.
USSR	6.8	18.5	31.3	41.7	43.4
Yugoslavia	35.7	71.4	108.6	125.0	135.1

Source: Motor Vehicle Manufacturers Association of the United States, *Motor Vehicle Facts & Figures* (Detroit: MVMA, 1990), which gives the data in terms of cars per person.

in relation to Poland's dependence on Fiat, to the fulfillment of hopes for material advancement, modernity, and comfort.

The constraints that Soviet political hegemony imposed on Skoda's technical experts point to another theme adumbrated above—the extent of coordination among bloc members toward automotive production, distribution, and other policies concerning the Socialist Car. Who decided how many Ladas would be exported to, say, Hungary or whether parts manufactured in one Eastern Bloc country would find their way into the engines or interiors of cars assembled in another? Presumably COMECON (the Council for Mutual Economic Assistance, founded in 1949) had something to say about this, but more definitive answers await further research.[25] Thirty years ago, seeking to explain the then near-contemporary turn toward pessimism among the Soviet middle class, John Bushnell noted inter alia that the increase in the number of Soviet tourists visiting other East Bloc countries gave rise to the perception that in standard of living and availability of consumer goods the bloc countries had surpassed the Soviets.[26] The data presented in table I.1 show that, with the exception of Romania, car availability certainly conformed to this generalization.

But if, as Wendy Bracewell has put it, Yugoslavia (or perhaps even more so, the GDR and Czechoslovakia) could be construed "as the West to the Soviet bloc's East," it is important to remember that the Soviet Union itself contained huge differences.[27] At eighteen cars for every thousand people in 1977, Azerbaijan placed in the bottom third of Union republics in terms of car density, whereas Lithuania's fifty and Estonia's sixty-one meant that those Baltic republics had a density greater than Poland's and Bulgaria's and roughly the same as Hungary's (as of 1975).

Table I.2 Density of automobile ownership by Union Republic

Union Republic	Cars/1,000 people	
	1977	1985
USSR	26	45
Estonia	61	96
Lithuania	50	93
Latvia	45	81
Georgia	35	71
Armenia	32	56
Turkmenistan	24	46
RSFSR	21	44
Ukraine	21	46
Belorussia	21	39
Kazakhstan	21	39
Azerbaijan	18	30
Kirgizia	17	34
Uzbekistan	16	36
Tadzhikistan	14	35
Moldavia	14	33

Sources: William Pyle, "Private Car Ownership and Second Economy Activity," *Berkeley-Duke Occasional papers on the Second Economy in the USSR*, no. 37 (1993), 49; and A. Arrak, "Ispol'zovanie avtomobilei lichnogo pol'zovaniia," *Voprosy ekonomiki*, no. 7 (1978): 134 (for 1977); *Izvestiia*, Aug. 14, 1988: 3 (for 1985).

Automobilities?

Car densities in the GDR and Czechoslovakia did not quite match Western European levels, though they approached them. There is another lens, however, through which to view the Socialist Car. Less quantitative than qualitative, it is called "automobility," a term that sociologists and geographers began employing in the 1990s to denote the private car's intrusion into and increasing domination over large sectors of the global landscape. John Urry, one of the first to use the term in its contemporary connotation, understood it as a "social and technical system ... which links together cars, car-drivers, roads, petroleum supplies and other novel objects, technologies, and signs."[28] More recently, Robert Argenbright has distinguished "automobilization" from automobility by subsuming under the former "process, particularly the physical aspects (i.e., vehicles, infrastructure, service facilities)" and reserving for the latter "the culture of driving and its mentalities."[29]

The most elaborate definition of automobility to date is that of Steffen Böhm et al., who suggest three dimensions: first, "one of the principal socio-technical institutions and practices that seek to organize, accelerate and shape the spatial movements and impacts of automobiles, whilst simultaneously regulating their many consequences"; second, "an ideological or discursive formation, embodying ideals of freedom, privacy, movement, progress and autonomy"; and third, "a phenomenology, a set of ways of experiencing the world which serve both to legitimize its dominance and radically unsettle taken-for-granted boundaries separating human from machine."[30]

Of the three dimensions, the second is the only one that would have caused Communist political authorities some problems. Organizing and regulating were core values, after all, and as for unsettling conventional boundaries between humans and machines, the alchemy of transforming flesh into metal had a storied career in socialist realist art and literature.[31] While movement and progress certainly fell within the orbit of officially endorsed Communist values, freedom (of an individual kind) and autonomy were more problematic. Even after the mass production of cars had signaled the abandonment of ideological objections to private car ownership, their availability could not be taken for granted, and such accoutrements of car-driver mobility as limited-access highways, motels, dependable road maintenance and service stations, and a host of other features of the "roadscape" taken for granted in the West remained rudimentary in the Eastern Bloc.

Yet as the geographer Tim Edensor argues, "automobility... is always situated in contextual conditions," especially "the contextualizing matrix of the nation."[32] The cultural values and meanings of the things around us and with which we grow up are, he continues, "part of the *way things are,* yet this masks the social and cultural relations out of which they emerge."[33] Some of the culturally embedded associations Edensor mentions in connection with cars—desire and sexuality, mobility, status, family-related activity, independence, adventure, freedom, and rebellion—did not exist or did not exist to the same extent in the Eastern Bloc countries as in the West. But the shortages and privileges, the waiting lists and high prices, the (largely male) sociability, and the special role truck drivers and mechanics occupied appear generic to East Bloc automobility, part of what Gatejel calls its "common heritage."

Tinkering, the subject of Kurt Möser's chapter, also figured as a common element of East Bloc automobility. Cars everywhere throughout the bloc "were geared to cater to the needs of being serviced, repaired, or modified by nonprofessional users." In the GDR, looking after one's own car actually was invoked by ideologists as a contribution to building socialism because it supposedly raised the level of "craftsmanly and polytechnical knowledge." Seen from another perspective, which

Rubin discusses, this dependence on *Eigen-Sinn* ("individual initiative, creativity and self-taught know-how") worked symbiotically with the rationally organized, planned economy at the same time that it contradicted the same system's pretensions to superiority. Automobility in the Eastern Bloc thus came with full repair kits, the clearest possible message to new car owners that their relationship to their machines would be an intimate one.[34]

Möser also notes that although both boys and girls received polytechnic education, tinkering remained predominantly a male practice. This difference undoubtedly reflected larger gender-based distinctions, but what about driving? Both Corinna Kuhr-Korolev's and Siegelbaum's chapters take up this question in the Soviet context, one with respect to cars and the other to trucks. Few Soviet women drove, but, as Kuhr-Korolev demonstrates on the basis of fascinating "auto-biographies," even among those who did not but whose fathers, coworkers, suitors, or husbands did, cars played a major role in their lives. Whether as co-owners or merely passengers, they derived prestige from their association with a car. In the case of trucks, we enter the realm of a profession coded as male but vulnerable to intrusions by women—for example, during the Great Patriotic War, when many got behind the wheel of a ZIS-5, a GAZ AAA, or other Soviet-made vehicle, and in the fantasy world of folk song and legend.

In these cases, boundaries were being crossed either metaphorically or in reality. The theme of boundary crossing does not figure prominently in this book but is worth noting here in two connections. One is auto tourism, which road associations encouraged in a "know thy country" spirit but which could also involve visits to other countries in the bloc and even neighboring countries outside it—at least in the case of Yugoslavs, for whom visas were not required. By the same token, expanded motel and camping facilities also accommodated auto tourists from Western countries, though how many and to what effect awaits more research. A second kind of border crossing occurred when the Socialist Car was exported. As several contributors to this book have noted, cars produced in one country found their way to others irrespective of the lack of spare parts (which were not exactly thick on the ground in the country of origin) and repair services. Consignments of Ladas arrived in Yugoslavia as early as February 1971, and in Bulgaria, Hungary, Czechoslovakia, and the GDR before the year was out; Trabants sold well in Hungary and Poland; and Skodas found eager buyers not only throughout the bloc but, as Valentina Fava notes, "in markets that followed the laws of capitalism." Along with the cars came scores of aphorisms and jokes about them, reflections perhaps of both wounded national pride and the captive nature of the market. "Why does a Skoda/Lada/Trabant have a heated rear window?" went one. "To keep your hands warm when pushing it." "Beware of loose women and cars made in Russia," East Germans told each other, and so forth.

Outside the bloc, probably no country had a higher proportion or range of socialist cars than Finland. Until the late 1950s, one could encounter East German IFAs and Wartburgs, Czechoslovak Skodas, Polski Fiats, and Soviet Pobedas and Moskviches on the streets of Helsinki and other Finnish cities. Largely because of severe restrictions on the import of Western cars, Soviet models made up about half of the total in the country. The Lada did fairly well in Finland during the 1970s, but by the beginning of the 1980s its reputation had plummeted (because of unflattering comparisons with its Western and Japanese competitors rather than any deterioration in quality).[35] The Lada's trajectory elsewhere in Europe resembled the Finnish experience except in Britain, where sales peaked in the late 1980s before succumbing to more stringent emission-control standards.[36] The off-road Niva and the Samara hatchback, both AvtoVAZ cars, struggled to find their niches. One would like to know more about the marketing of these and other Eastern Bloc vehicles not only in Western Europe but in the farther-flung countries of Africa, Asia, and Latin America. Just as some in the Eastern Bloc countries felt their purchase of a Fiat- or a Renault-derived vehicle brought them a little bit closer to the West, did those who took the leap of faith in buying a car from the Second World experience a little bit of socialism?

Finally, does it make sense to refer to an Eastern Bloc automobility as distinct from that which Urry, Edensor, and other social scientists have been writing about? If we take the six components that according to Urry "generate and reproduce the 'specific character'" of automobility, we can see that we are dealing for the most part with transsystemic degrees in kind. The first, the "quintessential manufactured object" of twentieth-century capitalism and the industry from which the concepts of Fordism and post-Fordism emerged, would not seem to apply except that the Socialist Car owed its existence to Fordist (but not post-Fordist) technology. We should be more cautious about identifying the Socialist Car as the quintessential manufactured object of real existing socialism for the simple reason that with the possible exception of nondescript ferroconcrete apartment blocks, the Eastern Bloc probably did not have a quintessential manufactured object.[37] Urry's second component—"the major item of individual consumption after housing which provides status . . . and preoccupies criminal justice systems"—seems apposite, although given the generally lower rates of car ownership, criminal justice systems in the East did not preoccupy themselves with traffic violations. The linkages with other industries, services, design and planning operations, and "various oil-rich nations"—Urry's third component—obviously were weaker, though as Le Normand, Beyer, Meier, and Rubin emphasize, integrated urban (and suburban) planning did take the Socialist Car very seriously, and unlike in the West, oil continued to flow. Indeed, the discovery of new reserves in the Soviet interior and oil's export *to* the West were what made the Lada possible. Still, unlike cars in the

West, the Socialist Car failed to generate a viable infrastructure around it; planned economies simply could not cope with all the details of such a highly sophisticated system. The fourth component—"quasi-private mobility"—is the only one of the six that probably should be weighted more strongly in the Eastern Bloc by virtue of the relative scarcity of other private or quasi-private venues. In fact, in addition to Möser's point that we need to view "usage" in a wider perspective, it should be acknowledged that the principal thing that is consumed in connection with cars is precisely this quasi-private mobility, and in the case of the Socialist Car that dimension loomed very large. The last two components—the cultural and environmental consequences of car use—though less extensive than in some Western countries, replicated Western patterns quite closely and, in the case of "major discourses of what constitutes the good life," obviously internalized them.[38]

The Eastern Bloc's version of automobility both replicated and departed from Western standards. So too did the car cultures and the "vernacular, generic motorscapes [that] stitch the local and the national together through their serial reproduction across space."[39] Refraining from wearing seat belts in order not to offend the driver (or if you *were* the driver, not wanting to appear unmanly); expecting to settle with the traffic police if stopped rather than going through complicated formal procedures; adorning one's car with bunting, dolls, or some other good-luck charm on the occasion of a wedding; removing windshield wipers after parking; being prepared to maintain one's own car; and a host of other practices comprised the cultures. The motorscapes ranged from isolated and dangerous to crowded and dangerous. In these respects, the world inhabited by the Socialist Car might be located conceptually somewhere between the First and Third Worlds, which is why the term "Second" seems appropriate.

Since the collapse of that world, the plants where workers toiled to produce the Socialist Car and the workers themselves generally have fallen on hard times. A few firms were swallowed by Western companies and modernized, but others have struggled to stay open, and still others succumbed to global competition and shut down. The cars themselves have achieved legendary status as objects of ridicule and nostalgia. In the case of the Trabant, the shift from one to the other happened "at an unbelievable pace and all at once" almost immediately after it had transported "Ossies" over the border.[40] *Kopeck,* a Russian film comedy about the original Lada (2101) that debuted in 2002, contains heavy doses of both.[41] In this collective history, the authors put aside both nostalgia and ridicule in the interest of trying to understand the Socialist Car in its own context.

Part One

SOCIALIST CARS AND SYSTEMS OF PRODUCTION, DISTRIBUTION, AND CONSUMPTION

1

THE ELUSIVE PEOPLE'S CAR

Imagined Automobility and Productive Practices along the "Czechoslovak Road to Socialism" (1945–1968)

Valentina Fava

In Czechoslovakia the automobile was not born socialist. After February 1948 the technicians who were involved in the development of the automobile industry had to take into account, on the one hand, the well-established productive practices that were the result of the complex, multilayered industrial history of Czechoslovakia and, on the other hand, the American model of mass production that at the time everyone considered the primary reference for the automobile industry.[1] What is more, almost fifty years of "automobility" had created high expectations among both the experts in the sector and the common people regarding how and when mass motorization would come about. Finally, in this young, industrialized Central European republic, starting from the first half of the twentieth century, the automobile, which was destined for exportation and racing, had become one of the symbolic manufactured products of the Bohemian "industrial tradition."[2]

This chapter examines the history of the automobile industry and of automobility in Czechoslovakia between 1945 and 1968, retracing the ideological and concrete development of the "people's car." It traces the changes in the organization of production that involved the main Czechoslovak auto producer, Škoda Auto of Mladá Boleslav, renamed AZNP (Automobilové Závody, Národní Podnik—State Enterprise Automobile Factory) after its nationalization. Then, through an analysis of the technical and strategic debate that accompanied these changes, it explores the way technicians active in the sector related to the power of the Party and its policy choices regarding industry and transport.[3] This documentation and some articles taken from the most important Czechoslovak automobile magazines, *Auto* and *Svêt Motorû (The World of Motors)*,[4] illustrate how technicians and planners

Translated from Italian by Brenda Porster.

attempted to make "socialist" a product as greatly desired as it was potentially subversive of the ideals of February 1948.

Indeed, between 1948 and 1968 the automobile represented for the Czechoslovak economic and technical bureaucracy a veritable Trojan horse, exposing planners and technicians to a close-up comparison with capitalism in regard to both the modes of organization and the product itself. As goods to be exchanged for hard currency, for the entire period under study Czechoslovak cars had great difficulty competing on the world market with products that were the fruit of Western automation technologies and with the increasingly aggressive marketing strategies used by capitalist competitors. As a product designed for domestic consumption, the people's car recalled the splendors of the first period of Czechoslovak automobility in the interwar republic led by President Tomáš Masaryk; at the same time, it represented a promise that the planners were not able to keep, since they did not manage to achieve levels of productivity comparable to those of capitalist enterprises.

The chapter explores four moments of particular significance in the history of Czechoslovak automobility:

1. The period between 1945 and 1948, including Alexander Taub's consultancy (Taub was an American engineer who, along with Czechoslovak colleagues, created a project to realize a "people's car for a people's democracy" according to the American mass-production model).

2. The launch of the first five-year plan (1949–53), which brought about the marginalization of automobile production.

3. Starting from 1954, the relaunching of the automobile as a symbol of socialist technology.[5]

4. Finally, the period of reform (1963–68), when the difficulties of the planned economy in coordinating production of an item as complex as that of automobiles became more and more evident, as the gap between official discourse about the automobile on the one hand and the reality of Czechoslovak plants on the other grew exponentially, undermining the image of the national industry's efficiency and confirming the criticisms of a technical-productive nature that were at the heart of the movement for political reform in the sixties.[6]

A People's Car for a People's Democracy: The Czechoslovak Road to Automobility and Its Rapid Abandonment (1946–1953)

On January 10, 1946, the magazine *Auto,* official organ of the Autoclub of the Czechoslovak Republic, inaugurated the New Year with an article by Jaroslav Frei entitled "What Will Be the Destiny of Our Automobile Industry?"[7] Below the text there appeared a photograph of the latest model of the 1942 Ford. The war had been over for only eight months, and after six years of German occupation in Czechoslovakia there was much discussion about the position and role of the new republic's automobile industry in the international context. Diplomatic and economic isolation seemed only a far-off memory, and the pages of *Auto* reflected the curiosity and enthusiasm of auto fans and of many technicians about novelties in the sector. Readers and journalists were aware of the changes the war had introduced in the automobile market and were informed about the state of auto production in other countries: the automobile, formerly a luxury for the privileged few, was becoming an object of common use. And Czechoslovakia anxiously awaited its "motorization boom."[8]

However, commentators diverged profoundly about how to take advantage of what appeared to be the great opportunity of the Czechoslovak automobile industry and about the goals of modernization itself. On the one hand, Frei held that in order to compete with France and England on the European market it was necessary to produce in the shortest possible time a completely new people's car with an engine no larger than 1,000 cc. On the other hand, only a few pages further on in the same magazine, František Kec, while agreeing with Frei about the need to take advantage of Germany's weakness, held that Czechoslovak production should be destined for the less demanding markets of eastern and southeastern Europe and that a small-engine car should not be introduced until later on.[9] The controversy concerned not only market outlets but also the organization of the industry and its recent nationalization, whose advantages were illustrated in an article of July 1946. According to the author of this article, the concentration of plants in a single productive unit dependent on a single central direction would guarantee cooperation among them, allowing the industry to overtake domestic competition and concentrate on producing large series of a single model.[10]

From the point of view of the foreign market, however, as Frei and others feared, this meant exposing the sector to a serious concentration of risk: if, in fact, the only model produced was not a success, it would be a catastrophe for Czechoslovak industry. What is more, the costs of this single model would never be so low as to make it attractive because of its cheapness. And it was unlikely that customers, especially foreign ones, would be satisfied. He wrote, "We mustn't forget that production is designed for consumers and that we cannot force them to buy what we have decided."[11]

After February 1948 very different considerations guided the development of the Czechoslovak mechanical industry. Yet between 1946 and 1948 it seemed possible to reconcile the needs of an efficient, modern automobile production—one inspired by new ways of organizing coming from the other side of the Atlantic—with the principles underlying the "socializing democracy" of the Košice Program.[12] In this context, the project of the Czechoslovak people's car and the reconstruction of the motorcar industry were entrusted by František Fabinger, a member of the National Economic Commission and director of KOVO (Generální Râeditelství Kovodêlného a Strojírenského Prûmyslu—Central Directorate of the Mechanical and Steel Industry), to an American engineer from General Motors, Alexander Taub.[13]

Taub's report, entitled "A People's Car for a People's Democracy," assigned the role of "motor" for the reconstruction of the country's economy to the auto industry.[14] To this end, he foresaw huge investments for the construction of a new plant equipped with the most modern technology available, which would allow the production of "the best possible product for the lowest costs," a car with a small engine that would not cost more than 23,000 crowns, equivalent to what the average worker earned in six months. According to Taub, Czechoslovakia would quickly have to reach the critical threshold of 200 cars a day for each plant in order to take advantage of the economies of scale and create a market that could absorb at least 125,000 cars a year. Taub envisioned a fully American-style modernity for the Czechoslovak auto industry, following organizational and strategic steps similar to those of the great American companies, from Ford, leader in the first phase of American automobility, to General Motors, which was better at grasping the potentials and nuances of a mature market. The Czechoslovak automobile industry should, in Taub's opinion, become a "robust newcomer" on the European market: not only was productive, organizational, and commercial modernization in line with the American model not incompatible with the principles and ideals of the Košice Program's socializing democracy, but it was, on the contrary, at its foundation.[15]

The publication of reports in specialized magazines on Czechoslovak technicians' journeys to America contributed to the idea that modernization of the sector was a "national undertaking," giving an almost collective dimension to the enterprise of planning the people's car (*lidový vûz*) and the plant that would produce it.[16] However, with the launching of the first five-year plan (1949–53) Taub and Frei had to leave Czechoslovakia, and the production of automobiles was transformed from the motor of growth to a "useless luxury."[17] As Evzen Löbl, the former vice minister of foreign trade, wrote in 1968, the fact that he had invited Taub, who had worked for Chiang Kai-shek and the American War Production Board, soon served to swell the dossier of accusations made against Rudolf Slánský, former general secretary of the Communist Party, and his collaborators. Among these was Fabinger, who was condemned in 1952.[18] During the first five-year plan, instead of receiving the planned investments, Škoda was despoiled of its best machines and spaces, which were given over to the production of heavy and military vehicles. In

1952 only slightly more than 6,000 cars were produced, compared with 24,463 in 1950, and production nearly came to a halt.[19]

The Automobile in Czechoslovakia during the First Five-Year Plan: New Tasks and Old Limitations

Thus the expectations created among technicians and motorists by the Taub affair were not met, and from articles in the specialized magazines we can grasp the dismay and perplexity, as well as the ambiguity, with which the subjects of the people's car and automobility were treated within official propaganda. Starting from 1951, the Czechoslovak Autoclub became the Union for Collaboration with the Army (Svaz pro Spolupráci s Armadou), and the articles published in *Auto* reformulated the aims of automobility as education for defense, road safety and sport.[20] The change thus brought Czechoslovakia into line with the Soviet precedent, dating from 1935, of placing automobility and automobilism under the supervision of an organization dedicated to defense preparedness. At the same time, socialist automobility was presented as being for the masses, as opposed to the upper-class, elitist version characteristic of Czechoslovakia in the period between the wars.[21]

The pages of *Auto* and *Svêt Motorû* illustrate the attempts to justify the industrial policy choices of the first five-year plan, focusing as they did on heavy industry at the expense of consumer goods: strengthening heavy industry would create the productive and material premises for raising the workers' standard of living, with the result that owning a car would no longer be a "marker of class," the prerogative of "exploiters" to whom "normal people" had to give way.[22] On the contrary, it would be a commodity "handed over directly to the workers," who would use it for practical and pleasurable purposes (as was already demonstrated by the increased availability of motorcycles).[23]

Finally, if the price to pay for the passage to a socialist mode of production was a certain delay in motorization, as was hinted at here and there, this would be compensated for by the collaboration between technicians and workers that would guarantee not only the quantity of output but also the renowned quality and perfection of Czechoslovak automobile production.[24] Though these articles seem packed with the rhetoric of "building socialism," it is perhaps worth noting that in Czechoslovakia even in the early 1950s the modernization of automobile production and individual motorization continued to represent not only an objective but above all a national undertaking, both for technicians and in popular opinion. To cite Tim Edensor, the automobile in Czechoslovakia was, for potential motorists and fans and also for the greater part of the Communist economic bureaucracy, a symbol of a historic system of production that boasted extraordinary efficiency and high quality[25]—features that had to be disassociated, however, from the experience of the First Republic of Masaryk.[26]

Although these arguments—often written in reply to readers' complaints about the delay in motorization[27]—were not answered with counterarguments by technicians, the limits and ambiguities of the Party's policies regarding the automobile were becoming evident. Indeed, the sudden change in priorities and the declassing of the sector decided in Moscow and at COMECON headquarters were fiercely contested not only by managers, technicians, and factory hands in general but also by top-level experts of the planning apparatus, the Ministry for General Mechanics (Ministerstvo Všeobecného Strojírenství—MVS), and the Economic Council of the Central Committee of the Czechoslovak Communist Party (Hospodářská Rada Ústřední Vybor KSČ).[28] Between 1949 and 1953, the factory of Mladà Boleslav was repeatedly accused of "excessive localism,"[29] and the attempt to bring into the shop the "Soviet system of industrial administration" (*sovětské řízení*) met with determined resistance. In 1951–52 the decision to move the production of the Tatra 600 to Mladà Boleslav, a choice that was totally nonsensical from a technical point of view, stirred up a conflict between the local Party cell, unions, and workforce on the one hand and the upper spheres of planning on the other.[30]

However, even the upper spheres—the engineers working for the Mechanics Ministry—did not seem to be in total agreement with the sacrifice of national production, which they accepted only as a temporary choice motivated by the growing international political tensions. Their attitude toward automobility and the individual use of cars was ambivalent, and their approach to the Soviet system, to which they opposed the long Czechoslovak experience in auto production, was cautious. In the course of the 1950s, however, there was an ever-widening gap between the competence of the technicians, who continued to use the know-how acquired in the United States in 1946–47 as their reference point for technology and production, and the actual working of the plants, with their outdated machines, old-fashioned methods, and limited production volumes.

In the shops the Soviet system of industrial administration may have determined the phases of production, but in their reports the technicians seemed to prefer a mixed model of efficiency in which there were some elements of the American model—especially special-purpose machinery and high-quality steels—a somewhat secondhand admiration for the supposed results of Soviet industry, and frequent references to the Czechoslovak industrial tradition. The latter generally meant the organizational practices and know-how that had favored the development of the automobile sector before World War II.[31] In light of all these considerations, the technicians pointed out the dangers of marginalizing the auto industry on the grounds that it represented not only a Czechoslovak tradition of which to be proud but also a key element in the balance of trade, since cars were by and large exported and therefore a source of foreign currency.[32] At the same time, they were rather skeptical about the possibility that the road to mass motorization could be taken up again when the time for Czechoslovak Fordism was finally mature:

> In theory, here we talk about the emergence of a new social class which, thanks to its new affluence, would want to and be able to buy and use a car, for example to go to work.... This will signify a radical change in the social organization of our state: the workers will be given the possibility to buy a car and take care of its maintenance by themselves. But when will it be decided that the time for this solution has come? However, since as we have already pointed out, the automobile production foreseen in the next two five-year plans will not affect the number of cars in circulation, nor will it lead to replacement of the car fleet, we prefer not to answer this question, as we feel that in light of these figures regarding production and sales, even when the right moment comes the necessary automobiles will not be available.[33]

The Relaunching of Socialist Technology (1954)

In January 1954 the people's car was already on the road again, at least according to proclamations found in the headlines of *Svêt Motorů*.[34] In 1954 the government began to be somewhat more favorably disposed to private motorization at the same time as it was paying more attention to winning consensus in the world of production.[35]

In Mladà Boleslav the rhetoric of socialist technology, which between 1954 and 1958 dominated the Central Committee of the Communist Party's discussions about technical and scientific development, seemed to give at least temporary answers to the deep dissatisfaction that had been smoldering among technicians and workers during the first five-year plan.[36] Socialist technology promised recourse to mechanization and automation, which technicians had long desired and saw as a symbol of modern automobile production. At the same time as it guaranteed growth in labor productivity and a reduction in physical exertion, it promised the workers and technicians more participation in the planning phase. Within this framework, at least according to the propaganda, "the new social class" that would benefit from the construction of the socialist "people's car" began to emerge from the shadows.[37] Thus it is not surprising that the late 1950s saw a return to some of the topoi characteristic of the debate on automobility immediately after the war and in the period just before February 1948. There was a feeling that mass motorization was about to take place in the countries of the new-formed Warsaw Pact as well, and after the unsuccessful attempts of the early 1950s the possibility of a genuine collaboration and international division of work among the COMECON countries seemed stronger. In these countries the improved standard of living would soon lead to a rapid increase in the demand for automobiles, a demand that would not have suffered from the crisis of overproduction that planners felt was already threatening capitalist countries.[38]

In accordance with this change in policy regarding the automobile sector, the government created the Ministry of Transport and Farm Machines (Ministerstvo Automobilového Průmyslu a Zemědělských Strojů, MAP). A conference of automobile industry experts took place at Mladá Boleslav in March 1956, only a few months after the September 1955 metalworkers' congress, during which the serious backwardness of the mechanics industry was denounced and the new lines of Party and government intervention were set out.[39] As a consequence the Mladá Boleslav factory and the proposals put forward by the technicians of AZNP almost a decade earlier found themselves the focus of planners' attention. Indeed, most of the papers presented at the 1956 conference were inspired by old reports of the Taub consultancy and by technicians' accounts of their 1947 journeys. At times, as in the case of the report on the body workshop, the authors were the very same technicians who had taken part in the American project.[40] Between 1955 and 1957 the newborn Ministry of Transport and Farm Machines formulated a plan for restructuring Czechoslovak automobile production: in 1962 a new plant would be completed, and 1964 would see the start-up of the production of what was considered the first Czechoslovak people's car, the MB 1000.[41] The new factory marked the passage from the methods characteristic of batch or small-series production to those of mass production, and the achievement of volumes of output that were significant, though still far below those of Western Europe: from 5,375 units produced in 1954 there was an upswing to 64,325 in 1962, and then, with the introduction of the new car, to 77,705 units in 1965.[42] This made it possible to increase the country's motorization significantly; though still below the European average, car density doubled, from a car for every sixty-seven inhabitants in 1956 to one for every twenty-nine inhabitants in 1967.[43]

The magazines emphasized this development in a growing number of articles dedicated first to the Škoda 440 Spartak and then to the MB 1100.[44] But after 1957 the role of the automobile changed: the growing demand became the "indicator" of the high standard of living achieved by workers in socialist Czechoslovakia.[45] In an article significantly entitled "Motorists Facing the Elections," in which the "facts of Hungary" were also alluded to, we find these words:

> [W]e have achieved our greatest success in the consumer goods and food industries. Compared with 14,116 motorcycles produced in 1937, during the bourgeois republic, in 1956 there were 112,990; while in 1937 there were 12,634 autos produced, in 1956 there were 25,068. . . . [W]e could go on like this endlessly, but the most important thing is that while in bourgeois Czechoslovakia only very few workers could

buy a car or a motorcycle, now in February almost 600 million crowns were collected in banks, meaning crowns for 36,295 automobiles. This is an indication of the high standard of living and culture of our people.[46]

Instructions on how to reserve a car replaced articles on road education, and the taxes that still weighed on the automobile were justified by the need to build roads, petrol pumps, service stations, and other infrastructure.[47] In this optimistic scenario the one thing remaining was the liberalization of the motor vehicle market, as was already augured in 1960:

> Motorization [*motorismus*] is an intimate part of our economic life, influencing the population's living standard and cultural possibilities. . . . We have to take into account the increase in living standard and therefore the growing number of workers who will want to own a car. Today the number of those who have deposited in state savings banks the 20,000 crowns they need to buy a car, almost fifty thousand people, is high, but it is still limited by the fact that many people who would be interested are discouraged by difficulties in using the bonus and so have not even made a request. The time has come for this number to grow thanks to growth in production and, possibly, to a liberalized market.[48]

The Myth and Reality of the Czechoslovak People's Car

With growing demand, the investments in production and the modernization of the Mladà Boleslav plant wound up bringing to light the shortages and problems that automobile production, based as it was on a multiplicity of parts, components and materials, met in a centrally planned economy.[49] The technicians working in the automobile sector could not fail to see how far they were by now from the levels reached by the capitalist competition and what a huge task filling this gap would be. Between 1955 and 1964 planners made many attempts to solve the problems inherent in the production process and to improve the quality of the cars produced. In contrast to the years of the first five-year plan, they now were paying attention to suggestions coming from the plants and above all from Motokov, the state agency responsible for foreign sales of Škoda products. Nevertheless, the problems posed by the requirements of an efficient system of automobile production ultimately challenged the very foundations of economic planning and touched on such politically sensitive issues as the liberalization of the domestic market, the introduction of the market mechanism in price setting, and the use of marketing and advertising strategies for foreign distribution.[50] Despite the appeals to automobility, in socialist Czechoslovakia the automobile was meant mainly for export (in 1955, 9,441 out of 12,430 automobiles produced were exported, and in 1965 more than 49,000 out of 77,700). Difficulties in the division of labor in the COMECON and the need for hard currency meant that the most interesting markets for Motokov were the traditional markets for Škoda cars—Austria, the Scandinavian countries, Belgium, and Holland—markets that followed the laws of capitalism.[51] Thus a paradoxical situation emerged, one that was full of contradictions: the Socialist Car, produced in a system based on supply—the "political economy of communism"—had to be sold in capitalist markets, where it was demand that counted most.

What had been an indirect comparison with capitalist industry from the point of view of production methods all through the 1950s became a direct comparison if seen from the perspective of sales. Besides highlighting with precision the defects of socialist technology, the intense, continual comparison with Western capitalist industry had important consequences for industrial processes of technical learning (learning how to design a competitive car) and in the end convinced technicians to import commercial practices that challenged Party ideology.

From the late fifties on, Škoda cars—both the Š440 (Octavia), which began to be produced in series in October 1955 and continued until 1968, and the MB 1100, the people's car produced from 1964—gradually became less competitive against foreign brands. The fears expressed by technicians back in 1949–50 seemed to have come true, and innumerable criticisms and complaints came from Motokov and its distributors (in 1958 over four thousand complaints arrived from Sweden alone).[52] The needs and requests of foreign consumers were disappointed first of all by the low quality of the cars and then by the lack of service and distribution. This was discussed at the highest levels of the planning apparatus and succeeded where the needs of domestic buyers and the technicians' reports had failed.[53] Even so, problems with the coordination of planning, the result of difficult relations between Mladá Boleslav and its suppliers, persisted.

The situation was aggravated by problems in the organization of "cooperation" between companies and ministries and among the ministries involved in automobile production. At the above-mentioned automobile sector conference, experts denounced the absence of planned coordination between the AZNP and its more than one hundred suppliers, which among other things depended on different ministries. Until then cooperation had been a last-ditch resource to procure supplies that were not covered by the central plant or to make up underutilized or free productive capacity. Relations between the AZNP and suppliers were characterized by continual disputes about the quality of goods or failure to meet delivery deadlines, and the efficiency of cooperation was penalized by long and costly transportation or high production costs. The experts therefore recommended the specialization and consequent rationalization of plants producing component parts.[54] But the way forward seemed to be blocked. Reports on the construction of the new factory made clear just how much the very possibility of producing a people's car was seriously weakened by the delays and high prices of subsuppliers and by the central administration's inability to remedy the situation.[55] The introduction of economic productive units (*vyrobní hospodářské jednotky*, VHJ) with the reform of 1958 did not solve the problem; on the contrary, the bottlenecks already present in the years of the first five-year plan now occurred at the plant level rather than at the ministry level as before.[56]

Market Research on Installment: The Springtime of the Czechoslavak Automobile Industry

The crisis of 1963 was the start of the real reform movement for the Czechoslovak economy.[57] At Škoda it was met with a gradual radicalization of proposals for innovation and for reorganization of relations with the minister, but the main change regarded relations with the agencies in charge of Czechoslovak automobiles' foreign and internal distribution, Motokov and Mototechna From them came concrete proposals, born out of contacts with capitalist industry, with no particularly revolutionary ideas as far as politics or ideology was concerned, and inspired by the need to solve existing problems and to give efficiency and prestige back to automobile production. A new freedom to call things by their names emerged from the technicians' writings. Now that the bottlenecks that had previously impeded production had been eliminated, they were at last rid of the embarrassment and shame they had felt about a product built with great effort but difficult to sell and scarcely representative of Bohemian know-how.

The instruments of capitalism—the workings of the market, the calculation of price, the internalization of distribution and of research and development—were not an end in themselves but instead provided concrete solutions to enable company management to restore productivity and efficiency to the factory. As in 1946, assuring the efficiency of industry was the way technicians and workers could contribute to building the Czechoslovak road to socialism. And once more they did this by looking to the practices and technology used beyond the Eastern Bloc.[58]

In their search for modernity and efficiency, however, they introduced ideas that risked going beyond the barriers of socialist ideology. In June 1967 Mladá Boleslav hosted a conference on marketing and it application in the AZNP.[59] The objective was to clarify the definition of marketing and of public relations, illustrating the forms of market research and the role of advertising, and to give explanations of how to apply marketing to the automobile sector and to "create a positive image of both the producer and the product and to influence the customer before he decides to buy." The conference also devoted much attention to the question of prices: "how to set suitable prices . . . how to judge when it is possible to set a price higher than that of the competition."[60]

A careful reading clearly shows that the simplification of the distribution process "following the model of other industrially developed countries," improvements in the maintenance of Škodas (including service and access to replacement parts and repairs), and the complex mechanism of price formation were studied in response to problems of exportation and to accommodate the tendencies of the international market and not in response to the pressing demand coming from the domestic market. Along with the need to take measures regarding body works and perhaps optional features, the most radical proposal concerned the role of Motokov and the desirability to make it a division inside the AZNP, responsible for all the questions connected with trade and distribution—not only sales but also service, advertising campaigns, and so on. At the same time, planners contemplated a decentralization of distribution and service at the regional level for the domestic market; in this way "the company would transfer only part of the distribution without having a monopoly on sales—on the contrary, it would be competing with Mototechna, Obchodní Dům and so on."[61]

However, the introduction and study of marketing strategies and innovative distribution systems were a sign that things were going too far: the rejection of flexible mass production and mass marketing had been a fixed point that differentiated the socialist from the capitalist auto industry. Although by the 1950s the Sloanist principle of "a car for every purse and purpose" had slowly won favor in capitalist Europe, beyond the Eastern Bloc the car was and had to remain a utility good—resistant, useful, and unsophisticated—one that taught technical skill and discipline and was produced according to the canons of "exaggerated Soviet Fordism."[62] The reference point was still, though with some updating, the Ford Model T: motorization was to come about through a single model, and the market would be created thanks to low sales prices, low production costs, and a maximum of standardization, as in the United States in the first decades of the twentieth century. Besides complicating the production process, the proliferation of optionals and models implied a recognition of the consumer's individuality and the need to meet individual needs and tastes.[63] As the growing literature on consumption under socialism shows, this sort of recognition risked taking on ideologically subversive connotations and evading the planners' control.[64] In Czechoslovakia the decision to increase the number of models on offer "to please even the fussiest motorists, the ones who haven't liked our cars up to now" re-evoked the deleterious, elitist automobility of the 1930s, a target of ideological darts all through the 1950s.[65]

And actually in 1967 the potential Czechoslovak consumers who were starting to make their voices heard and their desires count were increasingly in agreement with the needs and demands originating in the world of production as the following interview shows:

> *I:* At the beginning of the spring, the director of Mototechna said that in two or three years cars will be sold on installment. What do you think?
>
> *D:* According to habits valid in commerce and in the world, I could answer your question by saying that this will happen when supply exceeds demand. But I know that the TV viewers expect another answer: first of all, let us analyze the evolution of demand and supply in recent years. As the diagram for demand since 1963 shows, demand exceeds supply and grows very quickly; this leads to a growing number of reservations that we have not been able to satisfy, a growing number of people interested in having a car who have not received one. We cannot know yet how the supply will evolve; of course, the evolution of demand will also depend on the price of cars. The retail prices and their variations depend on the economic situation of our country and are without doubt also influenced by production costs. This is obviously the business of the producer and of relations between producer and subsupplier. We try to produce as best we can and at the lowest possible cost, but the evolution of demand will also depend on other factors such as, for example, the automobile tax, the price of petrol, the quantity, quality, and cost of repairs and replacement parts, the state and development of the infrastructure network, and a series of other elements. Another element no less important will be the rate of growth of the standard of living, and with it the growth and differentiation of earnings. From all that I have said, we can see that the variables to consider to answer the question on installments are many.[66]

The response to contradictions in the plans for the development of the Czechoslovak automobile industry, to the uncertainties and hopes inspired by the Czechoslovak road to socialism, was soon given by Soviet tanks, and they also brought a new automobility with them. Indeed, after August 1968, motorization for individual use was briskly pursued by the planners.[67] Despite continued productive problems, the Škoda found (at least temporarily) less fussy consumers in COMECON markets. A few hundred miles away the VAZ plant, inaugurated in 1970, showed for the second time and mutatis mutandis the only possible road for the socialist auto industry: import the most advanced technologies of Western automation without yielding to the perversions of capitalist consumption in order to produce a car that the consumer, to quote Henry Ford, could paint "any color that he wants so long as it is black." Such a car would, in the best Fordist tradition, distract the workers and in the Czechoslovak case the entire citizenry from involvement in political or union activism.

2

CARS AS FAVORS IN PEOPLE'S POLAND

Mariusz Jastrząb

Works on the functioning of centrally planned economies have proved that allocations of both investment and consumption resources often occurred in chaotic ways. Historians have already demonstrated that distributive decisions were often uninformed, made on the basis of common sense, precedents from the past, or intuition and not in accordance with scientific methods of planning. It has also been established that the centrally planned system left much room for bargaining and informal influences.[1]

Despite all the ills of its economic system, the socialist state had to create the prospect of satisfying consumer needs in order to encourage people to work. Socialism represented a promise of material advancement. Therefore, the state had to deal with the consumer appetites of its citizens, accepting some of their desires and disallowing others, redirecting consumer demand, and playing with culturally construed images of affluence. Even under Stalinism the state was not uninterested in consumer needs.[2] After the death of Stalin, European socialist countries sooner or later drifted toward the concept of the welfare state. In seeking to legitimate their power, the leaders of Eastern Europe offered their subjects a certain deal: social safety and satisfaction of basic consumer needs in return for conformism.[3] Poland was no exception in this process.

In December 1970, after a wave of strikes that ended in bloodshed, Władysław Gomułka, who had been in power since 1956, was replaced as first secretary of the Polish United Workers' Party by Edward Gierek. Gierek remained in office until 1980. The Polish historian Marcin Zaremba coined the term "*bigos* socialism" (after a traditional Polish sauerkraut strew) to capture the liberalization of the political system and a warmer attitude toward consumerism in Poland under the new leadership.⁴ At the beginning of the 1970s real wages grew significantly after stagnating in the second half of the 1960s, and Western consumer goods or their domestic equivalents entered the Polish market. In line with these changes the ownership of a private car was gradually becoming an important element of social representations of a decent life.

Socialist states always had the ambition to educate their citizens and also aimed to teach them how they should behave as consumers. Until the end of the 1960s, Polish officialdom considered that making a car available to the average family was contradictory to the socialist ideal of rational consumption, but from the beginning of the 1970s the government decided to give a green light to mass motorization. The desire to purchase a private car was now viewed as legitimate.

In Poland, as in other state socialist countries, cars were in chronically short supply and belonged to the category of the most desired goods. The state, as the sole proprietor and distributor of the entire stock of new cars available for customers, controlled all output and official imports. The distribution of cars therefore could be used to achieve various goals. Cars could serve as rewards for efficient work and/or political activism. The imperfections of the official distribution system encouraged potential customers to look for patronage and protection to get a car. On the other hand, people able to influence distributional decisions could exploit their position and play their own games.⁵ Scarcity, the culturally conditioned importance of personal ties, and the discretionary character of administrative decisions opened the field for the development of patron-client relations.⁶

This chapter is intended as a case study. I will use two sets of archival documents from 1977–80 and 1983–85 to illustrate the practice of distributive decisions at the governmental level. I will show the mechanisms of allocating cars to private individuals in a governmental institution. The process of making those decisions was characterized by the lack of formalized rules of behavior. Their character demonstrates the personal rather than administrative nature of authority. Cars were given to people with certain ties to decision makers. Officials who allocated cars received demonstrations of submission, gratitude and loyalty, or, in some cases, personal services in return.

To fully understand why cars could be granted as favors for loyal or exceptionally useful subjects by those in authority, one has to be aware of the peculiarities of the relationship among the car, power, and authority in an economically underdeveloped country like Poland. These relationships appeared to be persistent in time and resistant to changes of political regimes, as they were rooted in the interwar period. Their vitality was powered first and foremost by the long-lasting scarcity of cars.

The Heritage of the Past

Despite heated discussions on automobilism in Poland before the Second World War, the number of registered cars remained low. During the Great Depression, in the early and mid-1930s, the number of newly bought automobiles was even smaller than the number of those being deregistered. As a result, in a country of nearly thirty-five million inhabitants the stock of cars in use dropped from thirty-eight thousand to twenty-five thousand between 1931 and 1936. In 1934 horse-drawn vehicles generated 80 percent of road traffic.[7] Roads were bad, local authorities responsible for their maintenance were chronically short of money, and limited resources of the central government went for the improvement of the rail network rather than for roads. State policy toward motorization meandered. The government feared that its expansion and ensuing increase in fuel consumption would hinder exports of crude oil. Cars and car owners were heavily taxed. Such a policy was in accordance with the perception of a car as a product for the elite, but it obviously hampered sales of new vehicles. On the other hand, the development of the motor transport was perceived as important for military reasons. The army insisted on the expansion of domestic production capabilities.[8]

In 1928 the Ministry of Industry and Trade (Ministerstwo Przemysłu i Handlu—MPiH) funded a state-owned concern, the State Engineering Works (Państwowe Zakłady Inżynierii—PZInż). In 1932 the PZInż signed a contract with Fiat to expand and retool its existing facilities and to produce several models of Fiat vehicles. As a consequence of the modernization, the car factory of PZInż reached the production capacity of three thousand units per year. In 1935 it started manufacturing trucks (Fiats 621, chassis of Fiats 618) and the next year passenger cars (Fiats 508 and 518). By 1939 the PZInż with a staff of 8,500 had become the second-largest engineering factory in Poland. In addition to cars for both military and civilian customers, the PZInż manufactured motorcycles, tanks, artillery tractors, and other vehicles.[9] The production program of the PZInż was a compromise between military and civilian requirements. The army needed first and foremost cross-country vehicles and trucks. Passenger models limited the company's dependence on small and irregular military orders.

High import tariffs protected licensed production of the PZInż against competition from abroad. Another protective measure was the requirement of government permission to open a car assembly plant. The output of the largest plant, owned by a rolling-stock potentate, Lilpop Rau and Loewenstein, that assembled General Motors vehicles, was eight thousand units between 1937 and 1939. The small scale of domestic production, taxation, and protectionist measures contributed to high prices and low demand for cars in the domestic market. Thus the total number of cars did not exceed forty-five thousand, and the number of passenger vehicles was lower than thirty thousand before the outbreak of the war.

Under such material conditions the automobile played a prominent role in the discourse about modernity. Polish intellectual and political elites were painfully aware of the civilizational distance between Poland and the West. The decade of the 1930s was marked by attempts to catch up in many fields. First, domestic plants manufacturing cars on a larger scale symbolized the ability of Polish engineers and workers to master complicated technologies and the capacity of the industry to develop even under severe capital constraints. At the same time, popular literature depicted the car as a harbinger of a new millennium, a promise of a better future and a cure for the majority of social ills. It was supposed to be the cheapest and most efficient means of transport, a machine that shrank distances, offered freedom of movement, and opened new opportunities to its user to participate in culture. Readers learned that the car would make the movement of goods cheaper, boosting business activity and creating a world free of poverty. The car could save human lives—because motorization of emergency services would allow rapid help to those in need—and even human souls because it would facilitate pastoral ministry in remote areas. The car was also described as a disseminator of learning, as it enhanced the development of technical skills. Finally, as one writer opined, the car "brings the nations of the world closer to each other, throws a much-needed bridge between them, makes it easier to become acquainted with foreign social institutions, cultural achievements or opinions, and this way contributes to the eradication of prejudices and hatred."[10]

Despite millenarian expectations for the future, the Poland of the 1930s was a society deeply divided across social and national lines. The car here and now, not in the future, was a status symbol. Car owners were usually landowners, industrialists, high officials, or members of the political elite. A car was a part of the world of the privileged. Those less fortunate looked at this world with a mixture of jealousy and condemnation. Economic hardships must have incited many to judge businessmen and landowners as exploiters, extracting other people's work under very harsh conditions, without adequate pay. Their cars were thus a part of a luxurious lifestyle built on suffering. The atmosphere of suspicion around those who could afford to buy a car was additionally reinforced by the state itself. For example, tax authorities, as a part of normal practice, examined their documents for potential tax evasions.

The situation after the war reinforced the belief that the car, potentially a tool for the complete transformation of everyday life, was a luxury toy, out of the reach of ordinary people. Although in 1951 the first Warszawas (a licensed version of the Russian GAZ M-20 Pobeda) rolled off the assembly line of the newly built Passenger Car Factory (Fabryka Samochodów Osobowych—FSO) in Warsaw, under Stalinism public transport and commercial vehicles had priority.[11] The climate for individual car ownership changed after 1956. In 1957 production of a microcar (Mikrus, modeled on the German Goggomobil) began, but it stopped in 1960 after just 1,700 units. Also in 1957 the FSO launched its new model: Syrena (the Mermaid, after the coat of arms of the city of Warsaw), smaller and cheaper than the Warszawa.[12] Because both the Warszawa and the Syrena required a lot of manual work, the FSO's total output remained low, exceeding thirty thousand for the first time ever only in 1966.

In September 1957, the Polish government established the Motorization Council as its advisory body. The council consisted of scientists, public officials, managers of state-run motor enterprises, and representatives of the army. As early as 1958 the council voiced an opinion that it was necessary to start manufacturing a popular car and that it would be advisable to base the production on a foreign license. According to this view, the acquisition of a license would make it possible to start mass production within a relatively short time. Growth in the number of individual car owners would enable "saving social time, increasing general effectiveness and opening new opportunities of rest and recreation."[13] Nearly ten years passed before the recommendation of the committee materialized.

The number of motor vehicles grew quite fast in the late 1950s and 1960s. But people were still buying motorcycles rather than cars. Between 1954 and 1964 the total number of motor vehicles rose from 242,000 to 1,752,000, of which, however, only 430,400 were cars and only 211,200 passenger cars.[14] Sales to individual buyers remained low. For example, in 1965 private customers purchased only 34,700 cars and 160,000 motorcycles. The supply of automobiles produced domestically was limited—in 1965 only 11,800 Syrenas and 15,700 Warszawas were produced, of which nearly 6,000 went abroad. Home production was supplemented by official imports from other socialist countries. Private imports (2,300 cars in 1965) did not change the picture significantly.[15]

A car was still too expensive for the average family. In the mid-1960s the Warszawa was priced at 120,000 zloty and the Syrena at 72,000 zloty, an amount equal to average wages for sixty-four and thirty-nine months, respectively. According to a survey from 1965, incomes of families who owned cars were 65 percent higher than the national average. Ninety percent of them already had a TV set and a refrigerator and nearly 100 percent a vacuum cleaner.[16] Buying a car was therefore a decision of those families who already possessed all the modern appliances available at that time and still had some financial reserves. Thus, possessing a private car was popularly regarded as the privilege of those working on construction contracts abroad, receiving large sums of money by inheritance, or lucky enough to win the lottery. The system of sales was simple: one had to pay in advance and wait.

Toward Mass Production and Mass Distribution

Domestic car production increased in the late 1960s. In 1965 Poland signed a licensing contract with Fiat for the 125 model. The first licensed cars rolled off the line in 1967. The FSO manufactured 51,000 Fiats in 1971, 60,000 in 1972, and 117,000 in 1976.[17]

In the late 1960s, the ruling elite still feared the conflict of values between official egalitarianism and the emerging prospects of individual car ownership. The problem of how ordinary people would react to seeing cars in garages of their more prosperous neighbors was still treated seriously. The situation became delicate with the acquisition of the Fiat license, as the Polski Fiat 125p was expensive—initially 180,000 zloty, which equaled roughly the average wages for eighty-five months. In 1971, the price was reduced to 160,000 zloty, which meant that an average Pole still had to work seventy months to buy it. Installment plans did not exist until June 1971. Even then the requirement to make a 30 percent down payment and the limitation of the maximum number of installments to twenty-four meant that cars were available only to relatively few. The reluctance of state authorities to make a 125 model more affordable demonstrates how this medium-sized and medium-priced Western car was *domesticated* in a poorer Eastern European country: it played the role of a cozy limousine. Despite prohibitive prices for Fiats, people still had to wait about half a year to buy them.

The development of the car industry was an element in the program of "intensive and selective economic growth" initiated in the second half of the 1960s by the first secretary of the Polish United Workers' Party, Władysław Gomułka. Decision makers were very much interested in the prospect of exporting cars. Sales in the domestic market should have secured a large profit margin for the state because "[c]ars are bought by a relatively small group of people with high incomes. If the state lowered the price, . . . we would have undoubtedly faced the phenomenon of speculative trade and various [illegal] maneuvers that had been observable many times under similar circumstances."[18] According to the official explanation, the high prices of cars ensured that the state budget rather than private speculators would receive profits that would go "for social purposes, among others to build schools, kindergartens, nurseries."[19]

Therefore, signing the first contract with Fiat did not mean a radical change in the official attitude toward individual car ownership. The government and intellectual elites seemed to believe that the private car would be used primarily for

Sunday trips to the countryside. Distinguishing between the use of cars for necessary (i.e., commercial, public transport) purposes and their use for extra comfort or fun, officials still exhibited a propensity toward favoring public transport and trucking at the expense of individual cars.[20] This created a situation in which mass manufacturing of a popular car was hardly imaginable.

Only with the second Fiat license did this situation change. To start production of a popular car was one of the key promises of the Gierek leadership. The second agreement, signed in 1971 for the 126 model, made possible the erection of a new car factory, namely the Small Engine Car Factory (Fabryka Samochodów Małolitrażowych—FSM) in Bielsko-Biała and Tychy. Within a few years the factory became capable of producing over two hundred thousand units a year. The first half of the 1970s also marks the first large-scale efforts to use cars to promote conformity. Gierek bought harder work in key factories with Fiats that were put on display in front of their gates and ceremonially distributed among their workers.[21] As early as 1967 the liberal journalist Andrzej K. Wróblewski had written, "A car is a child of stabilization. A car owner pays taxes and insurance premiums, he buys petrol and oil. Thus, he has to be a conscientious and efficient worker; he cannot afford any extravagances or fracases on the job."[22] And indeed, this might have been one of the reasons for the shift toward mass motorization.

The Coupon System

In Poland as in other Eastern Bloc countries in the 1970s, car ownership became an indicator of social status. Among the families of unskilled workers, only 2 percent owned a car in 1977, whereas for the families of white-collar employees the figure was 20 percent. Car ownership also closely corresponded to the level of education: only 2 percent of people who had not finished primary school owned cars, in comparison with 29 percent of those with higher education. Finally, those better educated and better-off owned more expensive cars. According to data from 1977, "among engineers and specialists a typical car is the Fiat 125p while among households of manual workers or farmers it is a Syrena or Fiat 126p."[23]

Fiat was to become the brand of socialist affluence in Poland. Retrospectively, the 126, a "small Fiat," is a symbol of Gierek's rule or even of People's Poland as such. Fiat licenses marked the beginning of the "good times" of stability and relative prosperity, for Gierek's decision responded to a deep longing in Polish society that newspaper columnists argued was "almost uniform."[24] Yet in 1977 as many as 42 percent of those who indicated their desire to acquire a car did not believe they would ever be able to purchase one, and another 40 percent thought this would happen in the distant future. Cars were objects dreamed about by many but available to relatively few.[25] In the second half of the 1970s the number of private cars doubled (from 1,041,600 in 1975 to 2,069,400 in 1979), but this did not satisfy all appetites.[26] Poland remained a country with a lot of potential car owners.

The authorities looked for new ways to respond to the desire for cars and concerns about their availability. The beginning of the production of the *maluch* (the toddler, as Poles called the Fiat 126) also meant a new sales system. The price of a 126p was set at the level of 69,000 zloty and announced to the public in 1972, before the first cars were available on the market. This price translated into twenty-five months of average wages, but at the beginning of 1973 the state-owned savings bank, Powszechna Kasa Oszczędności (PKO), started accepting *przedpłaty* (prepayments) for cars to be produced between 1977 and 1980. Within one week nearly 47,000 people opened savings accounts to set aside money to buy a car.[27] For those willing to save, the price was reduced according to the scheme presented in table 2.1. The system created an effective incentive to save. There is little doubt that the aim of channeling liquid assets into savings accounts was to stabilize the market for basic consumer goods. People keeping cash under their mattresses were encouraged to deposit it in savings accounts not only by discounted prices but also by drawings at the end of each year through which those who had paid full price could acquire automobiles without further waiting.

Although the authorities originally intended to accept no more than four hundred thousand prepayments, they allowed the system to expand. In 1981 the PKO opened nearly 1.6 million new savings accounts for both models of Fiats and for Polonezes manufactured in the FSO from 1978. In 1986 it became evident that the system was collapsing. The number of nondelivered cars exceeded 180,000. Payments as compensation to those who had not received preordered automobiles lasted well into the 1990s.

One of the reasons that the government was unable to deliver the promised number of cars to those who were saving for them was an extensive and chaotic system of allocating cars to various ministries, industrial associations, and other administrative bodies. Each of these institutions rewarded its own people with coupons

Table 2.1 "Prepayment" scheme for Fiat 126p

Year of acquisition of car	Advance payment in cash (zl)	Payment in monthly installments (zl)			
		Initial payment	Number of installments	Installment amount	Total
1977	63,740	5,000	47	1,300	66,100
1978	59,520	5,000	59	990	63,410
1979	57,780	5,000	71	810	62,510
1980	56,100	5,000	83	680	61,440

(*talony*) for cars. Despite the reserves created at the central and district levels, institutional players always claimed more cars than planned. They were, naturally, under pressure from below: the longer the delays in deliveries of cars for prepayments, the more attractive the possibility of bypassing the queue with the help of a talon.

Behind-the-Scenes Distribution

A pool of cars to be distributed among individual users was also at the disposal of the Office of the Council of Ministers (Urząd Rady Ministrów—URM). That it was possible to get a talon for a car from the prime minister's office was a public secret, at least among the upper strata of the Polish intelligentsia.[28] For many people, requesting an automobile from URM was their last chance after being denied by their "mother" institution. Allotting cars left few traces in the archives, probably because it was considered a trivial, day-to-day activity. Nevertheless, the records of the Office of the Council of Ministers held in the Archive of Modern Records in Warsaw contain four folders of files regarding allotments of cars to private individuals. Two of them contain petitions written between 1977 and 1980 to Janusz Wieczorek, chief of the Office of the Council of Ministers.[29]

Janusz Wieczorek remained in office for nearly twenty-five years, serving from August 1956 until his retirement in November 1980.[30] Although not a constitutional minister, he held the title of minister and participated in formal cabinet meetings. In the late 1960s the government met relatively rarely (six to eight times a year). In the early 1970s, during the first years after the change in power, the Council of Ministers convened twenty to twenty-two times a year, but as time passed the old pattern reappeared: the cabinet assembled in plenary session not more often than once a month. Thus, many important administrative decisions were delegated to the government presidium, a body composed of the prime minister, his deputies, and only a few of the ministers. Wieczorek also participated in this close decision-making circle.[31] His influence on real politics was thus greater than his formal position indicated.

The Office of the Council of Ministers prepared analyses and reports necessary for making governmental decisions. Its lawyers were responsible for drafting the government's rulings and legal acts to be sent to parliament. However, within the centralized political system, the office was more than an administrative unit subordinate to the council. It supervised various branches of local administration. The limits of its authority were vague, as its jurisdiction was not regulated by any legal act. For the same reason, although from a formal point of view the head of the office did not have any powers to make decisions in individual cases, the reality was completely different.

What has survived in the archive are documents from eighty-five petitioners, which surely represent just a small fraction of the original material. Wieczorek must have received a large number of requests for cars, although we do not know how many. We do not know either why these particular letters were preserved. Sixty-six of them went into the first and the remaining nineteen into the second folder. Fifty-nine were written by men and twenty-six by women. We can be sure that all requests that wound up in the second folder were denied. Among those in the first folder, twenty-nine received positive responses, and one was postponed to the next year. The fate of the remaining thirty-six cannot be determined beyond all doubt, although there are indications that they also were accepted.

Asking for a car was an individual initiative of the petitioners, but they also often submitted supporting letters from their place of work or a social organization in which they were active. No traces of any formal procedure for dealing with requests have survived. Sometimes those enfranchised simply confirmed the receipt of a coupon with a handwritten note on the original of their request, meaning they had been summoned to the office. Negative responses were sent within a few days, sometimes a few weeks from the receipt of a request. They were laconic and contained the following lie: "During the current year the Office of the Council of Ministers does not have any coupons at its disposal." Positive answers were sometimes communicated within a day but also after as long as nine months. Publicly known personalities could count on being contacted by phone.

Authors of petitions belonged to several distinct groups. Table 2.2 shows their professions. The most numerous were people working in the Office of the Council of Ministers. The specific feature of this group is that officials were outnumbered by those in auxiliary positions—technical staff and service personnel: plumbers, chauffeurs, or chambermaids from hotels for government members. People in low positions but with direct personal contact with those in authority could count on allocations. This conclusion can be supported by the data on military personnel: those who received coupons were officers or noncommissioned officers protecting government members or serving in the units guarding government premises.

Between 1960 and 1981 Wieczorek was the chairman of the Committee for Protecting Monuments of Struggle and Martyrdom (Rada Ochrony Pomników Walki i Męczeństwa), a government-sponsored organization responsible for memorial sites, cemeteries for war victims, and commemorative celebrations. He was also the deputy chairman of the official veteran organization, the Society of Fighters for Freedom and Democracy (Związek Bojowników o Wolność I Demokrację—ZBOWiD). That is why many of those who asked for cars were veterans. Many people who were still professionally active also cited their activities in the veterans' movement as an additional argument supporting their request for a car.

Table 2.2 Petitioners by occupation

Occupation	Number of petitioners
Artists and journalists	14
Employees of the Office of the Council of Ministers	28
Employees of other government bodies	2
Military personnel	6
War veterans	6
Managers	12
Engineers, doctors, and specialists	9
Scientists	5
Others	3
Total	85

Wieczorek was also the head of the Social Committee for Constructing the Monument-Hospital Center for Children's Health. The center was a large, top-flight pediatric clinic on the outskirts of Warsaw established to commemorate children who had lost their lives during World War II. The construction started in 1973. Outpatient units opened in 1977 and the hospital in 1979. The project was partly financed through public donations. The committee headed by Wieczorek raised funds for the facility and supervised its development. Doctors or specialists working on the construction of the center also figure among those asking Wieczorek for cars.

Cars requested most frequently (table 2.3)—small Fiats and Ladas—situated themselves on opposite sides of the prestige and price axis. They were asked for by people from distinctly different groups. Employees of the Office of the Council of Ministers (especially those in low positions), retired veterans, scientists, and specialists opted for smaller cars, often the Fiat 126 or a Zaporozhets. Actors, TV personalities, and managers tended toward bigger and more expensive ones, especially Ladas.

For the purpose of preparing table 2.3, if a letter writer listed a few makes of car in the same letter, I counted only the first one mentioned, assuming that the order of cars reflected the petitioner's preferences. One has to remember that lists of more than one car were not exceptional (there are twenty-seven in my material). People asking for Ladas wanted to be especially delicate. In their own mind they were asking for a luxury car. Therefore they were more apt than anybody else to suggest an alternative: if the Lada was not available, they were ready to settle for the Fiat 125, Polonez, Wartburg, or Zastava. Even taking this complication into

Table 2.3 Automobile preferences

Type of car	Number of requests
Polish Fiat 126p	18
Polish Fiat 125p	9
Polonez	3
Skoda	6
Lada	17
Zastava	10
Wartburg	5
Trabant	1
Zaporozhets	7
Fiat 128	1
Unspecified	8
Total	85

consideration, one can draw the general conclusion that foreign cars were asked for more frequently than those manufactured domestically. If we include Zastava and Fiat 128 in the foreign category (ignoring the fact that at a limited scale they were also assembled in Poland), the proportion is thirty domestic to forty-seven imported vehicles. People writing to Wieczorek looked for cars that were harder to obtain by regular means.

Substantiations of the requests for cars usually included remarks on the importance of the professional activity of the petitioner. Those in managerial positions in industry often made elaborate references to modern technology in their enterprises. A manager from a printing house in Warsaw argued, "I am a head of a newly established division of photosetting. The division I manage composes books and journals with the use of computer technology, working in a multishift system. Keeping the schedule of work and solving complicated technical problems require frequent professional consultations and interventions. It makes it necessary to be able to come to the workplace at any time."[32] References to modern technologies are not accidental. They reflect the official language of that time. The media and official speeches were creating the picture of the great transformation taking place in Poland. Allegedly, the country was overcoming once and for all the heritage of multicentury backwardness. Technocratic managers of newly built industrial enterprises were presented—and represented themselves—as role models rather than as political loyalists. The same was true with artists and scientists. It was the creative character of their work, not political matters, that made them eligible for cars. But this might not be enough. Petitioners looked for further arguments that could positively differentiate them from potential rivals. Therefore, they strongly emphasized their professional ties to organizations they believed were closest to Wieczorek's heart. That is why one of the authors felt obliged to underscore that "[d]uring my twenty-three years of work in the publishing house I was technical editor of nearly all the publications of the Committee for Protecting Monuments of Struggle and Martyrdom."[33]

To make their argument stronger, many petitioners combined descriptions of their professional work with information on membership in social organizations. This was to show they were close to the officially propagated ideal of citizenship. They demonstrated their eagerness to participate in "Gierek's great consensus," which allowed Poles of various convictions, guided by the Party, to work actively on the creation of a modern state. Several petitioners explicitly referred to their political activity to advance their cause. One of them declared, "From my earliest years I have been an activist in the revolutionary movement." He reported on his membership in the Communist Party of Poland before the war and a prison term he served[34] and then about yet another arrest and his years of detention between 1949 and 1955 that he attributed in his letter to "mistakes and distortions of Beriaism."[35]

Some of the writers took the opportunity to tell their life story. They usually stressed hardships they went through, very often including the horrors of World War II. One wrote, "During the Occupation, for my political activity, I was put in the Auschwitz Death Camp, where the Nazis conducted pseudomedical experiments on me. I am an invalid. . . . I escaped from Auschwitz and hid in forests for eight months."[36] Those who used their sufferings from the past as a major argument for a car usually built their stories around easily recognizable symbols of oppression. Communists with long Party membership wrote about Bereza Kartuska, a labor camp for political prisoners in interwar Poland, while others mentioned Pawiak—a political prison under the Nazi occupation—or concentration camps.

For some of the authors the life stories were narratives of strenuous struggle against disease or disability to conduct an active and productive life. Social integration of the disabled was not an issue attracting wide attention in the 1970s. Professional activity of people with special needs was by no means the norm. State policy leaned toward offering them less than modest pensions or, at best, some simple jobs. That is probably why an author from Krakow who asked for a car for his deaf-mute daughter found it necessary to assure Wieczorek that people with such a disability were capable of driving a car.[37]

In general, complaints about poor health are not rare in letters to Wieczorek (thirteen of eighty-five authors mention them). Syndromes impairing the ability to walk appeared most frequently. Apparently the authors believed that mentioning an illness of this kind would bring them closer to their coupon. In her request for a Wartburg, a translator from Warsaw who suffered from bone tuberculosis, after describing her surgeries, continued, "Limited ability to move and ensuing dependence on the help of family members significantly narrows my possibilities to live normally, to actively participate in society.... Car ownership will enable me to start active rehabilitation. Furthermore, it will allow me to pursue my professional career, which is my deep desire."[38]

Much space in the letters is also devoted to other personal problems of the petitioners, described as central to them but unsolvable without a car, like taking care of elderly parents living far away, transporting children to school, coping with the double burden of professional activity and household work, and keeping in touch with relatives. Requesters described themselves as hardworking people without sufficient financial resources to buy an automobile on the secondhand market or for hard currency.

To maximize their chances of succeeding, they depicted themselves as completely powerless to solve these problems. To emphasize the magnitude of their difficulties they used the language of submission ("I bear a humble request"; "I dare hope that Citizen Minister will deign to look favorably at my request") and helplessness ("You are my only hope, Minister").[39] Sometimes they described at length other attempts to get a coupon that had ended unsuccessfully and recollected or alluded to personal meetings with Wieczorek. Many petitioners listed orders they were awarded to show they had more rights to a coupon than other people. They also wrote extensively about the moral satisfaction they would derive from such a sign of appreciation, about how important a car was for them from a psychological standpoint and how deep their gratitude would be if they received one.[40]

Petitioners who already owned a car (there are at least twenty-four of them in my material) felt compelled to explain why they were asking for a new vehicle. They stressed objective reasons such as old age and wear and tear on their car ("The car I've owned since 1964 is in such bad technical condition that I was unable to extend its registration because of the hazard it poses to road safety").[41] As a rule, they swore that their application for a new car was not the result of the careless use of the old one. For example, "due to the lack of garage, despite paint protection, the Fiat 126, for which I received a coupon from You, Minister, in 1975, was destroyed by corrosion."[42] In this way authors signaled their awareness that their property rights to an object granted by a decision of a state official were not unlimited.

On the other hand, the letters confirm their authors' conviction of their entitlement to certain comforts of life. They (rightly) felt that to admit they had become accustomed to driving a car (or a certain make) would not undermine their chances to receive a coupon. "From 1957 I have always had a car with only short breaks," wrote a film director.[43] Another petitioner simply wrote, "Due to the fact that I got used to driving a Wartburg, I would prefer to stay with this make."[44]

Many petitioners believed they also could legitimately explain their request for a car with aspirations to spend their free time more comfortably. The most common explanation of this type related to a garden allotment outside the city, but more elite leisure activities also appear in the requests. A public official who asked for a Lada or Polonez argued, "I have a family of five, I am a yachter and I badly need a car of this class to be able to haul a trailer with a boat."[45]

THE second batch of requests from the 1980s is more homogeneous. It is composed of 131 requests written between 1983 and 1985.[46] All the petitioners are trade union activists. For union activists this was a special time for creating new union organizations, as in October 1982 all preexisting unions were dissolved. From the official perspective, revitalizing unions was an important sign of the return to normalcy after the period of martial law (introduced in December 1981, suspended in December 1982, and finally lifted in July 1983).

The majority of people who applied for cars in 1983–85 were salaried, employees of the trade union apparatus, usually at the level of a federation (association of unions from a given industry) or the District Alliance of Trade Unions. Petitions were addressed to Stanisław Ciosek, Paweł Chocholak, or Piotr Karpiuk. Ciosek at that time was the minister of labor and the minister for trade union affairs and from 1986 was also a member of the Politburo. Chocholak was the head of the Bureau for Cooperation with Trade Unions in the Office of the Council of Ministers, and Karpiuk chaired the Commission for the Management of Trade Union Assets, established after union activity had been suspended during martial law. As with the earlier petitions, we do not know why this particular set of documents survived in the archive.

The procedure of allotting cars in the 1980s was more formalized, which has to be interpreted as a legacy of 1980–81, when subjective distribution of automobiles came under severe criticism. In addition to writing a request, all petitioners had to fill in a special form with questions regarding their car ownership status. If they had previously possessed a car, they were supposed to write when and how they had bought it. They also were required to state that none of their direct family members owned a car. If the petitioner was saving for a car, he or she was supposed to produce a certificate from a bank confirming either the liquidation of the savings account or the extension of the saving period by at least four years. If no driving license could be produced, one had to promise to pass a driving test within a given period of time. The petitioner was warned that false statements were punishable by law.

In reality, those caught on some inconsistencies had to write additional explanatory notes, but they were not brought to courts.[47] Moreover, they usually received their coupons, although with some delay. In addition, those who failed the driving test could count on tolerance. The rule that a citizen was entitled to a new car not more often than once in four years was obeyed. I found only one case of noncompliance, but this concerned a person whose car had been stolen. The decision was made personally by Deputy Prime Minister Mieczysław Rakowski. This is not to say there was no room for informal influences. Some documents contain hand notes by URM officials such as "I promised him [a coupon]"; this indicates that independently of all formalities it was still possible to secure an allotment through personal contacts.[48]

The decision-making process was protracted. Many requests were fulfilled only after a year or even a year and a half.[49] That is why direct interventions by Alfred Miodowicz, the head of the All-Poland Alliance of Trade Unions (Ogólnopolskie Porozumienie Związków Zawodowych—OPZZ), were not uncommon. Unlike those in the earlier period, the cars allotted were almost exclusively the Fiat 125 (FSO 1500), the Fiat 126, and Wartburgs. Only two were Ladas, and they went to high officials: Commissioner Karpiuk himself and Jerzy Uziębło, deputy head of the OPZZ. This is a sign of economic crisis. The petitioners usually substantiated their requests by pointing to their long careers in the trade union apparatus or in other political organizations.[50] They emphasized their role in organizing new unions after martial law. Some even claimed they had risked their lives confronting Solidarity during the period of strikes and social protests in 1980–81. They wrote about their social activism and promised to use their cars in their union activity. The poetics of their letters reflect the political conflicts of that period.[51] For those union activists who were not paid, car assignments constituted a form of remuneration. As in the previous period, people who were about to retire wanted to see a coupon as a reward for a long professional career.[52]

In the 1970s Poland passed the threshold of mass car production. But cars were still scarce, and pressure on the official distribution system made it unreliable. Under such circumstances we can see a high official, Janusz Wieczorek, playing the role of a benevolent father. The recipients of his favors were people who could be useful to him in one of his many roles: for example, as a supervisor of the construction of the children's hospital or as head of the Committee for Protecting Monuments of Struggle and Martyrdom. He also showed benevolence toward URM personnel, which could simply have facilitated his everyday work. These favors were granted on the basis of direct face-to-face contacts, although people with no direct access to him could also count on a coupon.

The introduction of the formal regulations regarding car allotments and the bureaucratization of the process in the 1980s were intended to limit arbitrary decisions. In reality, the institutionalization of the decision-making process was fictional. Officials from the URM were still unconstrained in choosing who would receive their favors. The logic behind the distribution differed from that of the 1970s; it no longer had to do with building a private clientele but rather with mobilizing union activists in a difficult moment. In the 1970s a car could become compensation for personal sufferings or an award for creativity and technical and managerial skills. In the 1980s it was a prize for loyalty to and activism in a movement that was highly unpopular but important from the point of view of the state.

Polish historians have stressed the analogies between supplications made by peasants to their feudal masters and those written by the citizens of People's Poland to the authorities. Both cases contained a mixture of requests and grievances. Their authors humbled themselves before their masters and declared trust in them. The notion of supplication has been used most commonly to refer to Stalinist times.[53] Archival material shows, however, that in later decades the citizen assumed a similar pose in relations with an omnipotent, paternalistic official world. Letters to the URM should be analyzed as social facts. They were written and sent in this form and not in any other. It is true that their authors assumed a certain convention of writing. We will never know to what extent they truly were helpless and to what extent they only pretended helplessness to achieve their goals. But they did not assume the convention accidentally. Petitioners bowed before their master and appealed to his benevolence because they believed they had to. This behavior tells a lot about the nature of power.

The images found in petitions of an everyday life transformed into a problem-free existence thanks to a private car also are not accidental. They resemble images from before the war. Social consciousness evolved more slowly than material reality.

The distinctive feature of the paternalistic relations described above was that the lucky recipients never assumed full property rights to the object of desire they received. It was the benefactor who decided the boundaries of legitimate use. If the boundaries were crossed, the next request for a privilege could be denied. The state distributing cars among its subjects wanted to achieve many contradictory goals at the same time: to remove excess money from the market, to create an everyman car, to generate a strong incentive for work, to reward those politically loyal, and to earn dollars on car exports. As a result, it lost control over the distribution system that its agents at least partially privatized as they played their own games.

3

ALTERNATIVE MODERNITY?
Everyday Practices of Elite Mobility
in Communist Hungary, 1956–1980

György Péteri

This chapter addresses the failure of the state socialist social order to assert its systemic exceptionalism (a pattern of development distinguishing socialism from capitalism) in the field of modern mobility.[1] The Hungarian experience was that the infrastructure serving collective transportation and the latter's contribution to the aggregate performance of personal transport failed to keep pace with the explosion, from the end of the 1950s onward, in the growth of personal car ownership and the increasing role of private (individual) car-based mobility. In other words, the Khrushchevian ideas about the socialist use of personal cars did not fall on particularly fertile ground in Hungary. As in most other discourses reinforcing the self-understanding of the state socialist social order, at the core of these ideas was the wish (and claim) to assert economic rationality at the aggregate social level as opposed to the principle of private ownership. They emphasized not merely the collective means of transportation but, more important, the *collective use* of personal cars in the form of taxi and rental services offered by public (state-owned and/or cooperative) companies. Khrushchev's idea for the use of personal cars was nothing less than a gigantic system of car sharing that encompassed the whole nation. The understanding was that in this way all legitimate needs for individual mobility could be catered to at a much higher level of socioeconomic efficiency (fewer cars and a considerably lower level of car density) than in the capitalist regime of privately owned and used personal cars. As Khrushchev told a Western audience in the spring of 1960, "For us, the capitalist, private ownership-based use of the car is a path to be avoided. We will provide [for] our population in a socialist manner."[2]

Significantly, even while Khrushchev was in power, the reception of these ideas in Hungary amounted to what could best be described as repressive silence. Several

Soviet works propagating these ideas were translated and printed in Hungarian,[3] but Khrushchev's design for a Socialist Car was never discussed anywhere, either in the Marxist-Leninist ideological and agitprop literature or in the more professionally oriented discourses of economic and social planning. The first and only time it was actually considered, only to be summarily discarded, was in an essay inspired by the late-coming conservative Communist reaction to the consumerism unleashed during the 1960s. The argument against Khrushchev's suggestions stressed the need to maintain effective incentives motivating people to work—socialism (a social formation characterized as "no longer capitalism but not yet Communism") had to tolerate and accept inequalities in incomes and fortunes in order to achieve dynamic economic development. But these inequalities could not have the desired stimulating effects as long as those who had deservedly high incomes were unable to "wield their purchasing power" to buy cars, villas, and other trappings of wealth.[4]

This reasoning needs to be taken seriously because it reveals some aspects of the dilemma that Communist modernizing elites had to confront after Stalin: if to propel further development, individual performance and achievement were to decide one's social and economic position in a not-yet-Communist social order, how could they make sure that this development was not toward "capitalist modernity" but toward *socialist modernity*? If the socialist mode of consumption was characteristically collectivist and the bourgeois mode was individualist,[5] what were the chances that a socialist mode of consumption could survive under socialism if the desires of consumers with "large volumes of purchasing power" steered development toward individualist rather than collectivist patterns?

At the end of 1957, the total number of personal cars in Hungary was less than 13,000. Fewer than a third of these cars (3,980) were owned by private individuals. By 1970, the total stock of personal cars in the country had grown to almost 240,000, with an overwhelming share (over 89%) consisting of privately owned cars. Ten years later the share of privately owned cars was close to 97 percent within a total stock of over one million personal cars.[6] At the beginning of the short quarter of a century covered by this chapter, alternative paths to develop modern mobility could still have been considered and asserted by central planners. In 1960 the density of personal cars (number of cars per thousand inhabitants) was three in Hungary—forty times less than in France, thirty-three times less than in Britain, and eleven times less than in Italy.[7] Modernity as "motorization" via the growth of the number of personal cars in private hands was still only a distant possibility and not a necessity. With this background in mind, Khrushchev's idea does not strike one as at all untimely. In fact, it could not have come at a better time: it came when an alternative, distinctly *socialist* form of motorization—one that emphasized collective transportation yet met the demands for individual mobility through well-developed services rendered by taxi and rental companies instead of privately owned cars—could rightly be regarded as feasible. By the 1970s and 1980s, however, the inertia of mass automobilism had grown overwhelming. In the 1960s personal cars constituted the fastest-growing sector of personal transportation, and their share in the total of personal transport grew from a mere 4.3 percent in 1950 (and even less in 1960) to more than 26 percent by 1972.

In what follows I will try to find an explanation for the failure of the socialist mode of consumption to assert itself in the field of personal transportation in Communist Hungary between 1957 and 1981. I will do so by taking a close look at the everyday practices of mobility in what constituted the core of the Communist political class: the members of the salaried apparatus of the Hungarian Socialist Workers' Party (HSWP), from the level of district committees up to the "White House" of Jászai Mari Square (the Party headquarters where the apparatus of the Central Committee had its offices). Everyday practices in social elites tend to assert themselves not only as normative criteria for policymakers (themselves a significant part of the social elites in state socialism) but also as the single most important source of inspiration for the rest of society. There may be tensions, even antagonisms, between higher strata of the middle classes and the rest of society, but the former's preferences, tastes, and ideas about the good life, manifest in their everyday practices, never fail to impress the latter. Studying them can help us explain the emergence and consolidation of particular patterns of consumption under state socialism.

Sneaking Privatization and Attempts at Its Containment

One of the early reports about the matter of mobility in the apparatus is the August 29, 1957, resolution of the Central Committee Secretariat "on certain issues of Party economic work." The resolution mentioned as a problem not only that the "counterrevolution" of 1956 had decimated the means of transport at the Party organizations' disposal but also that the Party's cars (as well as its motorbikes and bikes) were being used for private purposes.[8]

Indeed, the illegitimate use of the Party's cars for private purposes—a "sneaking privatization" of the mobility attainable by cars although not car ownership itself—proved to have been a persistent feature of the whole history of the HSWP apparatus. Throughout our period the apparatus trying to maximize its private possession and use of the Party's cars was engaged in a tug of war with the Party's regulatory and disciplining authorities—the Department of Party-Economic and Administrative Management (Pártgazdasági és Ügykezelési Osztály—PGO), the

Central Committee of Revision, and the Central Control Committee—which tried to confine this urge to privatize. Resolute as it was in exercising its counterrevolutionary terror, the HSWP leadership made serious attempts from early on to distance itself from the prerevolutionary Stalinist regime of Mátyás Rákosi. One rather understudied aspect of these efforts was János Kádár's policies to assert and consolidate what he called "socialist legality" (*szocialista törvényesség*)—a Communist idea of the *Rechtsstaat*, a rule-of-law principle that was intended to be imposed not, of course, to bring the Communist party-state under democratic control but to discipline the various apparatuses of this party-state and force them to obey their own laws and norms defining the borderlines between legal and illegal, legitimate and illegitimate, moral and immoral. As a regime disciplining its own elites, Kádárism could not (and did not want to) prevent the members of these elites from promoting their own private interests, but it did want to keep the tendency to assert elite self-interests within confines so as to prevent it from generating social tensions and conflict.

At a meeting held by the PGO with its county department chiefs in May 1957, the economic department chief of the Veszprém County committee put the blame for the apparatchiks' illegitimate use of cars (and motorbikes) on the central decision that had canceled earlier regulations allowing, within limits, the use of Party cars for personal purposes. He was emphatic about his department's embarrassing predicament in its relation to the rest of the county apparatus, partly because it had to introduce unpopular measures against "lax work discipline" and "against the unnecessary use of cars [*megszüntették a felesleges kocsizást*]."[9]

The PGO in Budapest started early in its attempts to stem an escalation of malpractice in the use of cars. With reference to a government decree from February 1957 regulating the use of state-owned trucks for employees' private purposes at industrial firms, the PGO accepted that, in cases of extraordinary need (major family events, emergency situations, etc.), employees in the Party apparatus might use a Party car under the condition that they paid a cost price (1.50 forints per kilometer) for it. It also emphasized that access to the Party's cars absolutely depended on the Party work to be done and that private use of cars must not be seen by any functionaries within the apparatus as a benefit due to them.[10] According to a speech by the PGO's department chief, Pálné Laczkó, the abolition (very soon to be annulled!) of private use of cars as a due was one of several measures abolishing privileges enjoyed by members of the Party apparatus during the Rákosi era.[11] Significantly, she asked for the apparatus's understanding with reference to the Party's precarious position in post-1956 Hungarian society, and she almost explicitly promised to relax the restrictions as soon as the general economic and social situation had improved enough to allow people to become less attentive toward the privileges of the apparatus. Yet, she emphasized, "the essence of the issue is that party workers, descendants of professional revolutionaries, should live in a modest manner.... We should not allow the living conditions of the apparatus to be turned, yet another time, into counterrevolutionary demagoguery through misrepresentations."[12]

Even though the speech showed Laczkó's (and the higher Party leaders') pragmatic understanding of socialist legality, the heirs to professional revolutionaries did not regard living modestly, even in the short term, as an agreeable occupation. As Laczkó herself noted in another section of her speech, "Some members of the apparatus frequently use [the available means of transport] as their private property, i.e., they regularly travel with them even when not on official trips."[13] At a meeting of her own department half a year later, she explained what complicated her department's efforts to impose greater modesty on the apparatchik class: "It has been raised that we should be more modest. When it comes to providing the leaders, [however], no modesty is in sight."[14] A year later, in front of the national meeting of county committee economic chiefs,

> [s]he raised as a sensitive issue car use and listed a number of particularly bad examples. She said that, for example, in Bács County [members of the apparatus] had no access to cars for many work-related purposes, while cars were readily available for the county secretary, the second secretary, and the department chiefs when these decided to go hunting.... The situation is not better in Miskolc [Borsod County] either.[15]

Laczkó encouraged the county department chiefs to stand up against the "county secretary comrades" and tell them "they are entitled to private car use, but [it is limited to] 500 kilometers a month, and the limits of the maximum monthly work load [310 hours] of the chauffeurs must be respected." She then lashed out against those county secretaries who used 1,500 kilometers monthly for their private needs, covering up the illegitimate use by developing a logrolling relationship with their chauffeurs. In her intervention at the meeting she also referred to mounting pressure on her department from comrades who wished to use the Party's cars to learn to drive and was particularly irritated by the fact that even economic chiefs of county committees approached the PGO with such wishes on their own behalf. "You should forget about this, we will never permit this, and [we won't allow it] particularly for economic department chiefs—[for, if we yielded to them] how are they supposed to resist such demands from the rest of the apparatus [?]"[16]

In a report from October 6, 1958, Laczkó summarized the experience of PGO inspections carried out in the provinces in the following manner:

> Party employees often take advantage of the cars, even though they have no permission and they don't pay for the use of the cars. This kind of use springs simply out

of irresponsible love of comfort and the seeking of individual material advantage. According to our experience, in the cases of this kind of private use, it is not only party employees but also their relatives and other people not employed by the party who exploit the cars. According to our inspection of waybills of cars belonging to Bács-Kiskun's county and district Party committees, since last December, more than five thousand kilometers have been used for private purposes.[17]

This PGO report is one of many instances where the unholy alliance between party employees and chauffeurs in "joint drinking parties, the use of cars for private purposes, and breaches against traffic rules" were mentioned and criticized.

As early as mid-1958, the tendency of sneaking privatization of automobility offered by party cars had become manifest in transgressions of the HSWP's annual budget. A report from September 1958 noted that in sixteen out of the eighteen counties the limits of expenditure on cars stipulated in the annual budget had been exceeded. The PGO complained not only about the uneconomic, uncoordinated use of cars but also about the "encroaching illegitimate private use of cars" without the users paying for the costs. It also insisted on eliminating the excess spending by "frugal economic management and by bringing an end to private traveling [with the Party's cars]."[18]

The most common way of appropriating the Party cars for private needs seems to have been the manipulation of waybills set up for each trip made by the car. These documents were expected to clearly state the point and time of departure, the route, and the target station and arrival time of each trip; to identify all passengers by name; to reveal the exact distance covered; and to carry other official notices (e.g., permissions if required for the trip) that legitimized the use of the car. Meant to make chauffeurs' as well as Party workers' traveling accountable, waybills were easy prey to a broad scale of manipulation. Sometimes the setting up of a waybill for a trip would simply be skipped; on other occasions a Party boss might grant confirmation to cover up the chauffeur's private detours. The chauffeur would then willingly set up waybills about "official trips" that served the private needs of the boss and his family. In 1961 the PGO systematically scrutinized the waybills produced in the first ten months of the year by the Central Committee apparatus in Budapest. It found three "problematic" categories: (1) the ones that provided insufficient detail to reveal the actual destination or objective of the trip; (2) those that provided enough detail for one to surmise (but not prove) that the trips were made for private purposes; and (3) those in which "private use" had been explicitly mentioned but not in connection with the legitimate contingent available for private use by the functionary in question. The report includes a list of thirty-one functionaries whose trips, totaling 25,656 kilometers, fell into these dubious categories. During the same ten-month period, the *legitimate* private use of cars amounted to a mere 3,245 kilometers in the Central Committee apparatus as a whole.[19] Another memo of the PGO from 1960 concerning the use of cars at the Central Committee and its various organs added that it had been impossible to control the proper use of even the legitimate contingents available for private purposes (6,000 and 3,000 kilometers per annum in the case of Central Committee department chiefs and their deputies, respectively). The reason was that "the comrades fail to indicate 'private use' on the waybill, and one can only infer from the timing and indicated objective of the trip [that it served private purposes]."[20] The author of a report from a 1967 inspection of the central Party garage stressed how hard it was to draw the line, on the basis of waybills, between legitimate and illegitimate car use. Yet his description of what he found leaves no doubt that he too had to contend with sneaking privatization:

> The waybills don't always make it possible to see . . . whether or not the car use had been legitimate. [However], when the [biweekly] shifts of holiday makers take place [in the summer months] at the Balaton Lake, some seventy to a hundred Party cars converge on the major holiday resorts. Personal use and official trips mingle. A majority of workplaces do not keep records of the actual use of contingents available for private purposes.[21]

In other words, the comrades tended to use preprinted waybills intended for official work-related trips and not for trips that should have been made at their own expense. Thus, seeming modesty about exploiting formal entitlements to private use went hand in hand with extravagance when it came to making private trips under official pretexts.

From systematic study of the PGO documents it is quite clear that the tendency toward private appropriation of automobility by members of the apparatus was present throughout the period this chapter covers. I have found 120 documents either citing individual cases or summarizing the experience gained in the course of inspections of national, county, and district HSWP organizations. Observations of improper administration (by drivers and passengers) of waybills persisted throughout,[22] and there are good reasons to believe that suspicious waybills hardly indicated more than the tip of the iceberg when it came to the actual dimensions of the sneaking privatization of automobility. Symbiotic relations between Party bosses and chauffeurs[23] and careful coordination of official trips with private needs were effective means to cover up what actually was going on.

The Party's internal economic management had a real problem here. On the one hand, the attachment and loyalty of the apparatchiks to their Party was certainly affected by the accessibility of various perks and material privileges. On the other hand, many of these privileges were secured at substantial financial (and moral) cost to the Party, and the proliferation of semilegitimate or entirely illegitimate practices in resource use constituted a leakage in the Party budget, threatening the Party's economic stability as well as the legitimacy of its power. The costs of securing the apparatus's automobility tended to figure among the highest single items of expenditures. In 1968, 25.7 million forints (Fts) were spent on car costs in the whole apparatus of HSWP—more than 18 percent of the total expenditure.[24] In 1971 the apparatus operated 873 personal cars with total costs related to automobility amounting to more than 85 million Fts, including investments and costs of infrastructure (repair shops, garages, etc.). In the same year, the legitimate entitlements to private use of cars at the apparatus's disposal amounted to 396,000 kilometers.[25] Assuming a multiplier of 5.75 Fts/km,[26] the total value of these entitlements granted by the Party to its higher-level apparatchiks was 2.28 million Fts. The total of current operating costs of personal cars for the whole Party apparatus was 13 million Fts in 1972.[27] Therefore, we can assume that the formally sanctioned annual entitlements to private car use amounted to about 18 percent of total personal car costs. If we now assume that the extent of irregular use of Party cars for private purposes reached at least the level of the total of regular entitlements for private use,[28] we will understand the feeling of urgency with which the Party's internal economic management and the higher leadership tried to contain the sneaking privatization of automobility in the Party apparatus. Moreover, the costs of operating a large stable of personal cars proved not merely high but rather hard to control. For the year 1971, the gap between the planned and actual costs of the apparatus's automobility increased to an alarming extent (see table 3.1). Therefore, the ambition to contain sneaking privatization went hand in hand with the desire to tame and establish control over the dynamics of mobility costs.

Containment by Yielding: Legitimate Private Appropriation

One of the reactions from the regulators was to try to contain the tendency we have discussed above by yielding and at the same time setting limits. Only

Table 3.1 Mileage performed and costs incurred by the use of Party cars, 1971

	Mileage (km)	Unit cost (forints/km)	Total cost (forints)	Growth from previous year
Planned	2,200,000	4.92	10,830,000	—
Actual	2,563,146	5.6	14,250,190	141.3%
Actual as percentage of planned	116.5	113.0	131.6	—

Source: Hungarian National Archives (MOL) 288. f. 37/1971, 2. öe., fols. 30, 50.

for a very short period did the requirement of modesty lead to the cessation of legitimate entitlements to use Party cars for private purposes. Indeed, the regulations suggested by the PGO in July 1957 made no secret of the prevalent understanding according to which the private use of cars, for those above a certain level in the apparatus, should be an entitlement rather than an illegitimate practice. These rules, modifying the resolution of the Organizing Committee of the HSWP from February 20 1957,[29] distinguished among three categories of cars: (1) allowance (*járandósági*) cars, (2) personal use (*személyi használatú*) cars, and (3) official (*szolgálati*) cars.[30] The last category constituted the largest number, to be used exclusively for official trips by the great majority of rank-and-file apparatus members with no special privileges to use the cars for private purposes. Allowance cars were tied to the top of the apparatus elite: members and candidate members of the Political Bureau, Central Committee secretaries, and the first secretary of the Budapest Party Committee. They each had a car (and a reserve car) at their disposal with chauffeur and right to unlimited private use—the car and the driver were at their disposal day and night, including the weekends. Personal use was the entitlement of the chiefs of the Central Committee departments, the secretaries of the Budapest Party Committee, the first secretary of the Communist Youth Association, the head of the editorial board of the Party daily, *Népszabadság*, and the first secretaries of the county Party committees. Those entitled to personal use disposed of cars for private purposes up to the limit of six thousand kilometers annually—deputy chiefs of the Central Committee's departments had personal use up to three thousand kilometers.

In 1964 these entitlements were complemented with the right to make trips abroad paid for out of the officials' allowances. Approximately 160 to 180 high-status members of the apparatus were affected by this measure. For the chairmen of the Central Control Committee, the Central Committee of Revision, department chiefs of the Central Committee apparatus, directors of the Party Higher School and the Institute of Party History, and select others, the extension of their entitlement included disposal over the car together with a chauffeur. For the lower-level apparatus members, foreign travel was now permitted upon the condition that they had drivers' licenses and drove the cars themselves.[31]

The economic significance of the personal use entitlements for the Party budget as well as for the beneficiaries themselves is clearly shown by a statistical compilation summarizing "above-the-salary social benefits" in the Central Committee apparatus for 1964.[32] Among these benefits, the costs of personal use cars were the third-largest item (after subventions paid to kindergartens and holidays): they amounted to 0.5 million out of a total of 2.5 million Fts (over 20%). As a share of the total automobility-related costs of the Central Committee apparatus for 1964,[33] the costs of personal use were slightly above 7 percent. Seen from the beneficiaries' point of view, personal use cars constituted the second most important benefit in terms of annual cost-value per recipient. Subvention of kindergartens added 33,526 Fts per capita to the private economy of the recipients; personal use cars put an average of 12,214 Fts into each beneficiary's pocket, the approximate equivalent of two months' salary.

Surging costs of a sizable stable of personal cars owned and operated by the Party-state had forced the country's top political leadership by the early 1970s to reassess regulations. In accordance with a Political Bureau resolution of March 7, 1972, the Council of Ministers acted swiftly and introduced government decree 14/1972/IV. 22/Korm. sz., to become effective from July 1, 1972.[34] The objectives of the decree were (1) to restrict the personal (private) use of public cars, (2) to contain the growth of (and even to reduce) the number of public cars, (3) to achieve an efficient use of cars and chauffeurs in the public sector, and (4) to encourage the use of private cars in the service of the state.

The HSWP followed suit, and the Secretariat of the Central Committee adopted a resolution on July 7, 1972, that was modeled by and large on the government decree.[35] Like the government decree, the resolution modified the previous regime of entitlements, aiming to reduce the total mileage available for personal use from 396,000 to 312,000 kilometers. Issues pertinent to car use by the Party's top leaders were not discussed in the resolution.[36] Personal use cars (with unlimited private use) were the entitlement of the chairman of the Central Control Committee; department chiefs of the Central Committee apparatus; first secretaries of the county Party organizations and the Communist Youth Organization; chief editor of the Party's daily, *Népszabadság;* chief editor of the Party's theoretical journal, *Társadalmi Szemle;* and directors of the central Party institutions (higher Party school, Party history institute, etc.). Limited personal use within six thousand kilometers and daily commuting between home and workplace were granted to the secretary of the Central Control Committee; the secretaries of the Budapest Party Committee; and the chief editor of the Party's journal, *Pártélet.* Personal use limited to four thousand kilometers and daily commuting between home and workplace were granted to the deputy department chiefs of the Central Committee apparatus, the deputy chief editor of *Társadalmi Szemle,* and the secretaries of Party committees in the five largest provincial cities of "county status" (Szeged, Debrecen, Miskolc, Györ, Pécs). Beneficiaries of personal use limited to three thousand kilometers per annum (without the right to daily commutes between home and work) were the secretaries of county committees, deputy directors of central Party institutions, secretaries of the Communist Youth Organization's Central Committee, and the chief secretary of the Pioneers Association. Daily commuting between home and work with the Party's car was permitted to the first secretaries of Budapest's district committees, the department chiefs of the Budapest Party Committee, the secretaries of the Central Committee of the Communist Youth Organization (and their first secretary in Budapest), and the chief secretary of the Pioneers.

The PGO did not prove particularly restrictive when it came to implementing the resolution. Quite a few members of the apparatus were granted exceptions to the newly introduced restrictions. Entitlements such as commuting service between home and work were restored to them after the resolution had taken it away; the resolution deprived Party bosses in the districts and department chiefs in the Budapest Party Committee of their earlier rights to personal use (limited to three thousand kilometers), but the PGO increased the so-called social allowance available and accepted private purposes other than extraordinary family events (serious illness, death, etc.) as qualifying for the private use of Party cars.[37] Like the beneficiaries among high-level state functionaries, even Party apparatchiks with entitlements to private mileages and commuting between home and work were offered the possibility to relinquish their dues in exchange for an annual cash redemption. In the first year following the resolution, this redemption was two Fts per kilometer. In the course of the next five years up to July 1977, 59 out of 168 high-level functionaries relinquished their entitlements for cash.[38]

From the data available, it seems quite obvious that major economies could not be expected and perhaps were not even really intended through the new regulations concerning legitimate private use of Party cars. For one thing, these entitlements mainly concerned a rather limited circle of Party functionaries in the higher levels of the *nomenklatura*. In this respect, the rules are of interest because they better highlight the true nature of both the legitimate and the illegitimate private appropriation of automobility with Party cars. Particularly the entitlement-into-cash conversion speaks clearly about Party cars as means to serve the *needs for private mobility* of the apparatus elite rather than, or at least just as much as, the pressing mobility requirements of the work of "professional revolutionaries." This comes into even sharper relief when we consider that the same elite that gave rise to the tendency toward sneaking privatization and cherished career ambitions, fueled by dreams about ever more generous privileges and entitlements as they advanced upward in the hierarchy, also exhibited a remarkable resistance to the efforts of the PGO and the top Party leadership to impose a taxi system on their car use and, even more, to make them rely on collective transport.

Who Is Afraid of Car Sharing?

Another policy to contain sneaking privatization was the imposition of a so-called taxi system. This system directly confronted some aspects of sneaking privatization in that, to the extent it was observed, it prevented individual Party bosses and various units of the Party apparatus from taking cars into their exclusive possession. Cars and chauffeurs were supposed to be pooled and assigned various tasks by local PGO units in a rational manner to achieve optimal utilization of the resources of mobility in the service of Party work. For in the PGO's view, an all-too-large number of the Party's 873 personal cars were being operated in the exclusive service of particular persons and organizational units, one indication of sneaking privatization. Party bosses were unwilling to relinquish their "right" to "their" car at any time and found the idea of having to share it with other members of the apparatus quite unattractive. Therefore, one of the central objectives that the HSWP Secretariat pursued in its resolution of 1972 was to secure a general breakthrough for the taxi system. Carpooling and car sharing in the central, county, and city Party committee apparatuses became major criteria for the inspections carried out by the PGO in the 1970s.

The PGO tried to assert the principle of car pools and car sharing early on. A PGO report, summarizing countrywide experience gained from a series of inspections, stated in October 1958 that car use was highly inefficient in the provinces because of a lack of coordination between the different departments (and the Party bosses) of county committees who exercised exclusive "ownership" over "their cars."[39] A circular sent out by the PGO to all Party organizations in June 1959 emphasized, "We have already spelled out our view in this question: there can be no proper economic management of the use of cars until the distribution of cars is brought under central management."[40]

The situation prevailing in this respect at the Central Committee apparatus was actually worse than in the provinces. The November 1960 report of the PGO on car use in the Central Committee was emphatic in claiming that the rather steep annual increases in the total mileage performed by the Party's cars were largely the result of loose discipline in the apparatus, with several cars, each carrying one or two passengers only, going from the White House to the same provincial city on the same day.[41] In December 1960, the Secretariat of the Central Committee tried to deal with the problem in a resolution obliging the Central Committee apparatus to pool the cars at its disposal and to use the pool in a planned manner, through advance applications.[42]

Lack of coordination and exclusive rights exercised over cars by Party bosses and various departments proved to be chronic problems.[43] PGO representatives scrutinizing car use by the Central Committee apparatus of the Communist Youth Organization in 1963 bumped into a large number of irregularities, among them the recurring phenomenon of several cars going to the same places at the same time, indicative of the lack of coordination and failure to exploit opportunities for car sharing. It must have come as little surprise that also in suspicious cases, like the caravans of cars headed to Balaton Lake during the summer months, they noticed a complete lack of car sharing, planning, and coordination.[44] A PGO circular to all department chiefs of the HSWP Central Committee apparatus from 1965 reveals the persistence of the problem in the top layer of the apparatus. Dezső Lakatos, PGO chief, called for greater frugality in the use of the Party's resources and particularly more organization and coordination in the use of cars as they were the single largest item of current operating expenses.[45] The appeal apparently failed to work—early in 1965, the PGO announced "some measures of economy" to be carried out by the Central Committee apparatus, among them that no more than one car could be earmarked for and stand by at the disposal of each Central Committee department. This car should cater to all the department chiefs' needs as well as those of the rest of the department for trips within Budapest. All other cars that until then had been earmarked for the departments were to be pooled under central planning and coordination on the basis of advance applications from the departments. In addition, the apparatus had to apply well in advance to the PGO, which would then secure proper coordination and car sharing and arrange for the cars at the central Party garage for all trips to the countryside.[46] Two years later, an inspection carried out by the PGO at the Transportation and Technological Company (the name, after 1957, of the central Party garage in Budapest), led to the conclusion that although there had been a temporary reduction in the total mileage performed by the cars of the Central Committee, in terms of *rational* use of cars (coordination, car sharing, exclusion of illegitimate use of cars for private purposes, etc.), no improvements had occurred whatsoever.[47]

A 1977 general review of the automobility (*gépkocsiközlekedés*) situation in the apparatus also emphasized that "the understanding [that] 'it is my car' is haunting here. The consistent implementation of the resolution is decisively dependent upon how the number one [*elsö számú*] and leading comrades relate to this issue."[48]

In spite of the pervasive and lasting resistance to the taxi system, the PGO produced just as many reports about advances and successes achieved in this respect, particularly in the second half of the 1970s. These probably give a correct impression to the extent that during the second half of the 1970s a substantial segment of the Party cars in Budapest as well as in the counties had been successfully integrated into a collective system of central coordination and car sharing. The reason for this can hardly have been the submission of the apparatus to the system of pooling and sharing; rather, it was the fact that by then the Party's cars had lost much of their significance as the means of automobility for members of the apparatus. Instead, a massive reliance on their own private cars had been evolving, particularly after the Secretariat's resolution of 1972, "solving the transport problems of the party," a subject to which we now turn our attention.

Who Is Afraid of Collective Transport?

Nothing is more telling about the preferences and desires of the apparatchiks in the world of modern mobility than their practices in relation to the means of public (collective) transport. Collective transport was an important front for the PGO and the higher party authorities in their efforts to keep the costs of apparatus mobility within limits. Yet no other single policy of the PGO was as much of a failure as its series of attempts to persuade the central and provincial apparatus to rely on collective transport when feasible.

As early as 1958, the economic chief of the Budapest Party Committee, complaining about the all-too-few and worn-out Skoda cars at the districts' disposal, mentioned that "it is hard to get the comrades to accept relying on other means of transportation too."[49] The Central Committee of Revision, in its report on the Party's economic management for the first half of 1958, called attention to the opportunity for economies through using public transport instead of cars. It noticed that while the Central Committee apparatus had spent close to 2.5 million Fts on operating its cars during the first half of 1958, its spending on railways and buses was less than 20,000 Fts.[50] Scrutiny of the waybills for July and August 1958 revealed that conspicuous numbers of kilometers per car (up to three hundred per day) were used for trips *within* Budapest, where the apparatus had at its disposal the country's best local network of public transportation. The report on budget spending during the year of 1957 stated that a large part of the stipulated costs for transportation by means other than party cars (railways, buses, airplanes) had not been spent.[51] Political employees of provincial Party committees often had better reasons to insist on the use of cars,[52] but even in this context what impressed the inspectors was "the refusal [*elzárkózás*] to use anything else (railways, bus)" but the cars.[53] A report from the inspection of the Central Committee apparatus of the Communist Youth Organization in 1977–78 urged the apparatus to reduce its use of highly expensive *túra taxi* (long-distance taxi service), "all the more because for trips between Budapest and Miskolc and Budapest and Szeged there are means of collective transport (fast trains) available."[54] Both in the national Party budget and in the Central Committee's annual budget the posts devoted to the use of collective transport regularly closed the year with funds left over.[55]

A statistical compilation from 1967, shown in table 3.2, makes the structure of apparatus mobility visible through a longer period. Considering these as well as the data for the 1970s, we can say that reliance on collective transport was never a significant avenue for apparatus mobility and that, in the course of the history of state socialism in Hungary, this alternative literally withered away.

Table 3.2 The structure of mobility in the Central Committee apparatus, 1959–67

Year	Number of political employees in the apparatus	Car use (in thousands of kms)	Calculated cost of car use (at 2 Fts/km)*** (A)	Collective transport costs (in thousands of Fts) (B)	B/A (%)
1959	205	2,535	5,070	221	4.4
1960	215	2,620	5,240	230	4.4
1961	206	2,566	5,132	211	4.1
1962	220	2,412	4,824	159	5.4
1963*	222	2,371	4,742	161	3.4
1964	235	2,394	4,788	124	2.6
1965	245	1,970	3,940	153	3.9
1966	230	2,098	5,196	127	2.4
1967**	220	929	1,858	51	2.7

Compilation dated 30 August 1967, MOL 288. f. 371/1967, 4. öe., fol. 157.

* From 1 October 1963, data exclusive of the car use of Politburo members of approximately 250,000 kilometers per annum.
** First half year only.
*** The multiplier of 2 Fts/km is relatively close to actual costs in the very beginning and all too modest for the last two to three years of the period covered, when the actual costs were somewhere around 4 Fts/km.

From the Failure of Sharing Public Cars to the Success of Sharing Private Costs

We have seen three policies deployed by the PGO and the highest party leadership in their attempts to contain the rising costs of automobility and to put a stop to sneaking privatization. None of these policies can be said to have achieved the desired effects to a satisfactory degree. The tactics of yielding and thus restricting could work only to the extent that malpractice in waybills management was rooted out and proper accountancy of the use of entitlements (and related mileages) was secured. As with many other well-intentioned norms and rules, even the taxi system could be effective only if properly enforced. Since evasion of carpooling and car sharing went unpunished, however, this policy proved a poor deliverer too.

The most pathetic loser, however, was the policy of making the apparatus opt for public transport instead of using cars. Behind the singular failure of this policy we find not only the rather open resistance of the apparatus class, who strongly preferred individual automobility over collective timetable-dependent transport, but also the fourth important component of the 1972 resolution of the HSWP

Secretariat: the decision to encourage members of the apparatus to use their private cars in carrying out their work duties. The material incentives attached to this policy were so attractive and the initiative appealed so powerfully to the private interests and profound individualism of the members of the apparatus class that it practically swept all competitors off the table.

Chauffeurless Driving

Reducing both the number of chauffeurs employed in the Party's service and the number of Party cars was seriously considered early on as a way of cutting costs. The previously cited dismissive reactions of the late 1950s to applications from members of the apparatus to drive the Party's cars themselves were replaced by a cautious but increasingly permissive and even encouraging attitude by the late 1960s and early 1970s. "Chauffeurless driving"—Party cars driven by the apparatchiks themselves—became an expanding phenomenon beginning with the Central Committee apparatus in the late 1960s. In 1971, 15 percent of the total mileage (2,563 km) covered by the Central Committee apparatus was driven by the Party workers themselves, without chauffeurs. The cost of a chauffeurless kilometer in the Party car was 25 percent less than the unit cost of a car with chauffeur.[56] The attainable economies were, of course, a powerful impetus for the Party leadership to export to the provinces what was initially a privilege of the crème de la crème of the apparatus class. In a circular to all economic chiefs of the HSWP's county organizations, the PGO department chief, József Kozári, gave the green light to the county and district organizations to allow members of the apparatus, from October 1971 on, to drive the Party's cars on their official trips.[57] The 1972 resolution of the Central Committee Secretariat extended this policy to all members of the Party apparatus.[58]

In light of the modest but promising results of the first "experimental" years,[59] the PGO (and, behind it, the Party leadership) decided to promote this form of car use by measures calculated to appeal to apparatchiks' individual interests. (1) Apparatus members driving Party cars themselves were offered, for their private use, 10 percent (from February 1980, 15%) of the mileage they clocked while engaged in work, or they could from February 1980 opt for receiving cash payments at the rate of 0.50 Fts per kilometer as a bonus. (2) The PGO also offered to pay members of the apparatus, upon successful completion of the driving test, 50 percent of the cost of driver education fees. This latter measure was said to have evoked a particularly enthusiastic response on the part of the apparatus.[60]

The growth of chauffeurless driving in the apparatus continued, in both absolute and relative terms, until 1976. Thereafter, however, no more major advances were made in this respect, and the tendency leveled off. As a report summarizing the experience of inspections made in the center as well as in the provinces in 1976 put it, "We witness year after year the growth of reliance, for official purposes, on private cars. The demand for cars without chauffeur [however] is losing its momentum [*mérséklödik*]."[61]

Indeed, what in 1972 appeared as a minor contribution to the total automobility of the apparatus (slightly more than 1.5% of the total mileage clocked in Party cars), by 1976 had grown into a major component of the total mileage accumulated in the service of the Party: private cars owned by members of the apparatus ran almost seven million kilometers (around 75% of the performance of Party cars), transporting the professional revolutionaries to wherever they had to go in their official capacities. In 1976, there were "nationwide, approximately two thousand comrades using regularly or in periods their own cars in taking care of their tasks."[62]

Private Cars "in the Party's Service"

In its pursuit of lowering costs by reducing the number of Party cars and professional chauffeurs, the most successful policy measure taken by the PGO was undoubtedly the inclusion of private personal cars owned by members of the apparatus among the party's means of mobility. An intense interest in apparatus circles to acquire private cars had been present from the early days of the Kádár era. The PGO's internal newsletter, *Ügyrendi Értesítö*, carried a message to the economic departments of all county and district Party committees, urging them to inform "comrades asking about how to buy a car" to "turn with their wishes directly to the Ministry of Postal Affairs and Transportation."[63] While this piece of news reveals earlier practices by which the apparatus assisted its members in acquiring private cars, we should immediately add that in the early years the PGO discouraged rather than encouraged use of private cars by apparatchiks in their work. Nor was it ready to assist "the comrades to take driver's education by using party cars [or], in any form, by using the money of the party."[64] Both the pressure from the apparatus to get help in its efforts to obtain private cars (and to use them with reimbursements from the Party) and the PGO's restrictive attitude persisted into the 1960s.[65]

The lust for cars in the apparatus made an important breakthrough in 1963 when a resolution of the Central Committee Secretariat accepted "that comrades employed by the Party may, in performing their duties, use as means of transport their own cars and [that] the Party will reimburse them for such use."[66] Yet no considerable expansion was experienced in the course of the 1960s in this respect, probably because of strong worries in higher Party and government circles that the use of private cars in public service in exchange for reimbursements out of public funds might generate substantial additional incomes among the beneficiaries, which were considered either illegitimate or simply undesirable because of the inflationary pressure they might provoke.[67]

The real boost, in the form of powerful arguments, for apparatus mobility with private cars came from the discourse of reform economics. At the core of this discourse was the idea that no unavoidable antagonism existed among private-individual, group, and larger social interests. Indeed, reform economists defined the very task of macroeconomic and social planning as creating an institutional and normative environment that would enable the socialist social order to harness all the energy of individual interests to promote macro-objectives of general welfare. This was certainly the argument used to propose an "optimal combination of market and central planning," the "new economic mechanism." Similar arguments were deployed to promote an expansion in the use of private cars in public service.

The HSWP's Central Committee of Revision carried out an investigation in 1966 of the use of private cars, beginning with various companies (printing houses, publishers, the central garage, etc.) attached to the Party. The investigation, conducted by László Gács (managing director of the country's only savings bank and member of the revision committee) and Márton Béres, covered a five-year period (1962–66). Signed by Gács, the report concluded that the use of private cars for public purposes should be encouraged because (1) the economies achievable at the macroeconomic level were more important than the "profit" gained by car owners, (2) the possible misuse of such a system would cause much less damage than the actual illegitimate use of public cars and the theft of spare parts and gasoline, and (3) it would substantially ease the shortage of professional chauffeurs and personnel in various transport-related services.[68]

Five years later, in its proposals to improve "the material appreciation and working conditions of the political employees in the Party apparatus," the PGO promoted the ideas of making it possible for apparatus members to drive the Party's cars and granting favorable credit conditions as well as privileged access to buying cars for party functionaries, provided they promised to use their cars for purposes of official work.[69] Before the 1972 resolution of the Secretariat, however, the official use of private cars belonging to members of the apparatus had not reached significant proportions. In the Central Committee apparatus, for example, only four functionaries used their own cars occasionally in their work, with an accumulation of 1,438 kilometers over the whole year of 1971.[70]

The 1972 resolution on car use of the Central Committee Secretariat greatly facilitated the apparatus's reliance on private cars. It provided a mighty new impetus toward apparatchiks' acquisitions of private cars by (1) rewarding higher-level functionaries who relinquished their entitlements to Party cars for private purposes by offering support for their private car acquisitions (independently of whether or not they promised to use those cars in their official work) and (2) securing exemption from queuing and advantageous credit conditions for functionaries who committed themselves to use their private cars for official purposes. The resolution gave priority to provincial salaried Party secretaries and the political employees of district (*járási*) Party committees and Communist youth organizations.

The 1972 resolution triggered a veritable avalanche of car acquisitions in the Party apparatus nationwide. In the course of the second half of 1972 and 1973, 1,080 cars were bought by members of the apparatus with the help of the PGO. The county committees reduced their stock of Party cars by 62 (11%).[71] In the same period, the Budapest central Party garage rid itself of 23 cars, and even though the total distance traveled in Party work increased from 22.8 million kilometers in 1972 to 23.5 million kilometers a year later, the total cost of automobility in the Party apparatus remained at the 1972 level because private car use grew from 130,000 kilometers to more than 2 million kilometers between 1972 and 1973.[72] A report on developments in 1974 reveals that the PGO supported the purchase of 1,134 private cars by the apparatus, while the number of Party cars in the county committees dropped by 100 by the end of that year.[73]

Reports from the counties indicated a rapidly increasing motorization of the Party apparatus through the spread of private car ownership. Those from 1972 and 1973 tell only about very few apparatus members owning and using private cars in service. Thereafter, however, the numbers of car owners, those taking driving courses, and those using their own cars in work grew at a spectacular tempo. In Veszprém County, fifty-three political functionaries used their private cars regularly for official trips. The county committee also outdid itself in organizing the servicing and repair of the private cars belonging to the apparatus in the committee's garage.[74] In Pest County there were fifty-two political employees at the Party committee who regularly used their own cars for work-related purposes in 1973–74. In 1975 the number of private cars used in official work increased to 56.[75] The 1974 report from Szabolcs County told about an increasing number of private cars used in the Party's service (driven a total of 206,000 kilometers in 1974), although it was also remarked that while several functionaries drove the Party's cars themselves, quite a few of those who had received subventions and support to acquire driver's licenses as well as cars did not seem to wish to use their private cars in service.[76] In Hajdu-Bihar, too, the number of new private cars acquired with the Party's help (fifty-five functionaries bought such cars in 1973) grew faster than the mileage of private cars performed for the good of the Party (a mere 100,830 kilometers done by "forty-two comrades" in 1973, instead of the 235,000 kilometers budgeted and planned for).[77]

Besides subsidized driver's education, exceptionally favorable credit conditions, and the possibility of purchasing cars without having to stand in a queue for years as all other citizens in the country had to do, the availability of the Party's garages and repair shops that serviced the apparatchiks' private cars at special subsidized prices substantially increased the propensity of the apparatus to acquire and use private cars in Party work. By 1977 the results were absolutely convincing: the Party managed to reduce its stock of cars from 948 in 1972 to 740 by September 1977. Whereas the mileage covered by Party cars dropped by 30 percent, the total mileage used for the purposes of official work shrank by only 7.5 percent because of the enormous contribution of private cars. "Today, in the country as a whole, 1,800–1,900 comrades use their own cars regularly or intermittently in doing their work," announced a proud PGO chief to the national meeting of economic chiefs in the Party apparatus. They covered 6.2 million kilometers, equal to the annual average performance of 190–200 professional chauffeurs.[78] The Party leadership no longer had any doubts about being on the right path and wished to continue encouraging the use of private cars in the Party's service. It did so partly by repeating the annual car sale campaigns. In these campaigns the PGO received from the Ministry of Domestic Trade a contingent of approximately 1,200 personal cars, which it then distributed among applicants from various county committees and the Central Committee apparatus. Through this shortcut access the members of the apparatus thus had a considerable advantage over regular citizens who had to wait months or even years, depending on the demand for the particular model, after paying in full for the car. The PGO also had a special arrangement with the National Savings Bank for credit on exceptionally good terms to benefit the apparatus. It carefully monitored price developments affecting the costs of owning and driving private cars and adjusted reimbursements accordingly to maintain the interest of members of the apparatus in using their own cars in work. Last, they wished to promote the use of private cars in the Party's service by organizing "the ongoing servicing and repairs of the functionaries' cars in the repair shops, garages of the county Party committees, and the Transportation and Technological Company [in Budapest]."[79]

THE higher Party leadership was happy about the emerging new mix of Party cars with or without chauffeurs and private cars as contributors to the total annual mileage deemed necessary to take care of the apparatus's work throughout the country. In terms of cost development, increased contributions from private cars were encouraged because the reimbursements required to sustain the interests of the apparatus never came even close to the costs of running the Party's own car fleet. On the contrary, while the expansion of the use of private cars took place, the leadership exercised renewed efforts to curb the total costs of apparatus mobility by imposing restrictions on the composition and use of the Party cars: it tried to reduce the entitlements to private use, it tried to minimize the number of expensive Western models in the Party's car fleet, and it continued efforts to stem sneaking privatization. In these efforts as well as in its general desire to keep costs under control, the leadership never missed an opportunity to point out to members of the apparatus all the personal-private advantages they derived from the symbiotic relationship with their Party in the field of mobility. The PGO chief, László Karakas, was not shy about pointing out the new regime's achievements since 1972. Nor did he hide his understanding of the mutual interests of the apparatus at large and the central leadership in sustaining this regime:

> The continuous and flexible implementation of the [1972] resolution further improves the transport situation of the apparatus at the same time that we can reduce the number of cars [owned by the Party] and the personnel required for car transport.
> The possibility secured to buy a car without queuing and the favorable credit conditions granted for the apparatus bring with them substantial change in living conditions too. We may safely claim that thanks to these measures an improvement in living standards has been achieved.[80]

Indeed, the new regime managed to secure the transport performance required for Party work and at the same time enable the Party apparatus to enjoy the fruits of individual-private mobility through the wholesale conversion of costs of Party cars into costs of reimbursements for the use of private cars. In light of developments in the course of the short decade following the 1972 resolution, the PGO was correct in its claim that

> essentially, the apparatus's demand for mobility has by the integration of private cars been solved.... The efficient utilization of the work time of the political apparatus operating in the districts has been improved. Those traveling on assignments can use their time more flexibly and efficiently. *The imposed need of having to wait for one another has ceased to exist. Through the utilization of private cars even the leisure time of the functionaries has increased considerably.*[81]

The same report noted also that "encouragement to use means of public transportation has been met by the resistance of the Party employees." But this was no longer a serious concern of the Party leadership. The new regime of 1972, reconfirmed in the Secretariat's resolution of February 4, 1981, managed to strike an economically feasible balance between the irresistible desire among the apparatus class to enjoy all the physical and sociocultural advantages that private automobility seemed to offer, on the one hand, and the imperative felt by the higher Party leadership to contain sneaking privatization for the sake of budgetary stability as well as legitimacy, on the other.

We have seen that the everyday practices of apparatus mobility were a major force behind private car-based mobility at the expense of both collective transport and collective forms of utilizing personal cars. The social group involved in these practices constituted the very core of the state socialist political class and the most politically powerful segment of the social elite. The values of this elite, as they manifested themselves in everyday life, did have an impact on the rest of society. Commoners may have been profoundly suspicious when they were listening to political speeches or had to read various texts of agitation and propaganda, but they perceived the message immediately when they saw the high level of motorization of the political class in terms of both the large stock of public cars at their disposal and the conspicuously high density of private cars in their circles. They might have had doubts about the legitimacy of their rulers, but they could follow them without hesitation when it came to their ways of everyday life, and they certainly subscribed to their understanding of what a good life was like.

Few among the Hungarian population would have felt prompted to revolt against Communist rule again if the Kádár regime had decided to develop on a large scale the infrastructure of collective transportation and a Khrushchev-style system of national car sharing to cater to the needs of individual mobility. It is hard to imagine that the chances of survival for state socialism would have been smaller if it had wished to distinguish itself by giving priority to the development and maintenance of an up-to-date system of collective mobility, or if state socialist elites had satisfied their own needs for mobility by relying on collective transport and car sharing. The choices made by these elites during the long 1960s are of considerable historical significance in that they contributed to and confirmed the inability of the state socialist social order to emancipate modern social and economic development from capitalist patterns. It was in the everyday practices of elite mobility that the question of whether state socialism could assert an alternative modernity antithetical to capitalist modernity was decided. These practices constituted probably one of the most important social mechanisms for bringing about the convergence of socialism with capitalism.

Part Two

MOBILITY AND SOCIALIST CITIES

4

PLANNING FOR MOBILITY

Designing City Centers and New Towns in the USSR and the GDR in the 1960s

Elke Beyer

The international dream of free-flowing traffic circulating through the city organism and of individual mobility as a sign of progress has had a powerful impact on urban planning ever since the 1950s and 1960s. Traffic planning was given high priority in the (re)definition of urban structures on both sides of the Iron Curtain. The shared agenda of an international expert community on how to design urban space as an efficient tool for communications informed the thinking of professional planners in capitalist and state socialist countries alike[1] at the same time that countless individual citizens of both camps aspired to car ownership as a personal means to negotiate urban space. Planning for this new mobility played a decisive role in attempts to make over war-destroyed cities, restructure large cities, and create New Towns. This chapter focuses on one aspect of this global phenomenon: how planning for mobility, especially automobility, shaped designs for city centers in the USSR and the German Democratic Republic (GDR) during the 1960s.[2] In this decade, shortly after architectural research and the building industry had been geared to the mass production of housing, the definition of an ideal Communist city and its social epicenter[3] resurfaced on the agenda of both countries' architects and planners. Communications and transport infrastructures became of primary importance for the allocation and organization of city centers.

This chapter concentrates on the evolution of urbanist debates in the architectural press and the urban design practice of the USSR and the GDR in the 1960s. It takes the first All-Union Conference on Urban Planning held in Moscow 1960 as a point of departure. Its end point is marked by confirmation of the exemplary general plans for Togliatti in 1968 and Moscow in 1971. Both plans represented official approval of a definitive model for the modern Soviet city—a model that benevolently integrated and provided for an increase in individual automobile traffic. The fragmentary realization of these plans in these and other Soviet cities must be attributed to limited capacities and, ultimately, political interest in the field of urbanism.[4] In the GDR, the new impulses from Moscow were echoed in the "General Principles of Planning and Design of Socialist City Centers" edited by the Bauakademie (Construction Academy) in 1960. This document attempted to set guidelines for the renewed construction of city centers, an attempt advocated in the (overly) ambitious Seven-Year-Plan of 1959.[5] Modern spaces like the Alexanderplatz in Berlin and the New Town of Halle-Neustadt were designed and built together with substantial road infrastructures in a costly "center euphoria" still in evidence in the 1967 "Resolution for the Accelerated Continuation of the Buildup and Reconstruction of City Centers" that anticipated the twentieth anniversary of the GDR.[6] This phase of architectural production lasted until 1971, when Erich Honecker took over from Walter Ulbricht as general secretary of the Communist Party and shifted state investment to desperately needed housing projects such as the Berlin-Marzahn estate (discussed by Eli Rubin in chapter 7 of this book).

Thus, in both countries, the 1960s stand out as possibly the last moment of serious debate among architects and planners about designing an all-encompassing city model for a Communist future. Their blueprints not only took important cues from decidedly modernist positions as set down in the Charter of Athens and from Le Corbusier's urbanism—as Brigitte Le Normand argues for the case of Yugoslavia in the next chapter—but were equally inspired by the Soviet functional urbanism of the late 1920s. Some of them came remarkably close to the utopian visions of mobility and environmental technology drawn up by postwar avant-garde architects such as Archigram in Britain, Paul Maymont and Yona Friedman in France, and Kenzo Tange in Japan. A complex picture of cultural transfers, adaptations, and shared urbanist models ranging from the Soviet constructivist heritage of the 1920s to the megastructures of Japanese "metabolists" of the early 1960s emerges.[7] But rather than pondering which architects could claim the copyrights of certain formal solutions, this chapter is concerned with conceptions of space and "utopias of usage" at the root of urban planning.[8] First, the ideas for the reconstruction of the city of the 1960s are situated in the context of socialist urbanization and contemporary architectural debates on mobility in the state socialist countries and in the capitalist world. Second, the chapter traces how central urban spaces were engineered and represented as spaces of movement—from high-profile interventions in capital cities like Prospekt Kalinina in Moscow and the Alexanderplatz in Berlin to the emerging centers of New Towns like Zelenograd, Togliatti, and Halle-Neustadt.

The Socialist Reconstruction of the City: Urban Space As a System of Mobility

The production of space in the cities of the USSR and the GDR in the 1960s was an extraordinarily dynamic process.[9] As the Soviet urbanist V. A. Lavrov summed up the planners' agenda in 1960, "Mass construction of housing on virgin soil and the gradual reconstruction of the central part of the city are two aspects of the same task: the fundamental transformation of our cities."[10] The consolidation of state socialist societies after the war and after Stalin's death implied a rapid pace of urbanization and augmented living standards. The construction of new housing estates in the periphery and a gradual reduction of working hours contributed to an increase of everyday and leisure mobility, furthered by a slowly proceeding automobilization.[11] These new demands on traffic planning received considerable attention in the theory and practice of urban planning in the USSR and the GDR from the late 1950s, part and parcel of the claim to organize life according to rational, scientific principles. The creation of New Towns and the expansion of existing ones, combined with efforts to improve national transport systems in terms of railways, highways, and airports, encouraged many citizens of the USSR and the GDR to associate socialist urbanization with a higher degree of personal geographic mobility. In contrast with the coercive mobilization of Stalin's time, the notion of individual, comfortable, technically advanced mobility on a par with the imagined smooth flows so crucial for capitalist car (and jet-set) culture emerged from the mid-1950s onward in both public and expert discourses in the Soviet Union and the GDR.[12] Individuals and policymaking bodies strove according to their means and abilities to translate their ideas and requirements for mobility into an everyday reality of the city space. This proved to be an often inconsistent process, subject to interest conflicts and negotiations between the multitude of actors within the state socialist society and the planned economy.

Beginning in 1954, the building industry and the architectural profession of the USSR (and of the GDR, following suit) underwent a fundamental restructuring in the wake of Nikita Khrushchev's call for rationalization, industrialization, and elimination of excesses.[13] Priority was shifted from architecture as an artistic endeavor to building as a means to satisfy basic needs. Nevertheless, the urbanist prospects opened up by industrialized mass construction soon motivated politicians, planners, and architects in the USSR and the GDR to put a new emphasis on the conception and planning of centers. The urbanist principles of the Stalin era, developed in the Soviet Union since the 1930s and imposed on GDR architectural production in 1950 for a short but significant period, had focused on political representation, producing towering structures, central squares, and central thoroughfares designed as backdrops for the slow, compact movement of demonstration marches. Gradually these notions were complemented and superseded by a more complex understanding of urban space. Centers began to figure as junctions in the urban systems of logistics encompassing both the supply of social and service infrastructures and traffic.[14]

In 1960, within fourteen months of the first All-Union conference on the building of transport infrastructures, the first All-Union Conference on Urban Planning (*gradostroitel'stvo*) convened in the Kremlin.[15] Its 2,500 participants included delegations of architects and building professionals from the GDR, Czechoslovakia, and Poland. The conference speakers claimed that the technical prerequisites for the mass construction of housing already existed. But they underlined a lack of knowledge about urbanist interrelations and the implications of this new type of development, pointing to the more far-fetched goal of a fundamental transformation of cities on the way to Communism. Complementary to the provision of housing, they asserted that it was necessary to redesign urban structures at large on a scientific basis. In the first report to the conference, V. A. Kucherenko, president of the State Committee for Construction (Gosstroi), advocated comprehensive regional planning for a functional disposition of space, the "proper organization" of a system of civic centers, and the creation of a sophisticated, high-capacity system of roads and transportation, specifically mentioning the need to build urban expressways.[16] He thus staked out the claims for an urban model that was to determine the theory and practice of urban planning in the state socialist countries in the next decades: the city—or rather, the urban region—as a functional system of production and reproduction, structured by nodes of supply and supervision serving as social epicenters, implying and creating a high degree of mobility of people, goods, and information as a base for the "harmonization" of living conditions.

But Kucherenko's report also mentioned some factors that made the implementation of this ambitious model look rather remote, if not utopian: he pointed to the absence of institutions capable of pursuing a coherent urbanist policy over and above the particular interests of certain ministries and industries, to the underdevelopment of "the science of urbanism" entrusted with such far-reaching forecasts about the future society, and to the insufficient training provided for young cadres in this field. He also frankly stated another crucial problem: though urbanists were supposed to look ahead twenty-five to thirty years or more and to proactively create the material and technical preconditions of Communism, the social needs and technical possibilities of this ideal future seemed rather hard to predict. His GDR architect colleagues who discussed the Soviet conference materials in subsequent colloquiums on urbanism held in Weimar and Berlin echoed this concern, cautiously "underlining the necessity of scientific and exact forecasts of the conditions of living, housing, and also of our building in the future."[17]

So long as their respective governments pushed forward ambitious seven-year plans, any such reservations were swept away by increased efforts. In the course of the 1960s, architects, urban planners, and construction engineers of the central research institutions established a new body of research and theory, or at least guidelines, on urbanism and prospective problems in architecture and not least transport issues.[18] Authoritative multivolume manuals and textbooks appeared, addressing questions of both the composition and the structure of the city—that is, attempting to balance representational and functional aspects of urbanism.[19] The approach to city centers in the general literature on urbanism and in detailed monographs on the subject (authored by prominent figures such as Nikolai Baranov, head of the Central Research Institute for Urbanism in Moscow, and Hans Schmidt, head of the Institute for Theory and History of Architecture at the GDR Construction Academy in Berlin) is instructive. Such works begin with the desired social contents and communications. From these they develop functional requirements and an aesthetic program for a modern *and* socialist urban space. In the early 1960s, elements of Stalinist urbanism such as the central *magistral'*—the main thoroughfare and ceremonial axis for demonstrations and parades—were still incorporated into this program by Soviet and GDR experts, but these were discarded in the second half of the decade. "Generosity" and "spaciousness" were advocated as key qualities of the new urban landscape, conducive to the development of new people with new tastes and new forms of social interactions—an echo of the enthusiasm of the 1920s about the transforming power of man's physical surroundings.

But first and foremost, planners assigned generous spaces to the roads and traffic intersections deemed necessary to avoid the "collapse" that traffic had caused in the cities of capitalist countries with a much higher rate of motorization.[20] Employing a frequently used modernist metaphor, they conceptualized the city as an organism requiring adequate circulation channels for its healthy development: a system of scientifically categorized pathways of movement ranging from pedestrian areas connected by quiet alleyways to access and service routes and finally to the main traffic thoroughfares of local and regional significance, leading to a national system of highways. In introductory and concluding remarks the literature on traffic planning recognized the role of public transport in socialist urban mobility, but its discussion of traffic problems and acceptable solutions focused mainly on the car and corresponding road system. Pedestrians featured only as an endangered species needing to be isolated on reservations. Of trams little was said except for a perfunctory defense that this "cheap and most efficient means of transport" "has to remain the main public means of transport for a long time to come."[21]

Juxtaposed with an informed critique of the problems arising from individual motorization was a strong fascination with the images and technical details of infrastructures of automobility. It was shared in publications addressed to an expert audience but also between expert authors and lay readers—for example, in the popular treatise *Traffic in the Modern City* published by GDR traffic planner Wolfgang Weigel in 1968.[22]

Car-oriented traffic planning in the United States and Western Europe received considerable attention in such publications. Urban expressways and multilevel intersections, whether in Chicago or in Düsseldorf in the Federal Republic of Germany, figure in plates as impressive engineering achievements and are described down to the details of measurements. Automobilization and the substantial transformations of the built environment related to it were not presented as undesirable per se. Rather, traffic planners expressed confidence that it was possible to learn from the engineering feats performed in service of individual motorization in capitalist countries without importing the problems related to them. Their negative effects on the cityscape could be checked, they asserted, by the

4.1 "Traffic in the modern city." Cover illustration of a popular treatise by GDR traffic planner Wolfgang Weigel, 1968.

PLANNING FOR MOBILITY   77

all-encompassing urban planning inherent in a socialist system. This question of cultural and technological transfers between the socialist and capitalist camps in the field of architecture and urbanism deserves a short digression.

Learning from Foreign Experience

After Nikita Khrushchev's 1954 exhortation to learn from the capitalist countries what was needed to overtake them, in the architectural press of the USSR and the GDR—as in many other fields—the almost hysterical tirades against modernist architecture and urbanism of the late 1940s and early 1950s were quickly replaced by a business-like interest. During the 1960s an international expert community in the field of urbanism gained coherence through the meetings of the International Union of Architects, a range of international seminars organized by the United Nations that addressed questions of settlement and emphasized the mutual exchange of information. Numerous delegations of urban planners from western, eastern, and southern countries traveled to see what went on in their field in the Soviet Union. What they discovered was that despite limited opportunities for Soviet architects and town planners to travel, "foreign" planning and building occupied an important place in the curricula of institutes of higher education and research as well as in the programs of the state publishing houses. Specialists' libraries such as the House of Architects in Moscow and the Construction Academy in East Berlin made international literature, especially periodicals, available to interested professionals—who, according to contemporaries and as bibliographies and references show, eagerly absorbed them.[23] In the Soviet Union, where the linguistic barrier to English and French publications might have been considerably higher than in the postwar GDR, Gosstroiizdat, the State Publishing House for Construction, provided Russian translations of periodicals like *Architecture d'aujourd'hui*, the leading French journal on contemporary architecture and urbanism, as well as of the works of individual architects from Le Corbusier to Victor Gruen. Soviet scholars also published reviews of building technology "abroad" and of the architectural production of various capitalist countries. They devoted special attention to the building of New Towns, housing construction, and the reconstruction of city centers in connection with traffic planning and engineering. And they attentively studied designs for cultural centers and shopping centers, as well as new administrative and business centers in large cities like Paris and Milan.

A little series of drawings used by the already mentioned Soviet urbanist V. A. Lavrov in his 1964 book on the city and its social center illustrates to what extent specialists' concerns could even override political and ideological taboos. On the last pages of the extensive chapter on transport, right after a page-sized model

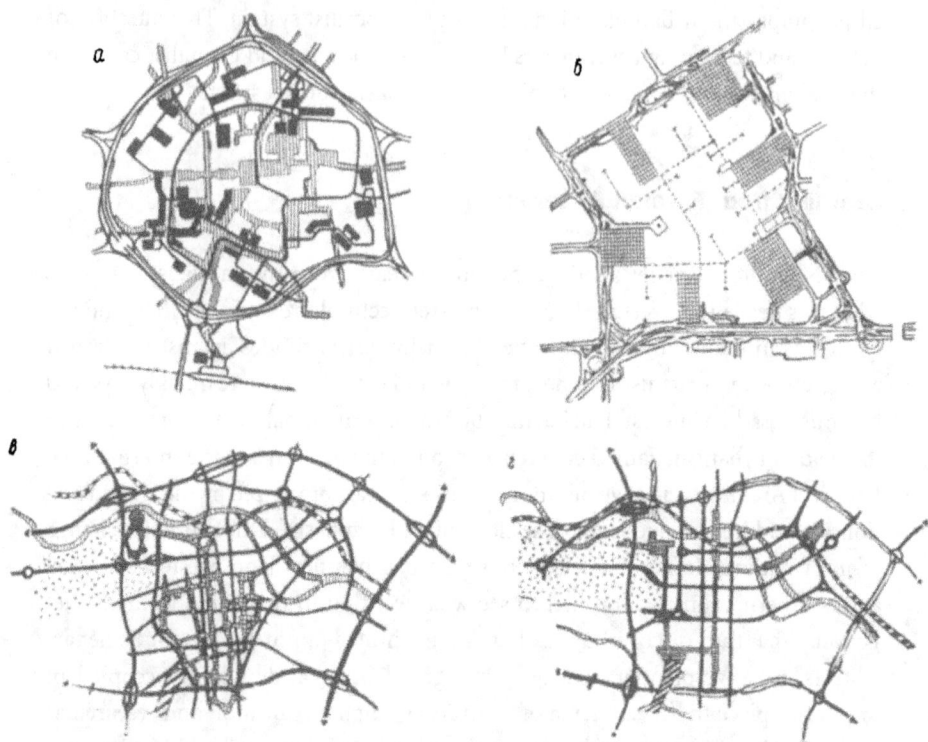

4.2 Comparative schemes of the distribution of parking lots and the organization of pedestrian movement in Coventry, Fort Worth, and Berlin. From V. A. Lavrov, *Gorod i ego obshchestvennyi tsentr* (Moscow: Stroiizdat, 1964)

photograph of Prospekt Kalinina, Lavrov discussed four unscaled "comparative schemes of the distribution of parking lots and the organization of pedestrian movement in city centers" identified only by place names.[24] These included (1) the reconstruction of the war-destroyed center of Coventry (UK) as a pedestrian shopping zone accessible via numerous parking lots and surrounded by an arterial ring road; (2) a comparable scheme for revitalizing the center of Fort Worth, Texas, by surrounding it with urban expressways and car parks doubling as heliports, drafted by Austrian émigré architect Victor Gruen (who became famous in the 1950s for designing the first regional shopping centers in Detroit's suburbs); and (3 and 4) entries for the competition Hauptstadt Berlin (Berlin Capital City) initiated by the West Berlin senate in 1958 for the entire central area of Berlin including the Soviet sector, which had caused outrage in the East as yet another proof of West German imperialist ambitions against the GDR. The featured project by British architects Alison and Peter Smithson (3) envisaged a network of expressways cutting through the center, bridged by a system of pedestrian plateaus on a second level and accessible by escalators. What is most suprising is the matter-of-factness Lavrov displayed in presenting these four projects without so much as hinting at the extent to which they promoted individual automobility, gave first priority to shopping and consumption, and furthered the transformation of the city center into a space dominated by commercial functions and offices. Restricting reference to such foreign urbanist solutions to purely technical matters like parking lots allowed these phenomena to be addressed without any discussion of their social significance or possible convergences with urban development at home. Architects' and urbanists' questioning of what was to be considered progressive in the capitalist camp and what was ultimately socialist about urban planning in the state socialist countries thus appears limited to "technical transfer without cultural diffusion."[25] The incorporation of traffic infrastructures comparable to those built and imagined in the capitalist countries in the actual design and building of city centers is a case in point.

City Centers as Spaces of Communication

The search for a new conceptual grasp of urban space also produced new representations of the city committed to a modern architectural language and spatial structure and physical spaces that defined the politics of space and everyday experience of the city. Traffic planning and transport infrastructures were of primary importance for the organization and design of space in the new centers. Though the urban design model of the "ensemble" remained valid, its eclectic neoclassicist interpretation gave way to a modernist one. This represented "a departure from the stage scenery of monumental ensembles of streets and squares to functionally and artistically diversified spaces of communication with a multitude of social facilities."[26] Spatial efficiency and flexibility for future expansion was to be achieved by basing the entire ensemble on a modular grid.[27] On the level of management, planning and construction activity, as well as urban mobility, was to be organized according to cybernetics—a science denounced as "bourgeois" only a few years earlier. The novelty of (partly) industrialized building methods displayed in the very heart of the capital cities, managed by flow charts and some early attempts at electronic data processing, meant that the construction sites themselves were highly visible demonstration objects for the creation of a new city by a socialist state that was mastering the scientific-technical revolution.[28]

The industrialization of the building industry resulted in the homogenization of building types and the urban fabric, but for the reconstruction of city centers more individual and remarkable solutions were sought via competitions. In the Soviet Union, Gosstroi initiated about fifty competitions for the reconstruction of city centers during the 1960s. In each competition, five to six collectives from different institutions participated, among them the offices of city architects, regional and central planning and reasearch institutes, and the Moscow and Leningrad schools of architecture—amounting to the involvement of several hundred architects in the search for an ideal modern center for a socialist city. The prize-winning designs published in the journal *Arkhitektura SSSR* all pursued the production of a complex civic centrality by creating ensembles of modern architecture and public spaces and making them accessible to all city dwellers by an extensive, high-performance, comfortable transport system including a network of urban expressways.[29] The strong orientation toward international modernism in architecture and urbanism cannot be overlooked in these designs.

In the GDR, the competitions for the socialist reconstruction of the center of Berlin held in 1958 and 1964 show how a modernist conception of architecture and urban space was gradually adopted by architects and political decision makers—and how planning for traffic and communication turned into a primary concern. Competitions and projects for cities like Chemnitz (Karl-Marx-Stadt), Leipzig, Dresden, and Halle developed in a similar manner in the course of the 1960s and were significantly influenced by traffic-planning concerns. Planning solutions aimed at an optimization of traffic flows and speed, mostly by proposing a functional separation of car, pedestrian, and public transport. Large spaces were allocated to moving and parking cars, and they often took center stage in descriptions of the new socialist cities, which could be read as promises for future mobility. Contemporary representations of the new city centers and public buildings—whether in the stage of project design or realization—evoked strong images of mobility, often automobility.

The composition of urban space explicitly addressed the perception from a moving car, integrating large traffic infrastructures into the experience of urbanness and centrality.[30] The high profile of ample spaces for the fast movement of cars spoke of an understanding of automobilization and road structures as attributes of a desirable modernity.

The Alexanderplatz in Berlin, constructed between 1965 to 1971, stands out as an example of planning "under the burden of traffic," in the words of the architect Dorothea Tscheschner, who was involved in the design and construction of this flagship project for the twentieth anniversary of the founding of the GDR. The 1964 urban design competition for this area was preceded by the definition of a very car-friendly traffic solution.

This solution meant connecting the four main traffic arteries—by bridging/opening up the bottleneck between Unter den Linden and Karl-Marx-Allee/Frankfurter Allee (formerly Stalinallee) and connecting them to the (eastern) main station via Alexanderstrasse and to the yet-to-be-constructed highrise housing

4.3 The new cinema International as a mere backdrop for cars parking in the center of East Berlin. Photo from a 1965 picture booklet on Karl-Marx-Allee. From Walter Stiebitz, *Karl-Marx-Allee: vom Strausberger Platz zum Alexanderplatz* (Berlin: Verlag für Bauwesen, 1965).

4.4 Traffic Solution Alexanderplatz, Construction Site Board, Berlin mid-1960s. Photo Landesarchiv Berlin, F Rep 290, Nr 21543, by Ingeborg Lommatzsdh. Reproduced with permission, Landesarchiv Berlin.

along Leipziger Strasse, respectively. Going underground avoided traffic crossings and especially the crossing of car traffic, pedestrians, and tramway lines. Such a solution essentially conformed to textbook arguments of 1960s international planning literature about how to guarantee the undisturbed movement of vehicles. Thus a car tunnel and an extended system of pedestrian underpasses and subway lines became proudly featured elements of the new ensemble. Edmund Collein, head of the Institute for Urban Planning at the GDR construction academy, added to this the proposal of a giant flyover tangent to the northwest corner of the square—thereby facilitating intersection-free car traffic from Unter den Linden to Frankfurter Allee. This very remarkable understanding of the central magistral' turned into an elevated expressway would have effectively cut Berlin-Mitte in two. As Dorothea Tscheschner relates, it took arbitration from Moscow to cancel the plans for this flyover.[31] When completed, the Alexanderplatz consisted of a large pedestrian area with a department store, a hotel tower, and diverse street-level gastronomy facilities. But on three sides, wide thoroughfares separated it from the surrounding office blocks with street-level retail spaces and cultural facilities like the Press House, Congress Hall, and House of Teachers. Political will had it that no building was to shield the view across the six-lane crossing into Karl-Marx-Allee. In the 1990s, the dominance of traffic space served as a first argument for a new master plan establishing the total reconstruction of the area, including the demolition of nearly all the GDR buildings.

Yet perspective drawings by architects of the future Alexanderplatz show to what extent ideas of mobility and spaces of movement informed the design and architectural imagery. More than ever, architects designed spaces for movement, simultaneously facilitating and representing the circulation of diverse flows of people, goods, and information. Similar imagery was employed in sketches for Prospekt Kalinina in Moscow in the early 1960s. If one compares these drawings with later photographs, intentions and reality seem to successfully coincide: an undisturbed flow of car traffic moves parallel to the stream of pedestrians in a wide separate area providing cultural and consumption facilities.

The intricate network of semipublic and private spaces characteristic of the old Arbat neighborhood had been replaced by a modernist space with a clear-cut division between a motorized and a pedestrian public.

Even if Prospekt Kalinina and the Alexanderplatz did serve as locations for parades, festivals, and other state-organized convocations of the socialist citizenry, the new central spaces were not primarily intended as vessels for the organized movement of masses in political demonstrations. For everyday use, as a counterpart to separated, fast-traffic infrastructures, large areas of the new central ensembles were set apart and designed for the leisurely stroll, a pastime for individuals or small groups, as well as for window shopping. Their spatial organization was based

PLANNING FOR MOBILITY   83

4.5 Ideal separation of car and pedestrian movement on Prospekt Kalinina, Moscow 1974. Vieri Quilici, ed. *Mosca. Il nuovo piano del 1971 e la sua realizzazione* (Milano: Gabriele Mazzotta, 1974).

on a utopia of usage, the effortless appropriation of the city center by "the working people," implemented in typologies like ample open pedestrian spaces with seating, greenery, fountains, or shopping arcades but also by spatial arrangements facilitating the observation and control of any movement. Narratives of mobility like space travel and tourism became tangible parts of the city center in the shape of monuments, buildings, and public art like the TV tower, the World Time Clock, and the House of Travel on Berlin Alexanderplatz and the monument to Sputnik located close to a central main traffic artery in Moscow. In the planning literature as well as in officially sanctioned representations like travel guides, photo books, and promotional film, the city center, with its new hotels, travel agencies, and attractive shopping destinations, figured as a place of temporary association for mobile subjects and as a hub for sought-after consumer goods. The multivoiced and futile protest of East Berliners in the 1990s against the above-mentioned plans to fill up the Alexanderplatz area with fifteen office skyscrapers to make it more "urban" may be interpreted as a sign that at least for a significant group of residents, this urban space was something they could identify with.[32] This attitude may not apply to today's Novy Arbat (as Prospekt Kalinina was renamed). Architectural guides of Moscow speak of it as a "foreign body" in the urban fabric, even if the area remains a popular shopping and leisure destination as well as providing central office space for countless institutions and companies.[33] Perhaps the difference lies in the fact that whereas the Alexanderplatz was strongly linked to the historical experience of constructing a better city after the destruction of the war, Prospekt Kalinina embodied the planned destruction of a beloved quarter in the service of traffic optimization and a top-down demonstration of architectural modernity.[34]

The high-profile and exemplary urbanist interventions in the centers of the capitals in the course of the 1960s materialized a specific understanding of a dynamic socialist urban landscape, manifesting itself in the design and representation of flows of public transport, of people, goods, and signals. Following models developed under capitalist conditions, urbanists aimed at incorporating individual mobility by car and designated considerable spaces exclusively for automobility. Yet in addition, central urban spaces achieved a specifically socialist character by providing truly generous opportunities for pedestrians to move about and to stay for a while, possibly but not necessarily frequenting the culture and consumption facilities entertained and supervised by the state. These public spaces were accessible to the majority by public transport—even if not in the most comfortable manner.

Cities of the Future: Dynamic Settlement Systems and New Towns

In the 1960s, the scientific organization of distribution and circulation within the existing city centers was seen as just a first step on the agenda for the design of an optimal city for the Communist future. As Kucherenko had stated at the All-Union Conference on Urban Planning in 1960, an all-encompassing regional planning approach was required to create a socialist (or even Communist) system of settlement clearly superior to the chaos stemming from the unplanned, unregulated urbanization taking place under capitalist conditions, largely as the result of automobilization. He and his counterparts in the GDR were quite explicit about the fact that the opportunities that a socialist system offered were not being exploited to the full with regard to urbanism. Architects and planners reclaimed more professional control of the urbanization process and demanded more political attention for their concerns, instead of ad hoc interference. They sought to reframe urban design as a science rather than an art, also in order to gain authority in the political process. The imaginary organism of the city was to be treated with a "scientific" approach on the assumption that it could be designed as a system, preferably with a fixed size and a fixed set of attributes. Numerous articles in the Soviet architectural press in the early 1960s testify to the theoretical search for this optimum city, calculated in terms of per capita requirements, economies of scale, space-time systems, cybernetic models of mobility patterns, and so forth. These endeavors were noted with due interest in the GDR, but no similar research projects were launched. Yet in both countries the integration of planning, social sciences, and design was advocated in order to determine the ideal built environment.

Research institutes and architecture schools were not alone in claiming to project a Communist ideal city from a scientifically established base of knowledge. Several informal groups and individual architects drafted urban visions for the future and put them up for discussion in the limited circles of professionals, especially at the Institute for History, Theory and Prospective Problems of Soviet Architecture directed by the young scholar Andrei Ikonnikov in Moscow.[35] The projects of the architect Viacheslav Loktev; the group New Element of Settlement (NER) formed by architects Alexei Gutnov, Il'ia Lezhava, and others; and the group Movement, including the artists Lev Nusberg and Francisco Infante,[36] all raised the promise of mobility in urbanism to yet another plane. They drafted plans for kinetic cities with flexible, movable structures, on earth or in outer space, and came up with the vision of a gigantic transport axis reaching across the Soviet Union from east to west as a backbone for new, disposable elements of settlement and industrial production.[37] Entries to the competition for the reconstruction of Moscow in 1965 envisaged transport-based megastructures—multilevel structures containing expressways, parking lots, and service facilities in a perfect circle around the Kremlin.[38] These designs and textual descriptions of urbanist models linked to them were quickly picked up and published in the architectural press in Italy, France, and the United States alongside numerous similar contemporary designs for cities of the future—for example, Archigram's "Walking City" and Yona Friedman's and Kenzo Tange's megastructure projects. They can be read as a shared reaction of architects to the prospect of apparently unlimited technological progress and human ability to create a fully controlled environment.

Meanwhile, the state planning and building commissions of the USSR and the GDR were taking a much more down-to-earth and rather schematic approach to

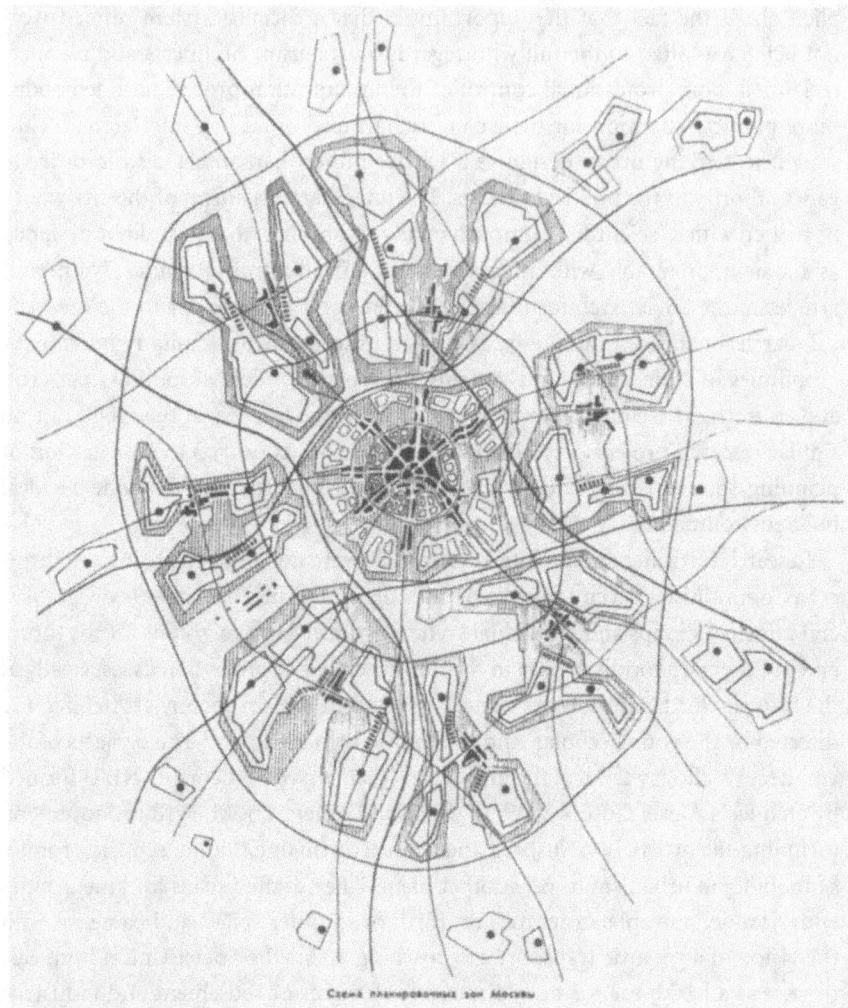

4.6 Scheme of the 1971 General Plan for Moscow. Vieri Quilici, ed. *Mosca. Il nuovo piano del 1971 e la sua realizzazione* (Milano: Gabriele Mazzotta, 1974).

socialist urbanization. The reconstruction of existing city centers and their outfitting for the future was to be complemented by the construction of a whole system of new civic centers. Thus, in order to govern the patterns of movement into and within the cities, a double move of planned spatial concentration and deconcentration was deemed necessary. The commissions prescribed rather rigid numerical parameters for the establishment of a tiered system for the concentration of functions in city centers. These centers were indexed according to population density, expected composition of age groups, and mobility patterns.[39] The tiered system of civic centers became the theoretical mainstay of urban and regional planning in the state socialist countries. As a prominent example of how this principle was expressed in planning for an existing city, the 1971 general plan for Moscow deserves some attention. It had been elaborated in the course of the 1960s in the office of the city architect Mikhail Posokhin and in the Institute for the General Plan of Moscow, supported by a competition in the mid-1960s.[40] The general plan envisaged the creation of a star-shaped system of subcenters surrounding the historical center of Moscow, linked by powerful transport arteries, in order to channel the movement of Muscovites and commuters, whether by car or public transport, away from the area inside the Garden Ring. The subsequent realization of this general plan was confined to some significant elements of the road system, but funds for the new system of centers never appeared. Thus, beyond mass housing production and insular flagship developments like the Olympic complexes and the pedestrian zone of the Old Arbat, it seems that providing for motorized traffic was all that could arouse urbanist action in Moscow in the 1970s and 1980s.

Meanwhile, according to planning theory, the tiered system of centers was to be extended from the scale of the housing complex to the scale of the nation as a whole. As housing complex centers and district centers were to complement the city center, satellite towns were to complement existing cities and newly developed urban regions the old industrial agglomerations. All were to be served by a correspondingly tiered road and long-distance transport system. This logistic model of assembling urban space assumed high geographic mobility of people and goods to start with—or rather, it was aimed at steering short-term and long-term population movements in order to gain control of the urbanization process and to avoid a traffic collapse of existing large cities.[41]

The construction of satellite towns, envisaged as complete urban entities providing work and housing as well as social and cultural facilities, had been advocated with renewed urgency by Khrushchev since 1954. One of the first was Zelenograd, built from 1958 onward with an ambitiously modern architecture and town layout thirty-five kilometers northwest of Moscow. As a center of research, development, and production in the field of electronics, Zelenograd was a closed city.[42] The town's center was formed by the intersection of three main arterial roads, separating a remarkable ensemble of cultural and administrative buildings from a shopping center and the central housing district. Transport within Zelenograd depended exclusively on buses or cars. A ride along its main traffic artery set within the green space of gently sloping riverbanks amounts to a sightseeing tour of the sculptural silhouettes of its modern public buildings, including the Institute for Electronics. The town center and the district centers of Zelenograd provide large spaces exclusively for pedestrian use, but its urban landscape appears intended for motorists.

Parallel to the establishment of satellites and new housing districts on the outskirts of large cities, the urbanization of more remote, previously rural or sparsely settled regions proceeded through the development of new industrial and research centers.[43] Soviet publications claimed that more than nine hundred New Towns had been built between 1926 and 1966.[44] In the 1960s, the planning of Soviet New Towns often amounted to drawing-board exercises for applying the tiered system of centers and linking it with an effective road system. A telling example is the general planning scheme for the Avtograd section of Togliatti by the team of Boris Rubanenko, which won a national prize in 1973 and subsequently provided mandatory course material for generations of architecture students in the Soviet Union and the GDR.[45] Aiming at a maximum efficiency of mobility and supply, the scheme distributed housing, services, and public infrastructure within a geometrical grid of wide esplanades that provided ample spaces for driving (and parking) cars.

The GDR, too, strove for the reconstruction of its settlement system at large. The situation was of course complicated by the drawing of national borders right across an existing, even if degraded, network of transport, urban, and industrial areas, especially in Berlin. The country's economic capacities had already been severely tested by the efforts to make up for the division and for the damage to transport infrastructures caused by war. Thus only four New Towns were planned and constructed in the GDR: Eisenhüttenstadt, Schwedt, Hoyerswerda, and finally Halle-Neustadt, built in the chemical triangle of Halle, Buna, and Leuna from 1964 onward. This "Chemical Workers' Town" was tied into a larger regional development scheme and linked to the huge chemical industries of Buna and Leuna by a fast local train line. Its layout followed precisely the system of tiered centers as elaborated above, but its chief architect, Richard Paulick, tried in vain to complete the ambitious central district with a Chemistry Tower and a multilevel pedestrian shopping zone composed around the backbone of a central arterial road connecting the New Town to the city of Halle.[46]

Zelenograd, Togliatti, and Halle-Neustadt are instructive examples of how planners' and politicians' visions of mobility were transformed into designs for cities and finally into urban reality. All of them were supposed to provide attractive and modern spaces for working and living, combined with fully equipped civic centers and made accessible by powerful transport infrastructures. They were designed to attract young and enthusiastically modern people, thus advancing geographic and social mobility in methodical progress toward the creation of a Communist urban space and lifestyle. Automobility—a certain level of individual car ownership and the provision of adequate road infrastructures—seemed to be taken for granted in this new urban way of life, complementing ubiquitous everyday pedestrian mobility and public transport. Glossy photos in journals and coffee table books celebrating the existence of these truly "socialist" towns often carry full spreads depicting car-exclusive spaces like elevated expressways or wide central traffic intersections, juxtaposed to images of clean slab-constructed housing blocks, happy people at work, and small children playing in their nursery schools.[47]

In retrospect, first-generation inhabitants often expressed ambivalent memories: on the one hand they were proud of belonging to a dynamic founding generation that had taken possession (and care) of the New Town, but on the other hand they regretted the lack of urban amenities, the supply problems, and especially the dysfunctions of the transport systems that resulted from long construction times. In the case of Halle-Neustadt, the vital streetcar connection to Halle running on a separate track of the elevated expressway was finally built in the 1990s, years after the demise of the GDR. The common everyday experience of crowded, cumbersome, and unreliable public transport even in model towns may have contributed significantly to promoting the ideal of an individual car.[48]

THE actual practice of designing and building city centers in the USSR and in the GDR resembled a process of bricolage from the planners' perspective—making do with available materials, construction methods, and state investments; developing tactics of mustering political support by using the appropiate architectural and spatial language; and displaying readiness to learn. Architects and planners even at the highest level of the state building administrations were painfully aware of the limitations of their position within the existing system of state socialism. Yet in the 1960s they displayed, at least in the USSR, considerable energy and creativity in dreaming up all-encompassing systems and schemes for future Communist patterns of settlement, which nearly always included fantasies of unrestricted movement by some high-tech devices even superior to the individual car—like monorails or helicopter transport. These designs were rooted in a firm belief in the opportunities a socialist system provided for urban planning and design if they could be fully exploited. At the same time, the professional community of architects and planners was reshaped from 1954 onward: they claimed authority as technical experts working with scientific methodology rather than as artists. On this level, the 1960s appear formative for the self-perception of belonging to an international expert community. Issues of transport and traffic planning lent themselves to the establishment of a scientifically derived body of urbanist knowledge and techniques that appeared to be politically neutral. Thus they make a pointed case for technological and cultural transfers across the ideological borders of the Cold War. Regarding the production of urban space, planning strove to meet the mobility demands of existing institutions, industries, and not least of urban dwellers in their everyday negotiation of space. On the other hand, planners sought to create new patterns of movement by establishing new focal points and new road

4.7 Reconstruction of Thälmann square in Halle as a traffic node between the railway station, the old town, and the thoroughfare to the new town Halle-Neustadt. From Gerald Grobe and Hans Jürgen Steinmann, *Zwei an der Saale: Halle/Halle-Neustadt* (Leipzig: VEB F. A. Brockhaus, 1979).

and transport links between them. Ultimately, the development of an integrated and all-encompassing Communist system of settlement that had still figured high on the agenda of planners during the 1960s faded away in the course of the 1970s and 1980s, leaving some traces in the form of traffic infrastructures that were not much different from those constructed under capitalist conditions.

5

AUTOMOBILITY IN YUGOSLAVIA BETWEEN URBAN PLANNER, MARKET, AND MOTORIST
The Case of Belgrade, 1945–1972

Brigitte Le Normand

In the recent flourishing of scholarship on cars and automobility around the world, a few key concepts have crystallized. Two are of direct relevance to the task of developing the history of automobility in European socialist states. The first is that the second half of the twentieth century has witnessed the emergence of a "globalizing car system," a product of postwar economic trends in which Fordist production and mass consumption have reached their apogee. The second and related concept is that although automobility is a global trend, the car cultures that emerged in each particular setting have also taken on a specificity that distinguishes them from cultures in other locales.[1] Thus we should approach automobility in Eastern Europe as both connected to global economic trends and manifesting itself in ways that are specific to the context of state socialism, as well as to the idiosyncrasies of individual socialist states.

The case of Yugoslavia is especially suited to exploring both the global nature of automobility and its specificity. Its development in this maverick socialist state was very much conditioned by Yugoslavia's participation in global economic trends. But where did its specificity lie? It seems clear that automobility in Yugoslavia and across the Eastern Bloc was shaped on the one hand by centralized planning forces that were skeptical of—if not outright hostile to—personal car usage and on the other by the existence of consumers who were ready to embrace personal car usage for the freedom and excitement that it promised. Yugoslavia, however, stood apart from its socialist neighbors by virtue of its experimentation with market socialism, which also had consequences for how automobility developed in this country.

One way of getting at how global, state socialist, and local factors interacted and affected automobility is to look at urban planning. In the case of Yugoslavia, car culture—at least in cities—emerged out of the competing visions of urban planners and drivers, the realization of whose fantasies was facilitated by the mechanisms of market socialism.

This chapter investigates the evolution in urban planners' attitude toward automobility from the adoption of Belgrade's first master plan in 1950 to the adoption of its second master plan in 1972. Belgrade's first postwar planners were resolutely modernist in their outlook. Envisioning the reconstruction of the city through the lens of Le Corbusier's Athens Charter, urban planners did pay close attention to mobility, but they conceived of it primarily in terms of efficiency. As a result, they did not encourage personal automobile usage, which they considered wasteful. The rapid rise in the standard of living in the mid-1960s was accompanied by the growth of mass consumption, an explosion in automobile usage, and the flowering of a middle-class car culture. Opportunities like car ownership, indeed, provided content to a middle-class identity in a socialist state that was not supposed to have such identities. By the late 1960s, when they began to consider the next master plan, urban planners had come face-to-face with their inability to control Belgrade's growth. No longer able to ignore the automobile, urban planners abandoned prescriptive planning in favor of trend management. However, rather than designing the city around the automobile, in line with global trends, they sought to reaffirm the central role of public transportation.

This analysis of how urban planners grappled with the automobile helps to elucidate not only certain dimensions of automobility in the context of state socialism but also the nature of state power in Yugoslavia. It argues that the authoritarian, even totalitarian, proclivities of socialist planners were no match for the power of the private automobile.

The First Master Plan: Mobility without Motorists

The case of urban planning in Belgrade, Yugoslavia's capital city, is uniquely suited to investigating the interactions between urban planners, drivers, and market socialism. Having been severely damaged by aerial bombardment during the Second World War, the city offered urban planners a broader scope for intervention into the urban landscape than was the case in other cities in the country. Because Belgrade's transformation began immediately at the end of the war, it also provides a wonderful snapshot of urban planning at the inception of the socialist regime, whose evolution we can then follow over time. Moreover, in light of the unpopularity of the first Yugoslavia, which had come into being after the First World War, Tito's regime invested a lot of effort not only in rebuilding the city but also in transforming its image. Urban planners consequently approached Belgrade's reconstruction with great trepidation and saw it as a kind of showcase for what socialism had to offer. New Belgrade, in particular, was seen as a kind of model city for testing cutting-edge planning concepts and construction technologies, which could then be applied in other Yugoslav cities. Thus, although Belgrade is in many ways unique, its planning influenced the planning of other cities.[2]

In the new socialist Yugoslavia, the task of rebuilding the capital city after its devastation in two waves of bombardments during the Second World War was given to Nikola Dobrović, a preeminent Yugoslav modernist architect who had trained and worked in Czechoslovakia in the interwar period. Although Dobrović lost his leadership role in 1948 when urban planning institutions were reorganized, his successor, Miloš Somborski, who had also been active in the avant-garde in the period between the two world wars, elaborated on Dobrović's central concepts. Under his direction, the municipal council's planning office (*uprava za projektovanje*) worked on the master plan that the municipal council adopted in 1950. The ambitious plan called for not only modernizing the existing parts of Belgrade but also building a whole new city center on the flood plains on the other bank of the Sava River, christened New Belgrade.

The team that produced the plan was composed of thirty-two architects and technical specialists in the fields of geology, sanitation, and transportation, with architects heading the project.[3] This composition reflected the widely shared view in Yugoslavia at this time that urban planning was fundamentally an aesthetic and technical pursuit. Urban planners saw themselves primarily as technical experts applying their expertise in an objective way and did not dwell on the ideological dimension of their profession. Contributions by urban planners to professional journals such as *Arhitektura* and *Arhitektura Urbanizam* attest to this self-perception. Party membership was not essential, and it seems unlikely that most employees of the planning office, aside from the top cadres, would have sought it. Additionally, most urban planners saw themselves primarily as practitioners rather than theoreticians, although at least three participants—Josif Najman, Stanko Mandić, and Oliver Minić—would later become professors in the Faculty of Architecture in Belgrade.[4] Urban planners in Belgrade also saw themselves as members of a profession that transcended national borders, and the planning team drew much of its inspiration from the international modernist movement.

The master plan it produced was very much shaped by the Athens Charter, the urban planning manifesto of the international modernist movement, which Le Corbusier wrote and published in 1943; it was based on the 1933 meeting of the Congrès Internationaux d'Architecture Moderne (CIAM) that had focused on the topic of the functional city. Because of this influence, the new plan for developing the city made mobility a priority. The Athens Charter preached the functional separation of different parts of the city into areas designated for housing, work, and leisure, giving mobility a key role in the functional city in facilitating the movement of goods and people efficiently to and from these areas. Le Corbusier and his followers argued that the automobile made the old urban forms unlivable, congesting city streets and threatening the lives of innocent pedestrians. Nonetheless, they saw the automobile as part of the larger machine age and consequently did not try to resist automobility. Rather, they advocated the adaptation of the city to the machine age through the separation of different speeds of traffic on the one hand and the implementation of a road network adapted to the automobile on the other.[5] In his 1935 design for the Radiant City, a theoretical model of the city of the future, Le Corbusier granted pedestrians total control over the ground level and elevated all vehicular traffic five meters above ground level, creating a grid pattern of straight, long avenues that varied in width between twelve and twenty-four meters and were specifically designed for the automobile. Round-point intersections were regularly spaced four hundred meters apart, accommodating high-speed traffic.[6]

The 1950 master plan for Belgrade, which was supposed to direct efforts for the following twenty years, reflected this modernist approach to mobility. Planners not only applied the functionalist approach to the organization of space in the city but no less ambitiously concerned themselves with Belgrade's place within the wider regional and even international transportation network, seeking to find the most efficient system possible for mediating movement to, from, through, and around the city.[7] Urban planners were clearly heartened by the key role given to them by a state committed to the central planning of resources.

The official publication explaining the master plan stated that, inside the city itself, the new internal street grid would be planned out on an orthogonal system, replacing the existing street pattern that had developed haphazardly over the centuries. This would be a differentiated street system, in which heavier traffic would be diverted to equally spaced main arteries. The planners established a hierarchy of street types with intersections placed closer or farther apart depending on the order of the street, disappearing entirely with the highest order roads, which would make use of over- and underpasses. The point of this differentiation was to optimize the speed of traffic within the city.[8]

This approach reached its apogee on the blank slate that was the new city center, which seemed in many ways a literalist adaptation of Le Corbusier's plan for the Radiant City. This settlement, completely designed for automotive traffic, was divided into vast blocks by broad principal roads (*magistrale*) and longitudinal roads. These blocks eschewed the traditional closed form that had predominated in Belgrade—in which a single building or series of buildings was placed along the perimeter, enclosing a courtyard—in favor of an open configuration, in which towers and slabs were freely placed and surrounded by green space. Inhabitants of this settlement would be able to fulfill their basic needs, such as buying groceries and sending their children to school, inside their housing community (*rejon*, later *mesna zajednica*), all within walking distance. To get anywhere else in New Belgrade—for example, to the leisure center planned on the riverbanks—or to access the old city center with its many commercial and cultural amenities, New Belgrade's inhabitants had to depend on these main roads, which, with their widely spaced intersections and complete absence of store frontage, were clearly not designed for pedestrians.[9]

New Belgrade did present, however, one major deviation from the Radiant City: it did not reproduce Le Corbusier's system for separating pedestrian and vehicular traffic. Such an involved scheme was likely beyond the new socialist state's budgetary means, but this omission also reflects the simple fact that urban planners did not intend to design a city for the automobile. Rather, they envisioned a city mainly serviced by public transportation—tramways, trolleybuses, and buses—as well as by a state-owned fleet of supply vehicles.

The rejection by Yugoslav urban planners of mass private automobile ownership was a direct consequence of the fact that Yugoslavia was a socialist state. In the period between 1949 and 1955, socialist policymakers in the country made rapid industrialization a priority, a choice that entailed focusing on investments in heavy industry and keeping salaries and wages low, which in turn pushed down personal consumption to a minimum. This had important implications for urban planning, including transportation. Fortunately, this orientation was compatible with the urban planners' modernist vision. Although Le Corbusier embraced the automobile, an approach that planners considered unsuitable for a developing socialist state like Yugoslavia, he also placed a great deal of emphasis on a collectivist approach to consumption. The Athens Charter was fundamentally a program for extending the benefits of modern living to all of society by maximizing collective consumption. Everyone, not just the wealthy, could enjoy a garden if gardens ceased to be private property and became public space, open to all. It would be possible to achieve this goal with existing resources if housing were made vertical and thus used up a smaller footprint of land, freeing up space for clean air, sunlight, and parks. Le Corbusier also argued that this project would require no additional financial resources, as no additional land would have to be purchased.[10]

Belgrade's urban planners latched on to the concept of providing a better standard of living to the entire population without additional cost through the collective use of space. It was on these grounds that they built apartment blocks instead of single-family homes, considered too costly for Yugoslavia's economy, and decided to put all their energy into public transportation rather than accommodating the privately owned automobile, which in any case the Yugoslav economy was not poised to produce in any significant number.

Thus the 1950 master plan for Belgrade was a plan for mobility without drivers or, more precisely, with only a small number of professional drivers (chauffeurs). Although the official publication about the plan provided some discussion of how the road system in the old city should be reconstructed to facilitate movement, there was no mention of personal automobile usage and the challenges that this particular form of transportation posed to the existing urban fabric. The sketches that accompanied the article on New Belgrade, whose avenues and highways were depicted as nearly empty, reflected this omission.[11]

Market Socialism, Consumerism, and the Emergence of a Middle-Class Car Culture

All this began to change in the mid-1950s, as part of the broader experimentation with market socialism. In 1955, President Josip Broz Tito announced that the state would reduce its capital investments and increase its production of consumer goods, a shift that was reflected in the social plan for 1957–64, Yugoslavia's version of a five-year plan. This projected increase in consumption went hand in hand with the emerging system of self-management. At the Second Party Plenum of 1959, Mijalko Todorović, a leading Party official from Serbia, explained that workers would be enticed to produce more by the promise of consuming more. Self-management gave this argument some plausibility as it allowed enterprises to keep a substantial part of their profits, some of which might be designated by the workers' council for salary increases.

Thus, beginning in the late 1950s, authorities officially began to encourage the population to spend on consumer goods, including automobiles. Overall consumption did in fact increase, by an annual average of 8.5 percent per year between 1957 and 1964. Zavodi Crvena Zastava, the factory whose international fame was secured by the Yugo, was poised to take advantage of the new demand that resulted from rising real wages. It had begun making cars in 1954 with the assistance of the Italian car giant Fiat, purportedly against the wishes of economic planners, who continued to obstruct Crvena Zastava's efforts to expand production. In market socialism however, the customer knew best. Crvena Zastava's yearly production jumped from 424 cars in 1956 to 1,935 cars in 1957, reaching 10,995 in 1961 and 25,960 in 1964.[12] Drivers endearingly called the car it produced the Fića, a diminutive for Fiat.

Moreover, Yugoslavs had access to a wide selection of imported cars, as advertisements for Škoda, Mazda, Wartburg, and Volvo in daily newspapers from the 1960s illustrate. Prospective drivers might also purchase foreign automobiles manufactured in Yugoslavia, such as the NSU Pretis, the product of a partnership between the German company NSU and the domestic Preduzeće Tito Sarajevo company. In 1968, *Borba,* the official newspaper of the League of Yugoslav Communists, reported that 110,000 new automobiles would be sold that year—56,000 domestic cars and 54,000 imports. The slogans used in advertisements to lure purchasers could have been taken out of any newspaper in a capitalist country, ranging from the pragmatic—"quality, security, comfort and economy" for Škoda—to the exotic—"road beauty from the Far East" for Mazda.[13]

The growth in automobile usage spawned a new market for other products and services. Jugopetrol, the state-owned petroleum company, boasted in the summer of 1968 that it would open up fifty-nine new gas stations by the end of the year.[14] Šumadija service center opened a new, expanded location in 1968 primarily to cater to increasing numbers of private automobile users. The new service center, which occupied a surface area of forty-one thousand square meters and was expected to employ five hundred people, offered both car maintenance and a sales office. Drivers could even take care of registration and insurance and buy spare parts and fuel all in the same place. As other chapters in this book suggest, car owners elsewhere in the Eastern Bloc could only have dreamed of this one-stop-shopping approach, which also entailed plans for a car wash to accommodate six hundred cars per day and a repair shop to house five hundred at one time. This giant operation would be run using modern managerial methods and technology. A "command bridge" would coordinate all activities using pneumatic tubes, intercom, and telephone.

Drivers who did not wish to leave their backyard to wash their cars might invest in a car wash automat for 14,000 dinars, with a down payment of 4,000 dinars, a sizable sum. The advertisement for this product was all the more remarkable in that it depicted not a luxury automobile but an ordinary car. The automat itself appeared to be located in the courtyard of a modernist apartment building, the very kind that was being built in New Belgrade. This scene not only associated automobile ownership with modern living but firmly located it within a middle-class landscape. It hinted at the possibility of integrating automobile usage into the collectivist consumption model, for readers encountering this advertisement might have asked themselves whether the automat in the image belonged to the car owner or was the property of the apartment building's housing community as a whole, available to all households for the care of their cars.[15] This ambiguity is important because it raises the question of whether the automobile was seen as somehow freeing the Yugoslav citizen from the constraints of the collectivist model.

It may seem strange to talk about a middle-class car culture in a supposedly classless socialist society. But in Yugoslavia, the existence of a system that encouraged workers to consume and promised higher levels of consumption eliminated the possibility of such a society. The opportunity to increase personal consumption did not present itself to all: only those who were productive, as measured in terms of profit, would have the chance to engage in conspicuous consumption. This was, in effect, a variant of the American Dream.

The appearance of media outlets devoted to the automobile also testified to the emergence of a middle-class car culture. The magazine *Auto: Jugoslavenska revija za automobilizam* began to appear on a monthly basis in 1968. *Auto* offered a predictable range of articles, from reviews of new automobiles to personality tests ("Is Your Steering Wheel Ruining Your Personality?"). The April 1968 issue also revealed an important aspect of this new car culture—its association with family travel. Articles dealing with this theme included "Our Signpost: Everyone to the Sea—Money or Hands Will Burn"; "Don't Forget the Brakes"; "Removing and Replacing Steering Wheels"; and "Our Advice: How Much Luggage Can You Put on Your Roof?"[16] An advertisement in a contemporary issue of *Borba* aimed specifically at automobile vacationers vaunted the qualities of Bulgarian highways, petrol stations, motels, and camping grounds.[17] These clues remind us that the explosion in automobile usage in Yugoslavia ran parallel to the growth in construction of weekend vacation homes, the so-called *vikendice* (similar to the Russian dacha and the Czech *chata*).[18]

Alongside this middle-class car culture there appeared a youth car culture. It included the officially sanctioned Academic Automobile Club (Akademski Auto Moto Klub) in Belgrade, a student-run affiliate, founded in 1947, of the Yugoslav Automobile Association (Auto Moto Savez Jugoslavije), which had its roots in the period before the Second World War. The Academic Automobile Club, which still exists today, trained student drivers and organized rallies, including the first Yugoslav-wide rally, which ran through Serbia, Bosnia Herzegovina, and Croatia in 1967.[19] There are hints, however, of a more rebellious car culture in Jovan Jovanović's *Mlad i zdrav kao ruža (Young and Healthy as a Rose)*, a 1971 cult film about a young criminal who returns to Belgrade after a prison stint and goes on a destructive rampage. During the opening credits of the film, the antihero cruises through Belgrade and across the Serbian countryside in a small car, perhaps a Fića. He projects an aura of rebelliousness at the wheel with his long hair and Union Jack-patterned shirt, occasionally dangling a cigarette from his mouth and taking a swig from a bottle of beer. Automobiles figured prominently in the film as the criminal element's mode of transportation of choice and as tools for spreading chaos. This was not your father's Oldsmobile or Buick. The film's depiction of wanton violence did not go over well with the authorities, and it was quietly removed from circulation after its premiere. Although this film likely did not play a role in popularizing a rebellious car culture, it may have reflected the existence of such a culture.

Motorists in Yugoslavia were largely brought into existence as subjects by market socialism. It not only provided them with the opportunity to buy vehicles but also promoted a variety of automobile fantasies that helped to define what it meant to be middle-class in Yugoslavia: washing the car next to the new apartment building, taking a vacation in Bulgaria, coming into contact with a beauty from the Far East. Were motorists willing to craft their identities within the discursive boundaries provided to them? The association of criminals and automobiles in *Mlad i zdrav kao ruža* suggests the possibility of another kind of car culture—an angry, rebellious, nihilistic culture that was not tolerated by the authorities. Encouraging citizens to form their identities was a bit like letting the genie out of the bottle.

The Second Master Plan: Mobility Reconsidered

Urban planners were slow to anticipate the growth in personal automobile usage that would come out of the shift in economic priorities from the late 1950s onward. New Belgrade, the construction of which had been suspended after the Tito-Stalin split and was renewed in 1960, provided a good barometer for the urban planning office's expectations of the present and future scope of automobile usage. Blocks number 1 and 2 of New Belgrade, which were designed in 1958 and 1959 and built between 1960 and 1963, were designed to contain a total of 12,425 inhabitants in 3,630 apartments. Planners set aside space for only 1,300 parking spots, or a ratio of roughly one automobile per 10 people. The real ratio proved even smaller, as the actual population of blocks 1 and 2 exceeded the original projections by 10 to 25 percent.[20] However, by 1966, when the conceptual plan for block 29 was adopted, urban planners had radically revised their expectations, anticipating a car ownership ratio of one car per 4 inhabitants.[21]

Urban planners had no choice but to recognize the challenge to the urban fabric posed by automobile usage. Automobile ownership had risen from 11.94 vehicles per thousand inhabitants in 1960 to 32.45 in 1965 and 81.8 in 1969. It would reach 180 automobiles per thousand inhabitants in 1973.[22] The most daunting challenge faced was how to deal with traffic in the old downtown core, which had never ceased being the cultural, commercial, and service center of the city in spite of ambitions to transfer its activities to New Belgrade. Moreover, in the 1950s and 1960s, population density in the city had increased as a result of the practice of building in previously unused parcels on city blocks. Additionally, nineteenth-century single-story buildings had been knocked down and replaced with modern high-rises. Whereas urban planners had made allowances, even if insufficient ones, for parking in the new housing settlements, very few projects to create parking were realized in the old city center.[23] This was partly a result of privileging housing construction over other types of construction because of the endemic housing shortage, but it was also due to urban planners' conviction that the country's economic means made automobile usage inappropriate. Unplanned growth on the city's periphery also likely aggravated the problem, as suburban inhabitants were just as likely to use their cars as to use public transportation to access the city center. The result was congestion of epic proportions—a classic case of automobility turning to immobility.

The chaos in the city center unleashed by automobile usage was compounded by the eruption of air and noise pollution. An article on hygiene in Belgrade published in 1969 highlighted the consequences of "the unresolved transportation problem, which aside from a direct endangering of life and health, has also created indirect problems endangering the hygiene of housing through air pollution and noise." The author cited a study that revealed that nearly the entire old city center suffered from intensive air pollution, attributed to industry, housing, and transportation.[24]

The first master plan had been designed as a useful tool for a period of twenty years, and by the late 1960s it had become clear that it needed updating. As the urban planning office of Belgrade (*urbanistički zavod*) geared up in 1967 to prepare a new plan, it was clear that the process would be very different than it had been twenty years before. Just as Belgrade was no longer the city that urban planners had confronted in 1945, so the planning profession had also evolved. Some things had not changed: the urban planners of the late 1960s continued to view their work as divorced from ideological questions, and the interest in global planning trends had only intensified over the years, as had the opportunities to travel abroad. Nonetheless, important changes had taken place within the profession, partly as a result of exposure to foreign urban planning trends. The profession had asserted its independence from architecture, building up its own professional institutions and establishing its own program at the University of Belgrade. Paradoxically, as it gained in self-confidence, it also broadened its scope to encompass the "science of man," incorporating social scientists and specialists in public health and public policy. In line with the development of self-management, there was an increasing interest in democratic planning methods. There were now substantially more women in the profession, although they were conspicuously few on the team charged with developing the new master plan. The team was much larger than the first, numbering eighty participants, including economists, a sociologist, and a specialist in municipal hygiene.[25]

When urban planners began to prepare a new master plan in 1967, they chose to make the problem of transportation a central concern. The official publication explaining the new plan left no doubt of this, showing numerous pictures of cars clogging streets, blocking sidewalks, and parked on public squares.[26] It is no coincidence that they sought out the technical expertise of planning specialists from Detroit's Wayne State University. These consultants brought with them knowledge of the "rational process" approach to planning. This approach perceived the city as a complex whole consisting of interconnected subsystems and posited that modifying an element in a subsystem had ramifications for the entire system; thus it was essential to estimate these consequences using computer modeling.

Quickly concluding that Belgrade's urban planning office was not sufficiently trained to properly use rational process methods, the Wayne State consultants adapted the theory to create a more limited procedure with a very heavy emphasis on transportation. The procedure consisted of three phases. In the first, different planners came up with fifteen concepts for the city's development, which would then be evaluated subjectively according to a number of criteria relating to transportation such as the relationship of work to housing areas, the existence of a multilevel road network, the location of public transportation terminals, the location of key infrastructure, the use of the river for public transport, the highway system, and the rail network. The two models judged most successful were then subjected by the consultants to a transportation study. In the second phase, based on the learning experience of the previous stage, the planning team created four new alternatives that it considered optimal for the relationship between land use and transportation, which it subjected to further analysis. Finally, the team devised a final alternative, which Wayne State University then subjected to comprehensive computer modeling, limited specifically to the issue of transportation.[27]

The details of the planning process are important because they reveal that, in spite of appearances, scientific modeling played less of a role than values in determining the content of the new master plan. After all, only one model was subjected to testing—the final model, which urban planners had developed through a process of subjective evaluation. Thus we should read the plan less as the outcome of an objective process than as a representation of urban planners' personal vision.

However, the new master plan was also shaped by a growing awareness among urban planners that, in spite of their continued commitment to collectivist modes of consumption, which they articulated most clearly on the topic of housing, they simply could no longer ignore motorists and their proclivities.[28] At the time of the adoption of the master plan, the rate of motorization was estimated to reach between 340 and 420 automobiles per thousand inhabitants, or one automobile per family, by 2000.[29] Instead of fighting against trends, they opted to try to manage them.

The new master plan abandoned the original concept of the 1950 plan to keep the city compact, adopting instead the idea of "inhabited islands in a sea of green." This was in keeping with European trends toward urban decentralization as a means of controlling growth, such as the Green Belt concept adopted in England in 1947 and the French model for the Villes Nouvelles located in the vicinity of Paris that was introduced in the mid-1960s. In keeping with these concepts, public transportation would continue to play the preponderant role in moving people around the city. The new master plan for Belgrade called for the creation of a mass rapid transit system, a metro consisting of two main lines.³⁰

The idea of mass rapid transit surely appealed to Belgrade's urban planners because of its collectivist nature, recalling the modernist argument that space and finances are used more efficiently when private resources are replaced with collectively owned alternatives. However, urban planners' accommodating attitude toward motorists is also worthy of notice. Rather than replacing automobile usage, the metro would work in tandem with it: they would build open-air parking lots next to metro stations outside the city center to encourage motorists to leave their cars behind when visiting the city center. Other positive and negative incentives were planned to ensure that 60 to 70 percent of traffic to the city center would be by means of public transportation. Planners did, however, plan to build parking garages on the edges of the city center for those who wished to drive in spite of the restrictions, as well as in secondary centers in the city.³¹

AUTOMOBILITY in Belgrade after the Second World War was the product of the confluence of two different visions: that of urban planners, who embraced a collectivist notion of mobility, and that of motorists, who embraced a more autonomous, individualistic notion. Urban planners ultimately lost the battle, unable to impose their will on a population of aspiring motorists aided by the new market mechanisms that made it easy to buy and maintain a car. In one sense, this story about a battle of wills between urban planners and motorists is particular to Yugoslav state socialism, illustrating its gradual transition from a centrally planned economy to a decentralized, perhaps even uncoordinated, system in which the logic of the market overruled official notions of the common good. This, clearly, is not a story that could be told in most Eastern Bloc countries.

What, then, was socialist about the particular form of automobility that emerged in Belgrade in the thirty years after the Second World War? Here, counterintuitively, we must again turn to the urban planners. They still retained much control in other areas that had repercussions for automobility, and they never confused the logic of the market with the concept of the common good, a distinction that was blurred in many planning offices across the world.

Turning to the first issue, although urban planners could not resist the onslaught of the automobile, they did play an important role in shaping the growth of the city in other ways. They continued to determine the form and content of new housing settlements and in this connection the location and size of shopping facilities. They persisted in designing neighborhoods according to modernist notions of rationality, seeking to ensure that everyday needs were met locally. Each of the high-density settlements they designed had its own local shopping facilities, and a local shopping center with more specialized shops was located in the vicinity. The construction of retail facilities often lagged several years behind that of housing, and once built, they did not always meet all the inhabitants' needs. However, urban planners continued to rely on this model, rejecting the supposedly inexorable logic of the shopping-mall suburb, so ubiquitously associated with the automobile. This is perhaps a testament to the limitations of market socialism, as retail stores continued to be part of the social sector, and their managers accepted subordination of their profitability to concerns about access. Although automobility had an important impact on the spatial organization of cities worldwide, this impact did not take the same form in state socialist cities.

Urban planners continued to hold on to a socialist-modernist notion of the good life, which sought to maximize access to municipal goods while minimizing cost through collective consumption. State socialist urban planners might have to contend with market forces, but they continued to distinguish between the logic of the market and the common good. The latter did not always win out, unfortunately. As Yugoslavia's economy sank in the global crisis of the 1970s, projects for a mass rapid transit system were shelved, demonstrating yet again the country's vulnerability to global economic forces and limiting urban planners' capacity to put constraints on automobile usage in the city.

6

ON THE STREETS OF A TRUCK-BUILDING CITY

Naberezhnye Chelny in the Brezhnev Era

Esther Meier

"All roads lead to KamAZ!" So proclaimed the newspapers in the 1970s as they sought to mobilize people for the large-scale project on the banks of the Kama. The truck factory KamAZ (Kamskii Avotmobil'nyi Zavod—Kama Automotive Factory) and the new city of Naberezhnye Chelny were one of the major projects of the Brezhnev era. Naberezhnye Chelny was renamed Brezhnev after the death in 1982 of Leonid Brezhnev, the USSR state and Party leader, and thereby became a symbol of an entire era.[1] In the 1970s and early 1980s thousands of workers from all parts of the Soviet Union came to Naberezhnye Chelny. They built KamAZ and a new town. They built the streets and the transportation system of a city planned to be a post-Stalinist model town, a "city of the future."

This chapter is about the streets of Naberezhnye Chelny during the Brezhnev era. It is about the vehicles that traveled those streets—the streetcars, buses, trucks, and cars—and the people who used those streets and vehicles. This model city of the future was designed to make good, in urban planning terms, on the promises the political leadership had given the workers in return for their participation in this large project. These promises included—in addition to an apartment of one's own,[2] an education, vacation time, and recreation—one's own car. In the Soviet Union, the way had been paved for motorizing the masses with the construction of the VAZ automobile factory in Togliatti, which began turning out the Zhiguli (exported under the Lada trademark) in the 1970s. Indications of a rising standard of living called for appropriate urban expression. What kind of everyday life was planned for the people of Naberezhnye Chelny? What was the transportation system like, and to what extent did planning take the use of private vehicles into account?

This chapter examines the symbolic significance of streets and how people took possession of them. For those living in the region before the new city was built,

Naberezhnye Chelny meant a transition from narrow, winding streets to broad, straight avenues. Streets are crucial to how a city is perceived, particularly in terms of the contrasting perceptions of the Stalinist and post-Stalinist city. People walked and drove along the new streets. How they got around in their city may also be inferred from the disjunction between planning and implementation, as well as from distribution policy.

KamAZ and Naberezhnye Chelny: A Short Introduction

KamAZ was established in the small town of Naberezhnye Chelny, or Iar Chally, as it is called in the Tatar language. The factory complex was located in the eastern part of the Tatar Autonomous Soviet Socialist Republic on the river Kama, some one hundred miles to the east of Kazan' and six hundred miles to the east of Moscow; within the Soviet Union, it was, geographically speaking, relatively central.

Construction commenced in 1969. Before 1969 Naberezhnye Chelny had had just under forty thousand inhabitants, mostly Tatars and Russians. In the Brezhnev era workers from all parts of the Soviet Union came to Naberezhnye Chelny, with Russians forming the vast majority. In its heyday in the early 1970s as many as forty thousand people were arriving every year. However, although a great many workers came, many also left when they found that their hopes had not been fulfilled.[3] Nevertheless, efforts to permanently settle workers were more successful in Naberezhnye than in other places with similar large-scale projects. Today Naberezhnye Chelny is the second-largest city in the Republic of Tatarstan with more than half a million inhabitants.

KamAZ and Naberezhnye Chelny were projects of the Soviet Union as a whole. As such, they were planned in Moscow. The central planning authorities (Gosplan, Gosstroi, and the Ministry of the Automobile Industry) took VAZ (Vol'zhskii Avtomobil'nyi Zavod) and Togliatti as their model. Togliatti was the natural choice, as VAZ had been the last major Soviet project in the automotive industry before KamAZ. Its construction had begun only three years before the advent of KamAZ. At that time, VAZ represented the most advanced state of technology in the Soviet Union. In addition, Togliatti, which was located on the Volga only two hundred miles from Naberezhnye Chelny, offered similar climatic and geological conditions. The architect Boris Rubanenko, who had planned Togliatti, was also commissioned to design Naberezhnye Chelny.[4]

But before the future could arrive with its broad, straight avenues, the past, with its narrow, winding streets, had to be erased. The factory and the new town needed space. The gigantic factory complex alone covers an area of sixteen thousand acres, equivalent to more than twelve thousand football fields.[5] Contrary to what Soviet accounts repeatedly claimed, KamAZ and the new city of Naberezhnye Chelny were not built in open fields. Builders had to first demolish the old Chelny, which consisted mostly of two-story houses, the bottom of stone and the top of wood. Several villages were also cleared away in the 1970s. Former residents either moved to newly created estates of prefabricated buildings or left the region. The Nizhnekamsk hydroelectric plant, construction of which began near Naberezhnye Chelny in 1963, submerged large parts of the region. The plant was one of the main reasons for the choice of Naberezhnye Chelny as the location for the truck factory. KamAZ and the creation of an artificial lake stretching to the Udmurt and Bashkir Autonomous Soviet Socialist Republics changed the region dramatically in the 1970s. Hundreds of settlements disappeared from the map. Many villages ceased to exist as a result of the migration to the major building sites.[6] Unlike the 1930s, the 1970s were not a period in which social and cultural upheavals were experienced collectively throughout the Soviet Union. But they were a time of radical changes at the regional level and in terms of individual experience, particularly for the rural population. For the people in the east of Tatarstan the 1970s turned out to be a period of profound change.

On the Road to the Future

One of the first things to be built in Naberezhnye Chelny was the street that now links the southwestern and northeastern parts of the city. Construction of the new city was begun in the southwest, the area where the old Chelny had stood. The building organization Kamgesenergostroi, which had been entrusted with the construction of the hydroelectric plant before it took on construction of KamAZ and the new city, had its headquarters there even before 1969. In addition, the buildings of old Chelny, before they were razed, provided accommodation for the workers. During the initial phase, this southwest area offered short traveling distances for workers and building materials. The centerpiece of the city of the future—KamAZ and the new city's center—lay farther to the east, however. A connecting road was built that cut right through the middle of the village of Orlovka. Before 1969, the inhabitants of Orlovka had been predominantly collective farmers who lived on the outskirts of the small town of Naberezhnye Chelny. Under the new development plan, the Orlovka area found itself in the middle of the new city. Orlovka was one of the villages slated for demolition to make way for this large-scale project.

The road from old Chelny through Orlovka to the northeastern part of the new city is one of Naberezhnye Chelny's two central traffic axes. The media celebrated

6.1 "The New Chelny," painting by Andrei Vashurov, 1976. Rausa Sultanova, *Iskusstvo novykh gorodov Respubliki Tatarstan (1960–1990 gg.). Zhivopis', grafika, monumental'no-dekorativnoe iskusstvo, skul'ptur* (Kazan: IJaLI im. G. Iragimova, 2001), 46.

this road, which links the old with the new, as the "road to the future." Andrei Vashurov depicted it in 1976 in his painting *The New Chelny*. In the foreground is Orlovka with its wooden houses and the Orthodox church, while the new Chelny, with its prefabricated buildings and the smokestacks of KamAZ, looms in the background. Orlovka is represented in dark colors, while the new city appears in white, bright and gleaming. The new city casts its radiance upon those parts of Orlovka that border on the city. The road thus connects darkness with light. It is traveled by trucks on which the building slabs have been loaded. The idea this is intended to convey is obvious: the city and industry, not the village or church, represent the future toward which one must strive. This future is transported on trucks.

The truck was, along with the car, the automotive vehicle of the "social contract."[7] Trucks and cars were both symbols of a rise in the standard of living. The centerpiece of the social contract was the construction of mass housing, which could be achieved only with the aid of trucks. This policy, which the political leadership hoped would have a stabilizing effect, also included the building of KamAZ. The social contract drove a Zhiguli and was transported on a KamAZ.[8]

But many inhabitants of Orlovka were not willing parties to this contract. For them, the trucks and the new road that cut a swath through their village were not harbingers of a bright future. Rather, they stood for the destruction of their past and present. The road was loud. The village's inhabitants were exposed to a noise level that they were not accustomed to. Nikolai Aleshkov, born in 1945 and raised along with his four brothers and sisters in Orlovka, remembers that his father complained about the noise.[9] In Aleshkov's 1981 poem "Ever Smaller Becomes My Circle of Friends," the asphalt-paved streets of Naberezhnye destroy nature and memory:

Сломают скоро старый дом в моей бревенчатой Орловке, и вся она пойдет на слом, чтобы в бетонной встать обновке.	Soon they will tear down the old house, in my wooden Orlovka, and the whole village is destined for demolition, to arise again in concrete.
Но где найти тогда исток любви и дружбы изначальной? Ведь речки детства измельчали в плену асфальтовых дорог.[10]	But where are sources of love and first friendship then to be found? How the little rivers of childhood have shallowed in the captivity of the asphalted streets.

Vashurov's painting and Aleshkov's poem have the same theme. But the Soviet cult of technology and progress was by no means undisputed in the 1970s. Like the proponents of the Village Prose movement—*the* literary event of the Brezhnev era[11]—Aleshkov rejects the ideal of industrialization and urbanization. The wide avenues that promise short travel times stand not for freedom but for confinement and captivity.

110　**ESTHER MEIER**

Modern Times

The planned alternative to old Chelny and the surrounding villages was a "modern city." The workers were promised a "modern life" (*sovremennyi byt*) for their participation in the project. And it was to look like this:

Stylishly dressed people stroll through the city; women in miniskirts stand alongside large cars. Paris and London are not the only cities that have these things—Naberezhnye Chelny has them too! Grandmothers in head scarves and stressed mothers with shopping bags and children are not a part of this picture. Young, slender people, post-Stalinist architecture, chic clothing, and cars were the symbols of a modern life with more consumer goods and freedom. How modern life was conceived owed less to the Soviet Union's real economic possibilities than to competition with the industrialized nations of the West, as will be shown below.

As the historian Monica Rüthers has noted, Stalinist architectural drawings usually showed only buildings, static and lifeless. Beginning in the late 1950s, these pictures became more dynamic, and people and cars began to appear. This shift reflected the changes in the visual culture after the death of Stalin. Light, dy-

6.2 Naberezhnye Chelny—the "city of the future": modern architecture, chic clothing, and big cars. *Arkhitektura SSSR*, no. 8 (1976), 13.

6.3 Naberezhnye Chelny—the city center. *Arkhitektura SSSR*, no. 8 (1976), 13.

namic images were necessary to evoke the carefree life that had been promised to a younger generation with no direct experience of terror and war.[12]

Figure 6.2 shows the plan for the center of Naberezhnye Chelny with a pedestrian zone lined by shops and cafés and laid over underground garages. Accompanied by his well-dressed wife, the Soviet man drives his own car from his own apartment on a shopping spree. This was the dream of Naberezhnye Chelny.

The Linear City: Driving on a Beautiful Highway

Though poems such as the one by Aleshkov could be published during the Brezhnev era, critics of the large-scale project had no lobby. The new Naberezhnye Chelny was built with tremendous speed. The city and its surroundings were made up of horizontally arranged functional zones designed according to a linear pattern:

> recreational zone
> residential zone
> protective zone with a transport strip
> industrial zone
> agricultural zone

Work began in the southwest on a linear residential zone that stretched along the future reservoir—the impounding basin was not flooded until 1978—toward the northeast. While the old town of Chelny stood on both sides of the Kama

6.4 Naberezhnye Chelny with the residential zone along the river Kama and the industrial zone (the square is KamAZ). *Respublika Tatarstan. Obshchegeograficheskaia karta* (Omsk: Omskaia kartograficheskaia fabrika Roskartografii, 2001). Reproduced with permission.

River, the new city was confined to the south bank. The planners designated the Kama and the large woodland areas adjacent to a recreational zone for the urban population. The residential zone bordered on the recreational zone to the north and to the south on the protective zone that separated the residential zone from the industrial zone. The three thousand-foot-wide protective zone contained green spaces and a linear corridor for public and private traffic—for buses, streetcars, and automobiles. South of the protective zone lay the industrial zone consisting of the KamAZ factory complex and a few other smaller industrial plants. To provide for the multitude streaming into Naberezhnye Chelny, an agricultural zone was created, completely restructuring the region's agriculture.[13]

The linear city model owes its origin to the Spanish urban planner Arturo Soría y Mata, whose work was published in 1883.[14] Various urban planners followed his ideas, but it was not until the Russian Revolution that the conditions existed for implementation of the linear city on a large scale. Nationalizing the land opened up entirely new possibilities for urban planners, who no longer needed to trouble themselves over matters of ownership. While the parceling of land prevented

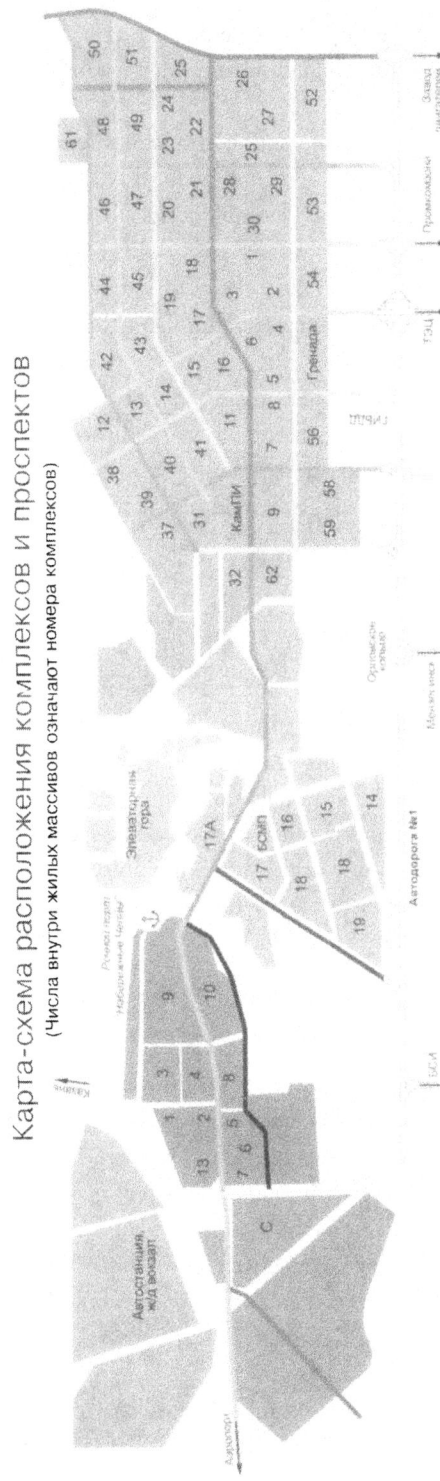

6.5 The residential zone with the microraions and the highway. *Naberezhnye Chelny. Karta-skhema goroda* (Naberezhnye Chelny: OOO "Grant-Trejd," 2001).

urban planners in Western Europe from giving free rein to their imaginations, planning in the Soviet Union could comprise large areas.[15] Utopian settlement patterns came to be realized.

The seminal work for the implementation of the linear city in the Soviet Union was *Sotsgorod* (*The Socialist City*), written in 1930 by Nikolai Miliutin, the chairman of the State Committee for the Planning of Socialist Cities.[16] The linear city model made its breakthrough in the early 1930s with Magnitogorsk, Stalingrad (Volgograd), and Zelenyi Gorod. In the wake of forced urban development under Khrushchev and Brezhnev, it was revived and implemented in Angarsk,[17] Novopolotsk, and Naberezhnye Chelny.

The concept of the linear city arose during the second half of the nineteenth century, a time when the negative consequences of industrialization were increasingly perceived to be a problem and solutions were sought that would get the workers out of the factory districts. The corridor structure that Miliutin developed ensured a division of the city into four functional areas—for living, working, recreation, and circulation—as the Congrès Internationaux d'Architecture Moderne (CIAM) was to call for in 1933 (published in the Athens Charter). It would protect the workers from the stresses of industry and traffic and allow them to live near recreational areas and close to nature. Proximity to nature, for that matter, was regarded as the realization of one of the core goals of Soviet planning: elimination of the contrast between city and country. As Miliutin wrote in 1930, industrial workers should be able to enjoy the advantages of country life—"air, forest, fields,"[18] while at the same time the rural population should have access to the advantages of city life—educational institutions, theaters, museums, etc.

Miliutin and his successors discussed the advantages of the linear city also from the standpoint of equality. The ideal linear city would offer more than just a separation of functions. Because the residents would all live at similar distances from the various functional zones, they would all be equally exposed to the negative phenomena of industry and traffic—and at least a rudimentary attempt was made to take wind movement into account—but would also have equal access to the recreational areas, water, and woods. By contrast, in a concentric settlement plan with a green zone around the city, exemplified by Moscow, only those who lived on the city's periphery were within quick reach of the woods. And unlike the "capitalist city," where according to the planners only the privileged typically had a view of the water while everyone else lived along transit lines or in the shadow of factory smokestacks, a linear settlement structure would be conducive to creating a city without preferential residential locations and hence without social segregation.[19]

The linear city was a model that promoted proximity to nature, but unlike the garden city movement[20] and more radical early Soviet plans—and notwithstanding Soviet planners' disapproval of megacities—it also did not preclude the building of large cities, which required rapid transport of people and goods. The linear settlement pattern was thought by its proponents to be especially suited for this purpose, even accommodating an increase in private traffic. The development of a rapid transit system would give structure to the linear city. The green zone and the traffic corridor with the highway formed the centerpiece in a sequence of functional zones linked to one another via vertical streets. The transport corridor would do more than just keep transit traffic out of the residential zone. It was also intended to have its pleasant side for travelers and passengers. The highway would be lined with trees. One would travel along a beautiful strip, enjoying the ride and a life that could only be described as wonderful. Or as Gogol wrote, "What Russian does not love a fast ride? [I kakoi zhe russkii ne liubit bystroi ezdy?]."[21]

The Microdistrict: The Freedom Not to Have a Car

The planners of Naberezhnye Chelny designed a city in which people could move about easily in their own cars, on the highway and on broad, straight avenues. The many pedestrian underpasses, which reduced the use of traffic lights, ensured fast progress from one point to another. The city also accommodated garages and parking areas. But an extensive bus and streetcar network was also planned to obviate the use of private vehicles. And planners also devalued the idea of a car as an absolute necessity by applying the concept of the *microraion* (microdistrict).

The residential zone was divided into microdistricts. Ideally no mere concentration of prefabricated buildings, a microdistrict was an autonomous unit in which all the facilities serving everyday needs were within walking distance. Each microdistrict in Naberezhnye Chelny was designed for eight thousand to twelve thousand people. The size of the microdistrict depended on the size of the middle school (*sredniaia shkola*) district. Each microdistrict theoretically contained one middle school, a kindergarten and nursery, shops, a public dining hall, and sports facilities.[22]

Let us take a somewhat closer look at the second microdistrict in northeastern Naberezhnye Chelny.

Note on figure 6.6 that 2–13 is a school, 2–14 a child-care facility. The schools and kindergartens were positioned in the microdistricts so that the children would not have to cross any streets. In the second microdistrict, the maximum distance from the place of residence to the day-care center was to be a mere 984 feet. Parents driving their children to the day nursery do not appear in this model. The distance to all the facilities serving everyday needs should not have exceeded 1,640 feet.[23] According to these plans, the modern life that the people

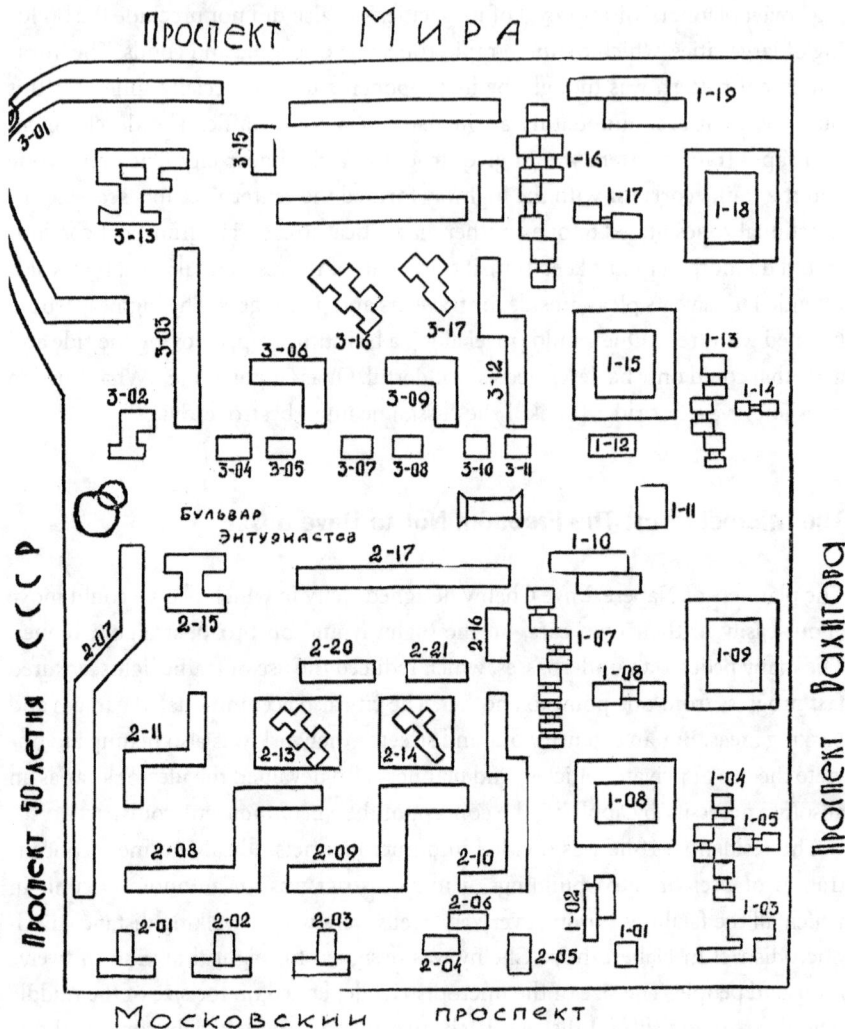

6.6 Microraions 1 to 3: The numbers on the map indicate complete addresses (3-03: microraion number 1, house number 1). *Vse o KamAZe*, no. 3 (1976), 64.

were promised—education, health care, and access to consumer goods—lay just beyond what were now their own flats. Such short walks could be achieved only by building tall and high-density housing.

Two to three microdistricts were grouped into one residential district (*zhiloi raion*). Thus microdistricts 1 to 3 made up residential district 1. Broad avenues bound all four sides of a residential district with parking areas planned to be mainly between the residential districts and the avenues. Those on foot relied on underpasses to travel from one residential district to another. In the residential zone the streets were arranged on a horizontal axis, the central street being the road to the future described above. The horizontal traffic routes in the residential zone and the horizontal transit street were connected to one another via vertically arranged streets, thereby creating a grid-shaped pattern. This was not, however, comparable to the street layout of many American cities with which we are familiar. The road network in Naberezhnye Chelny was far less dense, which, for the inhabitants, made a significant difference. It was not only because of the lower traffic density but also because of the street layout that the inhabitants of Naberezhnye Chelny were far less exposed to traffic nuisances than the inhabitants of American cities. The residential districts were closed to through traffic. Only emergency vehicles, delivery vehicles, and residents with cars could travel in them.

The Soviet man or woman might travel by car but did not have to, thanks to the combination of a linear settlement pattern with the urban unit of the microdistrict. This was the theory. In contrast to the Americans, the Soviet citizen was not dependent upon his own car and was therefore truly free. This concept of freedom could be applied only to the urban population, however, and it was applicable to them only if what was planned was also implemented, as will be discussed below. For the rural population, this construct was of little relevance to everyday life. In the 1970s even a regular school bus service was not something that could be taken for granted in some rural areas.

Getting around in Naberezhnye Chelny

At a time when the streetcar had disappeared from many Western European and North American cities due to mass motorization, Naberezhnye Chelny was designed to have a streetcar system. Urban planners in the West considered the streetcar old-fashioned and, because it was restricted to rails, inflexible, but the socialist countries adopted the streetcar after the war nonetheless.[24] The streetcar system went into operation in Naberezhnye Chelny in 1973. At the time, people rode to the "Teatral'naia" stop, but there was no theater. They could ride farther to the "Center" stop, where they would find themselves standing next to a mountain of piled earth. The streetcar ran, and the stops acquired their names, but what those names referred to did not yet exist.[25] The stops marked space. They were an invitation to the people to imagine the future city. What was and was not built, which plans were and were not implemented affected how the people of Naberezhnye Chelny lived during the 1970s and continues to do so today. How the people got around in their city may be inferred from the disjunction between the built and the unbuilt and from the means of transportation and their users.

According to the plans, Soviet parents did not need any means of transportation to take their children to the day-care center. But this plan worked only if the children got a place in the microdistrict in which they lived. In the 1970s thousands of children in Naberezhnye Chelny were on the waiting list for placement in day care. Implementation lagged behind planning, for one thing; for another, the demographic situation specific to Naberezhnye Chelny had not been taken sufficiently into account during the planning phase. Newcomers were predominantly young, and the birthrate was much higher than in the average Soviet city. Parents could be thankful if they got a place in day care at all, even if it was at the other end of the city.[26] The long routes diminished the value of the microdistrict concept and the freedom of not having a car.

The linear city idea itself was undermined. The dearth of child-care places led to bizarre solutions. In Naberezhnye Chelny, not only did much that was planned remain unbuilt, but some was also built that had not been planned, such as a group of kindergartens. Finding the land on which to build such a project was difficult. Land available for building in the residential zone had been set aside for structures envisaged in the general plan. The green strip, which planners had envisioned for traffic, was appropriated for construction of the kindergartens. Children played between KamAZ and the transit axis. The functional separation intended to protect people was abandoned.[27]

The money invested in Naberezhnye Chelny went primarily into the construction of KamAZ. What was left over was used for residential and road construction. The infrastructure in the microdistricts remained incomplete. There was a lack not only of child-care centers but also of libraries, theaters, sports fields, other recreational facilities, and shops. Large self-service supermarkets opened in Naberezhnye Chelny during the 1970s, though in a limited number. What was sought was often far away.[28] What remained unbuilt contributed to a situation in which people spent much of their time traveling from one place to another throughout the city.

They traveled along broad and straight avenues—just as they had in other cities during the Stalin period. And yet a ride down Gorky Street (Tverskaia) in Moscow was different from a ride down Prospekt Mira in Naberezhnye Chelny. It was the perspective from the street that revealed to the observer a crucial difference between the Stalinist and post-Stalinist city: unlike the housing superblocks of the Stalinist period, the microdistricts faced not outward toward the traffic axes but inward, away from the streets. While the apartment buildings in a perimeter block development were subordinated to the aim of creating imposing lines of sight along thoroughfares that converged at the center of power, the buildings of a microdistrict were grouped around a school and a kindergarten.[29] If one traveled along the Stalinist thoroughfares, one's view was drawn toward a single target. If one traveled along the post-Stalinist avenues, one was able to see into the microdistricts because of their asymmetrical and open coverage. The view from the street demonstrated to pedestrians, motorists, and passengers alike the opening of the post-Stalinist city, which Rüthers interpreted as symbolic of a more open society.[30] Planning, including traffic planning, was geared to the people's daily routine and did not give priority to creating a dramatic backdrop for power. The streets underwent a reinterpretation.

The Daily Struggle for Mobility

Let us proceed now to the means of transportation and those who used them. People traveled through the city, from the child-care center to the workplace, from the workplace to the shops, from the shops to their homes, and from their homes to their sports activities. Linear cities are long. Soría y Mata already knew this, but he saw the key factor in urban living not in distance but in travel time. In the case of Naberezhnye Chelny, the distance of eleven miles could, because of the linear street layout and the pedestrian underpasses, be covered in a continuous run and in a relatively short time. It became difficult if means of transportation were lacking.

Those who were lucky got a seat in a *marshrutka* (minibus). As already mentioned, up to forty thousand people were moving to Naberezhnye Chelny each year in the early 1970s. They came to a city in which the transportation system had yet to be set up. Before the streetcar went into operation, minibuses transported people. They were completely overcrowded and traveled irregularly.[31] Despite the central importance of work in Soviet theory, it was precisely on the route to work that the weak points of the linear city became apparent. Some of the routes to work were very long. Few worked on the link roads where they lived. "[A] worker's home will be situated no more than ten to twenty minutes' walk from his machine," Miliutin stipulated, but this was a utopian dream of the distant past.[32] The planners calculated for Naberezhnye Chelny a traveling time of no more than thirty to forty minutes from the home to the workplace.[33] This, however, could be achieved only under ideal conditions that did not exist. Workers came late to work. The lunch break was not long enough for a hot meal because, in the beginning, the cafeterias were often too far away.[34] The workers arrived back late from lunch. The workers in Naberezhnye Chelny broke the rules of job discipline not only because they drank too much or did not feel like working but also because they lacked the necessary mobility. And those who violated the rules stood little chance of increasing their mobility: those who came to work late were moved further down the waiting list for a car of their own or were struck from the list altogether (see below).

For many, Naberezhnye Chelny was not what they had hoped it would be. And they left. But even that was not easy—without means of transportation. Marat Abdullin came to Naberezhnye Chelny from Kazan in 1973 but left after a few months. "Getting to Naberezhnye Chelny was not difficult. But getting away from there was an impossibility. No buses, no ships, no railroad. Everything was overcrowded, tickets were unobtainable."[35] Today Abdullin interprets this as a deliberate measure to prevent people from leaving.

Disciplining the Drunk Worker

The streetcar system that went into operation in 1973 increased the mobility of Naberezhnye Chelny's inhabitants. Who, then, would drive his own car down the Prospekt Musa Dzhalil', and who would take the streetcar or bus? This matter was decided by Naberezhnye Chelny's two major industrial concerns—the construction organization Kamgesenergostroi and especially KamAZ. Power and the implementation of the social contract lay in their hands. They decided who received an apartment, a car, a vacation on the Black Sea.

Various incentives were created to mobilize the workers for the KamAZ and Naberezhnye Chelny projects. The crucial and, from a long-term perspective, most effective incentives were, first, the hope of having an apartment of one's own and, second, the prospect of education and social advancement. The first motive was shared in particular by those migrating from cities in which, even in the 1970s, it was not uncommon for two or three generations to be living in one room. The rural population was drawn primarily by the second motive. Secondary incentives included refrigerators, carpets, vacation trips, bonuses, higher wages—and cars.[36] This mobilization policy was not based on a tacit agreement, as researchers usually assume, but was anchored in labor legislation: "Blue- and white-collar workers who fulfill their work obligations successfully and conscientiously will receive preferential treatment when it comes to the distribution of privileges and concessions in the sociocultural field and in accommodation (stays at health resorts/vacations, improvement in living conditions, etc.)."[37]

But the waiting lists for coveted goods were not just an expression of scarcity. They were also a means of binding the workers to the factories. A large-scale operation such as KamAZ was able to function successfully only if it succeeded in permanently settling the workers. There was no interest in those referred to as "construction swallows," who would "fly" from one major construction site to another to reap the bonuses. The cars were not intended for them. A manual worker who wished to have a car of his own had to prove his loyalty to KamAZ. Aside from occupational qualifications—specialists were given preferential treatment—length of service was a crucial criterion for distribution.

As far as one can tell from the files, there were many apartments to be allocated in Naberezhnye Chelny during the Brezhnev era but few cars.[38] Many received their own apartments more quickly there than they normally would have in other Soviet cities. This does not appear to have been the case with cars. The car served as a symbol of modern life in the imagery used to promote the large-scale project to the public, and urban planning took it into account. But it was available only in limited supply. Automobility failed to materialize in Naberezhnye Chelny.

Cars, apartments, and vacations, however, were a means not only of mobilizing but also of disciplining the workers. Those who fulfilled their obligations successfully and conscientiously received rewards, and those who did not received penalties or had their privileges taken away from them: "[T]hose who violate public order will be harshly penalized, . . . and the incentive of getting a car withdrawn."[39] The main reasons for disciplinary measures were, first, arriving late for work or not arriving at all and, second, drunkenness; the second was one of the main reasons for the first. Workers were lying in drying-out cells instead of being at their workbenches. In 1977 alone, 14,649 people passed through drying-out cells in Naberezhnye Chelny.[40] The problem of alcoholism in Naberezhnye Chelny was categorized as "alarming."

Regular drunkenness was of course a good argument against giving someone a car. However, even those who took public transportation were not safe from intoxicated drivers. In discussions about the alcohol problem in Naberezhnye Chelny, the condition of employees of the municipal transport carriers attracted particular attention. Authorities removed 764 drivers from their positions in 1975 because they were not sober. Checkpoints were set up at which the condition of the drivers was scrutinized before and after their work shifts. Inspectors monitored the drivers along their routes. Not allowing alcohol at the steering wheel was a regular topic at meetings of the municipal transport carrier. It was thought that sports would provide a remedy. The bus and streetcar drivers boxed, practiced track-and-field athletics, and placed first in car rallies (with the Volga model GAZ-24). But all this was of little use. In 1975, 36 drivers had their driver's licenses revoked, 15 were dismissed, and 10 were sent to drug rehabilitation clinics. Compared with what was happening, however, these measures cannot be described as taking tough action. It is a good thing the streets were straight and wide.[41]

Socialist Cars in a Socialist City?

Naberezhnye Chelny was a city designed to accommodate an increase in private traffic without sacrificing the dominant position of public transportation. The car was a key symbol of the modern way of life in media portrayals, but traffic planning did not assign to it preferential status over buses and the streetcar. Private traffic was not the structure-defining element of planning familiar to Western Europeans in the period that saw the advent of mass mobility, the 1950s and 1960s. Although the Zhiguli created the conditions for mass mobility in the Soviet Union in the 1970s, this did not result in the adoption of earlier Western European models, which were themselves reversions to American models. Rather, the models in the East and West converged in the 1970s. The economic crisis made clear the limits of growth in the West, the case for environmental protection became more compelling, and the effects of automotive pollution on people and the natural environment became an important topic. As a result, public transportation assumed importance in the West again. At the same time, planning in the Soviet Union factored in an increase in private traffic in the wake of the new consumption policy.

In 1933 CIAM called for a radical break with historical city structures and for functional separation. Le Corbusier formulated and published this challenge in 1943 in the Athens Charter. After the war it was a guiding principle in urban and traffic planning in both East and West.[42] The principle of functional separation, however, could be implemented far more radically in Soviet cities than in capitalist cities. This was especially true of cities such as Naberezhnye Chelny, the planning of which completely ignored the region's history. Because of the more rigorous implementation of functional separation—though, as has been said, its implementation was not always consistent—people were far better shielded from the impact of traffic in a linear city than in many Western cities, though often they were forced to accept long travel routes. The models were similar in the East and West. How they were implemented, however, depended on how ownership and power were structured. Linear cities required central planning. They were built only in the Soviet Union and, in nascent form, in Brazil (Brasilia) and China (Shenzen). But the linear city model remains attractive to contemporary planners as well precisely because of the way it routes traffic. Experts continue to discuss possible variations of the linear city to this very day.[43]

Naberezhnye Chelny is a city constructed in a way that would not have been possible in the West. In this sense, it may be defined as a socialist city. But what about the cars that traveled its streets? What is peculiar to the Soviet car is less its social and cultural attributes than its place in the power structure. Acquiring a car was not just a question of affording it. The car was a means of mobilization and

6.7 Naberezhnye Chelny, 1979. S. A. Bogatko, *Tovarishch KamAZ* (Moscow: Plakat, 1979).

discipline, and it was a means of binding workers to the factories. However, cars were in short supply in the Soviet Union, a fact that severely limited their function as instruments of power. It made no difference to a worker whether he was denied a car because he regularly arrived late for work or was denied one even though he was never late for work.

Automobility failed to appear in the Brezhnev era, at least in provincial towns like Naberezhnye Chelny. A Soviet man did not drive his own car from his own apartment to the center of town on a shopping spree with his well-dressed wife and park in the underground garages. It was not only for lack of a car that he did not do this, but also because in Naberezhnye Chelny there was no center. Construction of the center, conceived as the epitome of the modern life, has not been completed to this day. The underground garages have never been built.

7

UNDERSTANDING A CAR IN THE CONTEXT OF A SYSTEM

Trabants, Marzahn, and East German Socialism

Eli Rubin

The Trabant is probably the most potent symbol of *Ostalgie*—that wave of longing for the return of certain aspects of the GDR that swept former East Germans and even West Germans in the two decades after the fall of the Berlin Wall. Before 1989, the Trabant, with its two-stroke engine, plastic fiberglass body, and terrible quality, was for many West Germans, and Westerners in general, the most potent symbol of socialism's incompetence and inferiority in comparison with their own world. The whimsical fascination with Trabis began as they started to disappear, along with the world that produced them. As more and more Trabants were replaced with Audis, Opels, or VWs or were even repainted, souped up, turned into traveling advertisements, or outfitted with subwoofers and disco lights for portable DJ setups, those few Trabis that still persisted seemed more and more out of place. The effect would have been the same, before 1989, had someone thought it useful to smuggle a Trabi to the West and drive it around; everything that had accompanied the Trabi was changing, becoming westernized. A Trabi parked in front of a Konsum store—a state-run store that sold common household consumer goods in the GDR—looked normal, but a Trabi parked in front of a Benetton that had taken over the same building space after 1989 looked bizarre and often comic. It is clear that context changed the meaning of the Trabant from a highly valued to a highly ridiculed to a fetishized object. But it is not clear exactly what that context was originally, which is one reason why a phenomenon like Ostalgie existed; as with most fetishisms, its origins had to be obscured to those experiencing it or the effect would wear off.

The purpose of this chapter is to restore some of the context to the Trabant by presenting it not so much as an automobile unto itself but as a system unto itself as well as a piece of a larger system of movement. The Trabant, as the quintessential

East German Socialist Car, was a piece of machinery that was defined as a nodal point of many constituent pieces of material and technology emanating from other currents in the East German *Volkswirtschaft* (people's economy). It was also part of a longer narrative of German and especially Saxon history. Its two-stroke engine, its plastic body, its boxy design, its upholstery, its owners' manual, and even the ways in which it was acquired and changed hands—all these defining characteristics of the Trabant were products of the socialist planned economy as well as the regional history of Saxony and Saxony-Anhalt, and they intersected in the body of the Trabant and the interactions between the car and its users.

But if the Trabant itself was a microcosm of the socialist planned economy and its southeastern German industrial heartland, it was also lost in a vast macrocosm of utopian urban planning that sought to transform the East German urban, semiurban, and rural landscape. Drawing from Corbusian notions of subjugating the automobile and the street to pure functionality in an effort to find the most efficient and rational system of moving people and things from place to place and reducing the interaction between person and car and person and street, the East German state folded the Trabant and the street more generally into what they termed a *Bewegungssystem* (system of movement). The Bewegungssystem was itself folded into an even more ambitious program of vast, mass-produced satellite towns and settlements built in the 1970s and 1980s. This chapter looks in particular at the housing settlement in far northeast Berlin—Berlin-Marzahn—begun in the late 1970s and continually built up until 1990. Marzahn was at once an attempt to solve what the Socialist Unity Party (the SED) saw as the most pressing need of the GDR—the lack of decent, modern housing in the country and especially in Berlin—and by far the most ambitious attempt to realize a Communist utopia on German soil. It was the largest mass-housing project on European soil, far larger and more ambitious in scope than the more isolated projects in the West such as the Märkische Viertel, the Gropiusstadt, and the Hansaviertel. It became a city unto itself, with four hundred thousand residents moving in between 1978 and 1990; more than that, Marzahn was a lived experience of Communist principles in city planning. It was, in short, the Eastern Bloc's answer to the Western example of the suburb.

The Western, especially American, suburb was inextricable from a particular notion of the car. The car was a nodal point. Cultural constructs such as gender, race, and class were threaded through it. So too was the car a result of economic and political preconditions like cheap fossil fuel and interactions between federal, state, and municipal leaderships and the auto companies (for example, taxpayer-funded expressways and sweetheart utility deals in which the metropolis bore the weight of the utility costs to the great benefit of the suburbs). Whatever else the car may have been in the postwar American world, it was certainly a keystone part of a solution to a problem that fundamentally challenged the industrial world, whether in Chicago or in East Berlin: how to continue to live with cities without necessarily having to live in them. Cities continued to be necessary for making money and making decisions, and yet they bore the weight of the ugly past of industrialization, with crowded slums, decaying infrastructure, and the collecting of society's unwanted. To leave the city and yet still profit from it—this was the importance of cheap gas, cars, suburbs, and federally funded highways. In America, cars cannot be understood apart from this context or from the heavily racist undertones of white flight that necessitated a car, a highway, and a suburb for so many Americans.

The Trabant as a System

The Trabant was "born" in 1957, a time when the Soviet world was undergoing a major sea change from a focus on production and heavy industry to more consideration of consumption and consumer goods, largely in response to the twin pressures of the West German "economic miracle" and the rise of Khrushchev in Moscow. Like many other industries and products in the GDR, the factory that produced the Trabant was not newly built but had been inherited from a prewar German industrial enterprise, or what remained of it, after war damage and Soviet dismantling had taken their toll.[1] The VEB Sachsenring Automobilwerke Zwickau had been founded in Zwickau, Saxony, by August Horch in 1904 and bore the Latin name for *Horch* (hark), Audi.[2] Along with the other auto factories in the industrial Saxon heartland, the Audi factory in Zwickau was sequestered by the occupying Soviet army, dismantled, and eventually reformed as part of the state-owned automobile industry, with the title VEB (Volkseigener Betrieb, or People's Own Factory) once the GDR came into existence in 1949. However, as in much of the industry of the GDR, change was slow to filter down from the top levels of the government to the actual products and processes of the factory floor. In contrast to much of the mythology of the new German state (and this was also true for the Federal Republic), there was no "zero hour" (*Stunde Null*) in the narrative of the postwar Saxon auto industry, the old Audi enterprise included. For several years, into the early 1950s, the Zwickau plant continued to make models that resembled the old prewar designs—as did the former BMW plant in Eisenach, which would eventually come to manufacture the Wartburg (East Germany's other car, more expensive and of higher quality and produced in much lower numbers than the Trabant). Many elements of the automobile industry in Saxony that predated the war lived on in the GDR, especially in Zwickau. Among the most important of these was the widespread use of the two-stroke engine (a simpler type of internal combustion engine, commonly used today in go-karts, lawn mowers, and golf carts). This was a tradition that dated back to its introduction in Saxony in 1911 by the auto manufacturer Hugo Ruppe from Zschopau.[3] Also native to Saxony and especially the so-called Chemical Triangle in nearby Saxony-Anhalt was the chemical industry, especially the Leuna, Buna, and Bitterfeld factories that had been so critical to the rise of the synthetic fuel, rubber, and plastics industries in the late nineteenth and early twentieth centuries. It was the ability to produce synthetic rubber, gasoline, nitrogen, and plastic material that made possible the production of munitions and vehicles during the First World War, when Germany was mostly cut off from the world's natural supply of rubber, oil, nitrogen, and natural materials by the Allies, who largely controlled the seas and the colonial sources of these vital resources. It was the region's ability to manufacture synthetics that enabled Hitler to flout the Versailles Treaty and the League of Nations and pursue economic autarky while at the same time rebuilding Germany's military might.[4]

In the era of the GDR, these two leftovers from the old Saxon and Saxon-Anhalt industrial base came to be highly useful. Indeed, the two-stroke motor and the synthetics industry seemed to fit the needs and character of the socialist economic order. The Zwickau factory continued the Saxon tradition of the two-stroke engine not only because of local familiarity or a nostalgic predilection for it but also because politically its advantages and disadvantages made more sense to the SED than the four-stroke, or "Otto," engine. Two-stroke engines are lighter and cheaper to produce, as well as easier to design in general. The country was having serious problems retaining its intellectual capital—much of the outflow of population from East to West in the years before the building of the Berlin Wall was driven by professionals and especially the "technological intelligentsia," including engineers and R&D professionals who had been previously drawn from the ranks of the bourgeoisie. Thus it was necessary to rely on technologies that were simpler and easier to teach and understand and the GDR embarked on an enormous campaign of bringing up a new generation of "cadres," that is, young men and women from the working class who were educated to be engineers and scientists.[5] It would be easier for them to learn the two-stroke engine. Another advantage of this engine was that it could be employed in any orientation (that is, it could be designed to be installed upside down, sideways, etc.) because it used motor oil differently than an Otto engine did. This made it more versatile, a key point in a planned economy that often lacked flexibility and had to find ways to maximize flexibility where and whenever possible. The two-stroke engine was lighter, meaning the supporting chassis could be lighter—vital for an economy that could not come by steel easily and would rely on wooden chassis at first and a plastic body later for the Trabant. The two-stroke was also much, much cheaper to produce, requiring less steel and less motor oil to run and thus providing great savings to the GDR's economy. The cost of these savings was having to endure the air and noise pollution for which the two-stroke engine was notorious. Street traffic in the GDR was characterized by the awful putt-putt sound of Trabants, described as a cacophony of outboard motors, as well as by the choking clouds of noxious light blue smog emitted by the engines.[6]

The use of plastic in the Trabant stemmed from the lack of drawn steel in the GDR, a result of the Mutual Assistance Control Act (known as the Battle Act for its sponsor, representative Laurie Battle of Alabama). The Battle Act, passed by the United States at the height of Cold War tensions in 1951, imposed an embargo on certain industrial goods to Eastern Bloc lands, especially goods that could have military use. The use of plastic was proposed shortly thereafter by Kurt Lang, the director of IFA (Industrieverband Fahrzeugbau), the umbrella organization that oversaw production of autos in the GDR. The first auto made using the two-stroke engine and a plastic body was the P70, which employed a shell made of polyvinyl chloride (PVC) hardened around three layers of paper and later cotton fibers, which was fitted onto a chassis made of wood.[7] This came to be known as "Trabiplast." In 1955 the "zero series" (that is, the first run) of IFA P70 cars was produced in Zwickau, drawing on the industrial processes for producing Duroplast (or Thermoset) well known in the area, as well as the familiar and inexpensive two-stroke, two-cylinder engine, with a total of 2,193 cars produced in 1955.[8]

At the same time, researchers at IFA, led by Dr. Winfried Sonntag, were developing a new model of car, the P50, which would be the first to bear the name Trabant. The P50 was planned to be smaller and lighter than the P70, although it would have a steel rather than a wooden frame. It would still have the Duroplast body, with synthetic PVC leather interior upholstery, and a two-stroke engine but one with three rather than two cylinders for slightly more power. It was designed to look more angular, more boxlike, more "modern." But far from being merely a third generation of cars from postwar Saxony, the Trabant P50 was both a result and a symbol of the change sweeping the socialist world as it came to focus on the mass production of consumer goods in an attempt to construct an alternative, socialist modern society to compete with the postwar West. The zero series of the Trabant P50 went into production in Zwickau in 1957, with a yearly production in 1958 of 1,750. But it was a car designed for mass production; in 1959 the Zwickau plant produced 20,040 P50s and in 1960, 35,270.[9]

In 1963 the GDR introduced a new Trabant, the P601. From 1963 onward, the P601 became the standard Trabant model until its production ceased in 1991.[10] The P601 became by far the most heavily produced model of Trabant—or of any car—in the GDR, and its even more angular and boxy frame, dull pastel monochrome colors of light blue, banana gold, light gray, blue-green, and cream, all in Thermoset plastic, formed the image of Trabant as it came to exist in the popular imagination. The car cost 7,450 marks.[11] Eventually, almost three million Trabant P601s were produced—though not all for the domestic market. In addition, not all cars produced or purchased in the GDR were Trabants—the former BMW factory in Eisenach began producing a "luxury" socialist car, the Wartburg 310—later the Wartburg 311—which had a steel body and a more powerful engine with twice the horsepower of the Trabant's engine and cost almost three times as much as the Trabant.[12] The Wartburg, however, was produced mainly for export to other socialist countries but also to nonsocialist countries as a way to bring in much-needed hard currency.[13]

The GDR managed to produce a steadily growing number of Trabant P601s from the mid-1960s until 1990, beginning with approximately 30,000 in 1964, climbing to over 100,000 in 1973, and reaching a high point in 1989 with almost 150,000. The production of Trabants was the GDR's answer to the push for mass-produced yet uniquely socialist consumer goods, but it was caught up in some of the most difficult contradictions of that push, including the fact that the more the GDR's planned economy produced consumer goods, the more demand it stimulated, and though it was able to rationally plan production, it was never able to control, plan, and forecast the desires of consumers. Thus it was that demand for the Trabant far outstripped the productive capacity. The infamous waiting list stretched up to thirteen years. Those who had placed their orders in 1977 experienced the cruel irony that their wait finally came to an end just as the Wall fell and Trabants became worthless in the face of suddenly available Western automobiles. By 1989 the ratio of those who wanted a Trabant to the Trabants available was 43:1.[14] In fact, the waiting list meant that in the GDR a used Trabant sold for more than twice the price of a new one,[15] and a brisk black market flourished in securing valuable spots on the list.[16]

The inadequate number of Trabants produced was paralleled by the pathetically small number of mechanics, garages, and replacement parts available. In fact, most Trabant owners either knew the inner workings of their car's pieces, parts, and especially two-stroke engine as well as most mechanics or knew someone who did. The latter were often paid in goods or other services for their help, a fact that contributed to the phenomenon of *Autobasteln* (see chapter 9 in this book) and to a vast gray economy. The manual for the Trabant P601 was unlike a car manual for most cars sold in the West, which usually focus on how to operate the vehicle and where the various buttons, switches, and levers are. It clearly depicted the name and purpose of every single gasket, valve, hinge, and so on of the car itself, with such detail that with a bit of determination and skill, any ordinary East German would have been able to take the car apart and reassemble it.[17] Reading the Trabant P601 manual was as much a basic course in automotive engineering as it was a user guide—and people needed such do-it-yourself knowledge because if their

Trabant broke down, they could not afford to simply get back on the waiting list and wait another thirteen years for a new one.

By 1989 more than 80 percent of the Trabants (and Wartburgs) produced in the GDR were still on the road, even though Trabants, and especially their two-stroke engines, were estimated generally to have a life span of only eight to ten years.[18] The simplistic two-stroke motor and the plastic body were advantageous. Far less complex than a four-stroke engine, the Trabant engine could in fact be fixed by nonprofessionals, and its basic design and physics were comprehensible enough that most people could improvise a replacement part of some kind if it was not possible to find a new gasket or hose or grill. In the case of a dent or even more serious damage to the car's body, the P601 manual itself went into great detail about how to repair rips and cracks in the plastic shell or the cotton substrate, with special emphasis on where to acquire cuts of extra Duroplast and how to actually glue new pieces of the plastic onto damaged sections of the body.[19]

In fact, the way in which the makers of the Trabi resorted to using Trabiplast and the ways in which people came to rely on their own gumption and creativity to keep their Trabants running are both classic examples of the phenomenon of *Eigen-Sinn*.[20] Eigen-Sinn is a counterintuitive concept on a number of levels because it posits individual initiative, creativity and self-taught know-how on behalf of workers in the GDR as the fulcrum of the entire system. For a collectivist system, it is amazing the extent to which factories (and stores, public services, etc.) stayed at least marginally functional in the GDR only because ordinary workers engaged in daily acts of near heroism to find creative solutions to breakdowns, faulty products, missing deliveries, poorly designed plans, etc. Workers often found ways to jury-rig machines, vehicles, or other technologies that did not work. Thus it was through extreme individual effort and highly idiosyncratic solutions (often unrepeatable and unpatented, unlike the Trabiplast) that the supposedly rational, systematic, planned, collective East German economy functioned at all. This attitude was not limited to workers in factories; many workers described by Alf Lüdtke and others as living according to a code of Eigen-Sinn were the owners of Trabis.

The Trabant as a Part of a System

The decision to begin planning a *Grossiedlung* (large settlement) or *Neubaugebiet* (new-construction area) in northeast Berlin stemmed from the palace coup that brought Erich Honecker to power as the head of the SED and effectively the GDR's state, replacing Walter Ulbricht. Honecker had made a strong case for his notion of "real existing socialism"—solving the pressing needs of people, especially in terms of housing, then and there rather then endlessly fiddling with new theories or experimenting with different structures of government and asking people to defer their needs—for a car, for a decent place to live, for some nice furniture—year after year. By the time of the Eighth Party Congress of the SED in 1972, which was the debutante festival for Honecker as the new leader and real existing socialism as the new philosophy of state, there were over one hundred thousand people in Berlin alone trying to find an apartment. East Berlin, like many East German cities, had borne the triple insult of having been bombed, having had urban combat in its streets that was far more intense than in the western areas of Germany, and not having the benefit of a Marshall Plan to help rebuild. Instead it had to endure the payment of reparations to and dismantling by the USSR. In addition, what would become the GDR absorbed the majority of the ethnic German refugees forced out of Poland and Czechoslovakia at the end of the war, most without a dime to their names. By the end of the war there was a shortage of 1.4 million apartments

7.1 Marzahn after completion, 1984. Courtesy Bezirksmuseum Marzahn-Hellersdorf/ Breitenborn.

in the Soviet Sector Zone (SBZ)/GDR. As with other aspects of the economy, the situation in housing reconstruction in the SBZ/GDR lagged far behind that in the FRG. Not only were relatively few apartments built between 1945 and the 1960s in the GDR, but those that remained were not renovated. This meant that a majority of GDR citizens lived in the same squalid working-class hovels that had defined proletarian life since the very beginning of large-scale industrialization in Berlin, or they lived in old rural houses that also dated back fifty or more years and were in desperate need of renovation. In 1961, for example, 10.3 percent of all apartments were officially condemned by the authorities as not fit to live in; one-third had no running water, and in smaller cities and towns like Neubrandenburg, only a third did have running water. Only a third of East German apartments had an indoor toilet, and only one in forty had central heating. More important than their poor condition were the links that these apartments and houses had to the past and to private property, both conditions that did not fit in the GDR's vision of a new, modern, socialist utopia. Almost exactly two-thirds of apartments and single-family homes had been built before 1918, and almost 80 percent were privately owned—only 12 percent were *Volkseigentum*—owned by the state.[21]

Thus it was at the Eighth Party Congress that the SED Politburo announced an ambitious apartment-construction program (the *Wohnungsbauprogramm*), which aimed to completely solve the housing crisis by 1990. The decision had already been made—in particular by the Berlin director of urban planning, Dr. Günter Peters—that rather than try to renovate the nineteenth-century slum buildings or build massive concrete slab buildings in the old city center itself, Berlin would build an entirely new satellite city in the rural northeast area of Berlin, centered around a medieval village called Marzahn. There, open, flat fields would be the tabula rasa for a quasi-Corbusian "City of Tomorrow." Indeed, the Marzahn project, originally developed in 1972 by the chief architect of Berlin, Roland Korn, and approved by Peters, the Berlin *magistrat* (city government), the State Planning Commission, and finally the Politburo itself, looked a great deal like Le Corbusier's City of Tomorrow. Like Le Corbusier's design, Marzahn was more than just a housing settlement; it was a total concept, with every conceivable need of the citizens planned in advance for the most rational and well-functioning form of living possible—the definition of the socialist system for the urban planners and architects, as well as the Politburo members, in the ascendant Honecker era.

Le Corbusier's City of Tomorrow was fundamentally based on the changes that automobile traffic had brought to the modern city and in particular on a totally different arrangement of the spaces in which living, driving, and working took place. The street, claimed Le Corbusier, needed to be abolished. Driving, as a function of getting from point A to point B, should take place in underground causeways built under the city. The surface should be reserved for green space and pedestrians. The old model of streets with houses and shops lining them was a vestige of the preautomobile city, according to Le Corbusier, when the slowness of travel necessitated a spatial connection between the residence and the travel capillaries and arteries. This had now led to several unfortunate things—the noise and air pollution of automobiles in the crowded city streets, the danger of accidents, and the fetishization of automobiles, parked as they often were in driveways or along the curb in front of a house or building, signifying the class and taste of the owners of the property. Le Corbusier proposed instead living towers, separated by wide swaths of natural green space, and with the places of work far removed. Working, driving, and living would be separate. Everything that a person might need would be placed within walking distance of his or her tower: from grocery store to school, from bakery to hair salon, the use of technology to build living towers and blocks would make for a *more* neighborly community. People would encounter one another as pedestrians, safely and without traffic jams, rude drivers, double-parkers, and so on to poison the general sense of humanity in the city. The smell of fresh air, rich with the greenery defining the overwhelming majority of the surface area of the City of Tomorrow, and the pleasant hellos and good-byes would draw people out of their polluted, isolated, unhappy shells.

Architects and urban planners in East Germany did not get their ideas directly from Le Corbusier—Peters himself claimed that the idea of rebuilding the ruined cities in the block-housing style with communal facilities (such as schools and restaurants) included in the design came from architects and urban planners who had been leftovers from the Bauhaus school of design or from Soviet literature that had been influenced by Le Corbusier's work (some of which was done in the USSR in the 1930s).

Attempts to realize Le Corbusier's vision of a city without streets or cars had already been made, most notably in the case of Brasilia but also (as Brigitte Le Normand discusses in chapter 5) in Belgrade. Elsewhere in the Communist world, much smaller-scale versions of the block-housing concept had been made in numerous places, usually as housing for a mass influx of workers to some enormous factory that had been built or augmented, such as Halle-Neustadt, the chemical workers' mass-housing settlement, and Nowa Huta outside Krakow. However, Marzahn was by far the most ambitious attempt to put this new kind of city concept into practice in the Communist world. Brasilia and other cities like it existed in the capitalist or quasi-capitalist world, which added a strong element of the unplanned and the unforeseeable—something quite antithetical to the notion of a perfectly planned-out city. But under Communism it would be possible to plan many more factors—who moved there, how many units would be built, how many stores and restaurants would be located in specific spots, where the tram lines were to go, and how much traffic and how many cars there would be—because of the kind of control the state had over economic means of production and distribution.

What had held Communist countries like the GDR back for so many years was primarily the prohibitive costs involved in building from scratch a massive settlement beyond the edge of the city. In fact, since the beginning of industrialization and the advent of urban slums in the working-class quarters of Berlin such as Prenzlauer Berg, Pankow, and Friedrichshain, numerous plans had been drawn up to resettle tens and even hundreds of thousands of Berliners "j.w.d." (*janz weit draussen,* or way out yonder—Berliner slang for "the boonies" or "the sticks"). Albert Speer himself had drawn up extensive plans to settle 445,000 people in modern housing projects outside the northeast edge of the city, including Marzahn (which would be renamed Ostachse as part of the farthest eastern extent of Germania).[22] Speer did not originate the idea either; plans for an expansion into Marzahn and Biesdorf to take some of the pressure off the crowded working-class slums had existed in the Weimar Republic,[23] and these in turn were based on plans for a resettlement of the population of Berlin dating back to the turn of the twentieth century.[24]

Yet the ability to feasibly settle large numbers of people out on the plains eluded various German regimes. Berlin's population was composed largely of the often exceedingly poor rural laborers, descendants of the German colonizers, who had been drawn by the city's industrialization. Their poverty was a testament to the infeasibility of moving large numbers of Germans into this particular Lebensraum. The fact that this population had to be housed in slums to make the growth of Berlin possible immediately raised the core problems of urban decay, filth, and revolutionary potential, all of which were set to play out in the *streets* of the slum districts. A true suburb, in the North American sense, was simply not economical. Whatever could be built in the j.w.d would not pay for itself.

However, by the late 1960s, that equation had changed, at least somewhat. Concrete-slab mass-housing technology had improved to the point where it was cost-effective enough to produce the number of apartments and other structures necessary to quickly mass-produce a new city. Though many designs had been passed around for prefabricated houses from concrete slabs dating back to the early twentieth century, the *Wohnungsbauserie 70*, or WBS 70 design—which came in five-, eleven-, and twenty-two-story versions—was the first that was cost-effective. The WBS 70 *Plattenbau* (as concrete prefab buildings became known) were churned out by an enormous factory that would mass-produce the concrete slabs in their various forms: window pieces, doorway pieces, inner wall pieces, floor pieces, roof pieces, etc. The technology to build these pieces efficiently and at low cost did not exist in the GDR or anywhere in the Eastern Bloc; for this reason Peters, now with a budget of almost a billion marks at his disposal from the city of

Berlin and the State Planning Commission, bought an entire factory from Finland, where the Plattenbau process had been perfected.

The plan called for three areas: WG (*Wohngebiet*—residence area) I, II, and III. WG I encompassed the southernmost third of the settlement and was referred to as the *Südspitze* (south point). The settlement was centered around the city hall; an open forum with a fountain; three public buildings to house a post office, a shopping center, and other service shops (cleaners, restaurants, hardware stores, etc.); two twin apartment towers twenty and twenty-two stories tall each; a school; a swimming pool/sauna; and a senior home, all built on the edge of a small natural pond called the *Springpfuhl* and all within a hundred meters' walk from the S-Bahn (the elevated public transit train)stop (S-Bahn Springpfuhl now). The entire settlement was connected to the main artery of East Berlin, Frankfurter Tor/Karl-Marx-Allee, through what had previously been the main country road leading out toward the eastern *Mark* (eastern marches or borders of the Holy Roman Empire) from Berlin, the Landsberger Allee. This was renamed Leninallee (today it has returned to Landsberger Allee).[25] Along its western side, Marzahn was bordered by the large industrial area where many of its residents would work. Almost all these workplaces were within walking distance of home. The S-Bahn line and the major traffic artery of Heinrich-Rau-Strasse (today called Märkische Allee) separated the living complex from the industrial zone along its western edge. Marzahn was bisected by another central artery—the Allee der Kosmonauten (originally named Springpfuhlstrasse, as discussed below). These two arteries, Heinrich-Rau and Allee der Kosmonauten, were as important for the building of Marzahn as they were for the future conduct of traffic flow through it, for they functioned as assembly lines for the so-called *Taktstrassen*. These were assembly teams made up of experts from foundation construction (*Tiefbau*) and above-ground construction (*Hochbau*) as well as engineers and other more technical utilities-installation experts. They all worked together on a housing block until it was finished, then moved on to the next block; the foundation workers built the foundation for the next block while the roofers finished up on the first one. A simple rail track was laid along Heinrich Rau and Allee der Kosmonauten, and a couple of enormous cranes were mounted on movable platforms on the tracks. They simply rolled down the tracks bit by bit, kilometer after kilometer, for almost eight years, until they reached the Ahrensfelder heights at the very end of Heinrich-Rau-Strasse and the end of the city limits of Berlin, finishing Wohngebiets II and III sometime in 1986.[26]

One of the guiding principles laid out in the original plans for Marzahn was that no residential building should be more than six hundred meters from a school, the S-Bahn, the shopping mart, a recreation field, or any other *gesellschaftliche Einrichtung*, or communal facility.[27] From the time of Le Corbusier's City of Tomorrow at least, the idea of housing people in tall blocks or towers was directly related to creating an integrated ground-level community, with lots of open, green, and communal space and with every conceivable necessity located within a short and safe walk. It was to be a "completely functional system."[28]

And for most newly arrived Marzahners, it was or was quickly on its way to becoming a completely functioning system. Marianne Fränzel, who moved into one of the first housing blocks on Luise-Zeitz-Strasse 99 in the Südspitze in 1977, needed "only ten minutes to the S-Bahn, which took seventeen minutes to get to the city center, so a total commute of a half hour."[29] The Kaufhaus "took another year and half to get built. Then three more residential towers were built, and there were stores on the ground level. Things moved along and got better. The library, the bookstore, and the café came along, and then with the shopping mart there was everything that one could want: towels, cassettes, radios, bed linens, shoes, and women's and men's clothing. It was lively at the very least."[30]

Tree planting was an important common activity for many new residents, both in the sense of redesigning the landscape according to standards of sanitation and pleasantness and in terms of the metaphoric value of putting down roots in brand new soil. And these roots were both Communist and personal, often both. The best-remembered—among Marzahners at least—tree-planting event was on September 22, 1978, when Sigmund Jähn, the first East German cosmonaut, visited Marzahn with the Soviet Cosmonaut Valery Bykovsky. The two had just returned from a space mission in the Soyuz space capsule and had been awarded the Order of Karl Marx at the Palace of the Republic by Erich Honecker. They then came to Marzahn directly, with an entourage of SED luminaries, to plant a maple tree each. This was followed by a guided tour of one of the freshly complete WBS 70/11 living units, block 60.17.[31] The event left a big impression on Marzahners—they renamed Springpfuhlstrasse, the main traffic artery alongside which the trees had been planted, Allee der Kosmonauten in honor of Jähn and Bykovsky, who were said to have had a special fondness for Marzahn and its residents. The cosmonauts left behind an official SED badge that they had carried into outer space and back, and they returned at least one more time in subsequent years to check on their trees and the residents of WBS 70/11 unit 60.17 and to say hi.

For the planners of Marzahn, the street and the cars to move along it were just part of a much larger, more complex integrated system. In fact, in the late 1960s, the German Building Academy (Deutsche Bauakademie, DBA), the government body most in charge of design and architecture in the GDR, began referring to the concept of a "movement system" (*Bewegungssystem*) in urban planning documents. Movement system was meant to include all the ways in which people and goods moved around—by car, truck, public transit, boat, and bike and on foot. The idea was that the most rational movement system unit should be chosen for each situation or

7.2a, b Trabants parked in Marzahn, seen from balcony of Plattenbau apartment, 1983. Courtesy Barbara Diehl.

project. Cars, as just one part of this system, were useful for transit from Marzahn to the city and back, but the layout of Marzahn discouraged their use there for such activities as going over to someone's place for a visit or going shopping. That was all designed to be done on foot. On the other hand, along the main thoroughfares—Leninallee, Heinrich-Rau-Strasse, and Allee der Kosmonauten—there was little possibility for pedestrians or bikers to appropriate the use of the road since there were no bike lanes, no shoulders, and in many places no sidewalks. There were tram lines for those who did not have Trabants, but these were roads specifically for car travel. Once one turned off into the residential areas, driving was possible only at a slow crawl, along twists and turns, in an effort to find a parking lot.

Of course, it helped to have this new city designed to maximize the efficiency of living without a car, since there was still such a backlog of Trabants. Most Marzahners took the S-Bahn to work; the walk was not bad, and the ride took only about fifteen minutes. For a suburb of sorts, Marzahn was built specifically with those who did not own cars in mind so that it would not be a place accessible only by car. Though almost a half million people ended up moving into Marzahn and its surrounding, spillover developments (such as Hellersdorf and Neu-Hohenschönhausen), about two-thirds of Berlin's population still remained within the historical city limits, including hundreds of thousands still living in the old slum buildings in Prenzlauer Berg and Pankow. This meant there were thousands of Trabis parked along the old streets, just the kind of situation Le Corbusier had not wanted. But it was clearly the plan of the regime to eventually move the GDR toward the Marzahn model of living spaces—if not entire cities cut from whole cloth, then large swaths of old neighborhoods torn down to make room for mini-Marzahns. By 1990, over half of all East Germans lived in a Plattenbau—the highest percentage in the world. Some of these were free-standing blocks that did not correspond to any kind of overarching concept of urban planning, but many more were built specifically for a kind of future in which people did not need to depend on driving and could get anywhere easily by foot if necessary, a future in which the Trabant would continue to be right at home.

IN addition to the concept of Eigen-Sinn, historian Alf Lüdtke has also coined the term *durchherrschte Gesellschaft*, or "thoroughly dominated society," in reference to the diffusion of power in the GDR. There has been much debate over the meaning of that term, however, and it has been used in many conflicting ways in the decade and a half since Lüdtke introduced it. It is not meant, by most interpretations, to be synonymous with the notion of an Orwellian state in which the ruling SED and its secret police, the Stasi, watched and controlled everyone and everything—though that has been a misinterpretation in the past. It is also not meant to imply that ordinary people "produced" power by taking advantage of the openings provided by the new ideological apparatus, though that did happen. Here, at least, what the term *durchherrschte Gesellschaft* implies is a sense of interconnectedness between the economy—the all-important planned economy—and the everyday life of people and the materials and places that constituted that life.

The Trabant was not so much an autonomous product or object, as many cars in the West seemed to be, as a manifestation of the various mechanisms at work in the socialist planned economy. The two-stroke engine, the plastic body, the motor

7.3a, b Allee des Kosmonauten, before and after construction of Marzahn. Courtesy Bezirksmuseum Marzahn-Hellersdorf/Breitenborn.

oil, the upholstery—these particular characteristics of the car could be explained only as part of a larger system of socialism. Moreover, the Trabant, even when taken as a unified object, could make sense only as part of the larger project of a utopian, modern urban planning vision, as a cog in the vast machine of moving people efficiently and rationally. When we look at Trabants now, we need to be able to see the plastic factories of Saxony and the two-stroke engines produced in the early twentieth century; we need to be able to see trams, S-Bahns, pedestrian pathways, and meticulously planned high-rise urban settlements. Only then does the Trabant, and its identity as a socialist car, make sense.

Part Three

SOCIALIST CAR CULTURES AND AUTOMOBILITY

8

THE COMMON HERITAGE OF
THE SOCIALIST CAR CULTURE

Luminita Gatejel

What seems to have survived the dissolution of the former Eastern Bloc with regard to cars is either their proverbial bad reputation or a nostalgic patina retroactively added to them. This chapter challenges these two dominant perspectives on Socialist Cars, one belonging to the Cold War context and the other to post-1989 Communist nostalgia. I aim to tease out the characteristic features of a so-called socialist car culture by dealing with the multiple usages, symbolic meanings, and conflicting perceptions of automobiles during late socialist times. The chapter looks at various constructions of the Socialist Car: it explores its becoming, its various shapes and curves. This procedure represents at the same time a way of looking at the automobile revolution in socialist countries. Empirical data will be used from three countries: the Soviet Union, East Germany, and Romania. The chosen countries correspond to three different approaches toward mass motorization inside the former Eastern Bloc. I argue that the Socialist Car gave rise to identical discourses and inspired similar popular cultural movements in all three countries, despite existing local differences and the uneven temporalities of its development.

At first glance, the Soviet Union, the GDR, and socialist Romania could not be more different. First and foremost, we encounter deep structural economic inequalities. Inside the Eastern Bloc the GDR, renowned for its long tradition in the automotive sector, met with Romania, an absolute newcomer in the world of the automobile.[1] On a political level, at least from the late 1950s onward, the two satellites had different relationships with the center. Moscow's most loyal ally, the GDR, was contrasted to Romania, the renegade state inside the Eastern alliance.[2] Apart from domestic pressure to expand automobile production, the Soviet Union as a global player had to take into consideration the success of private motorization in the Western countries. Therefore, the car played a distinct role in each of my case studies: in Romania it symbolized the enforced industrialization of a mainly agrarian economy, in the GDR it represented technological innovation, and in the Soviet Union it became a key figure in the Cold War battle to satisfy consumers.³ The GDR entered the era of mass motorization with two original car models, whereas Romania bought a license from the French car producer Renault. The Soviet Union's path toward mass consumption of cars represents a blending of these two models, combining local skills with industrial dismantling from East Germany and adding later imported know-how from the West. It should be emphasized that these distinct routes toward mobile societies shaped a common, astonishingly homogenous, socialist "automobility system." Here I refer to the famous definition of John Urry, who conceptualized automobility as "a hybrid assemblage of specific human activities, machines, roads, buildings, signs and cultures of mobility." Here it is not the car itself that is emphasized but the various interconnections inside this system.⁴ In other words, the externalities of the car—political decisions, patterns of work and leisure, models of retail and ownership, and everyday uses, all of which create a specific car culture—are my prime consideration.⁵

I start from the premises that the three case studies belong to a common sociopolitical and cultural realm that came into being as a result of multilayered cultural transfer processes. Without denying the dominant position of the Soviet Union vis-à-vis its allies, I prefer to follow Susan Reid and David Crowley and call this exchange an "asymmetrical" dialogue, which allows me to accommodate multidirectional aspects of the relationship between the USSR and the "people's democracies."⁶ Average citizens were connected via a very dense communication process with each other that shaped similar expectations. On a more structural level, the economic characteristics of socialist systems—rigid planning and retail services, the emphasis on uniformity rather than individual needs—led to many peculiarities of the socialist automobile system that were the same throughout the bloc. Another explanation for the commonalities can be traced to the so-called socialist consumption model, which the state educational apparatus propagated in all three countries. Apart from that, I want to stress the integrative function of the consumption and social policies of the 1960s and 1970s that homogenized socialist societies.⁷

With this in mind, the first part of the article traces the parallel advancement toward mass motorization in the GDR, the Soviet Union, and socialist Romania. The main focus lies in the national context and the specific conditions that allowed for the virus of mass motorization to spread throughout the entire Eastern Bloc.⁸ In a second step the chapter will bring the three countries back together so that common characteristics of the freshly motorized societies can be extracted. The range of commonalities—as the ensuing sections will show—reaches from car distribution policies and ownership symbolism to the implicit or explicit comparison of the "delayed" socialist automobile societies with the "more advanced" Western automobile cultures and the everyday uses of and interactions with cars.

Cars and Socialism

The vehicles of socialism were most prominently trucks and buses. Private cars seemed to be at odds with the collectivist definition of a socialist society. Nevertheless, motor cars were produced in and imported into socialist countries—as early as the 1920s in the Soviet Union.[9] After the war the considerations for a mobile society dramatically changed as the car became in more and more countries the epitome of a modern society whose members cherished its comfort and flexibility.[10] From the 1950s onward, socialist societies one by one entered the age of mass motorization. And cars, no longer seen as luxury items, became increasingly available.

The GDR was the first one to embark on this journey. The Nazi rulers created with the Volkswagen a new consumer desire, and the East German successor state found itself unable to resist this preexisting expectation among the population. The sudden success of the Volkswagen in the Bundesrepublik raised the pressure higher.[11] Despite economic hardships, augmented by the Soviet army's dismantling of industry and the rising tensions of the Cold War, GDR politicians and pressure groups plumped for a domestic automobile industry.[12] The embargo on sheet metal imports from the West put serious strains on automobile manufacturers, forcing engineers to look for a suitable substitute. Like their counterparts in the West, they considered synthetic fibers a panacea for future economic growth.[13] East German chemists and engineers combined their skills to find a viable plastic material that could be formed easily into a frame and at the same time be immune to weather conditions. The Trabant, made of Duroplast, embodied chemistry's prestige during postwar reconstruction. Celebrated in the press or sent to international exhibitions, it symbolized the success of the East German economy.[14]

In the GDR, where both politicians and citizens were constantly comparing themselves with the Federal Republic, no other option remained than to introduce private cars on a mass scale. East German officials even went so far as to ignore the signals from Moscow against private car ownership.[15] The alternative concept proposed by Khrushchev and articulated by the media throughout the Soviet Union was urban car rental centers. They touted this rental system as the embodiment of the socialist vision of a fair and economical usage of cars, shaping Soviet citizens' view of automobility.[16] Because of the negative attitudes among both the bureaucratic elite and the general population toward private cars, the change in favor of fully fledged mass motorization came as a surprise. With Brezhnev and Aleksei Kosygin in power, the motorcar sector became a top governmental priority.[17] A general fascination among the political elite with the technical innovations of the automobile revolution laid the basis for this change in policy. Additionally, increased productivity was justified with a boost in consumption.[18] As a result, in the newborn car city of Togliatti on the Volga, up to 660,000 vehicles were produced yearly. This meant a doubling of the existent automobile stock by the beginning of the 1970s.[19] Taking the Khrushchevian detour, the Soviet Union finally reached the point along the mass motorization route from which the GDR had started a decade earlier.

Domestic automobile production facilities in the Soviet Union, the GDR, and Czechoslovakia changed the nature of economic cooperation inside the Eastern Bloc. Reforms within the COMECON countries, starting in the late 1950s, stipulated that better cooperation among its members could be accomplished by avoiding direct competition. Reformers advocated specialization on certain economic branches within each "national" economy as the only viable solution. Following this logic, the supranational COMECON organization sought to prevent automobile production from spreading to other countries. The case of Romania, a country that turned into a motorized society relatively late, best exemplifies the failure of this policy.[20] In 1966 Romanian authorities signed a contract with the French automobile manufacturer Renault to purchase a production license. The first Romanian automobile plant was constructed in close proximity to the town of Pitești, where the Dacias, local variants of the Renault 8 and 12, were to be assembled.[21] The Dacia project represents the perfect example of a motorization plan "from above." Car ownership was a new phenomenon in the mid-1960s, a time when Romanian consumers seemed more interested in acquiring a less mobile shelter, such as one of the flats built extensively on the outskirts of towns. The population did not ask for automobiles as did the citizens of the GDR and the Soviet Union. Demand existed only in scattered form. The new car was simply given to people who at first met it with suspicion. The Romanian national car resulted from the political ambition of the ruling circles around President Nicolae Ceausescu. They were led by the ultimate goal of turning an agrarian society into a progressive, fully industrialized country overnight. With Romania we have the interesting case of a socialist regime taking up a modernization plan in order to catch up to and overtake not only the West but also the more developed brother countries within the bloc.[22]

Since socialism had failed to provide a more collectivist alternative to private motorization, and particular interests had overruled the master plan of COMECON for a strict economic division of labor among its members, the nation-state replaced the common market as the decisive point of reference for the future development of automobility. But although the Soviet Union, the GDR, and Romania were guided by divergent motivations and began their respective pushes toward mass motorization at different moments, each sooner or later stumbled over the same problems and witnessed similar accomplishments. The initial dissimilarities gave way to common characteristics of what I have called a genuine socialist car culture. It goes without saying that some local particularities prevailed, but I will focus on the common heritage of this culture.

Automobile Hierarchies

"Cars in socialist countries are simply means of transport and bear no signs of social distinction." This assertion was one of the commonplaces of socialist consumption discourse: objects should be cherished for their use value and not as status objects. However, reality looked somewhat different. In the Soviet Union of the 1950s the locally produced car models were arranged into the following hierarchical pyramid: at the bottom of the list stood (or rather crawled) the tiny Zaporozhets, built especially for disabled persons, followed closely by the small Moskvich, destined for the average buyer. Next on the scale was the middle-class Volga, the wheels for the nomenklatura. One position higher stood the Chaika limousine in which the high party and state functionaries were chauffeured, and on top, the ZIL, used exclusively during summits.[23] Instead of just one car for everybody, we find one model for each class, ordered along a strict hierarchy. The reason for this arrangement was simple: seeing cars passing by, one would immediately know who sat inside. Social status and car ownership were directly linked. The organization of automobile production in the GDR followed the same principles: one model for each car class and car classes reduced to an absolute minimum. The only things missing were the luxury brands. The GDR manufactured the small Trabant, along with the middle-class Wartburg for more distinguished clients.

This arrangement changed dramatically during the 1970s. In the Soviet Union it started with the mass production of the Lada. The Italian license did not fit into the class structure of Soviet automobiles; no social stratum or professional category received priority. The Lada was to become the most common car on Russian streets and therefore a true people's car, but its technology was more advanced than that of any Soviet car. In fact, all second-generation socialist cars bore the same features. The Polski Fiats, Soviet Ladas, Yugoslav Zastavas, and Romanian Dacias, manufactured on the basis of Western licenses, entered socialist markets like Trojan horses and brought with them the shine of a capitalist consumer culture. Let us examine the structural transformations that occurred in the car market when it absorbed these new car types.

These changes can be followed most easily in East Germany, a country where the range of available models was the broadest inside the bloc. Access to cars imported from other socialist countries contributed to the transformation. In time, as new car types became available, so did new preferences. What only a few years earlier had been the epitome of automotive quality turned into an outdated product—maybe best represented by the plastic Trabant, which had been prized as an outstanding technical achievement but eventually became a laughingstock in the international community of drivers. Generally speaking, preferences turned in favor of the second generation of automobiles, which had more powerful engines and more up-to-date styling. The older generation of cars could not keep up with the appeal of models originating from Western licenses. As several letters to the authorities show, East Germans ardently cherished these new cars.[24]

It remains a paradox that in spite of this development, national cars retained their position as the most sought after. Although the more modern foreign cars were openly admired, car buyers regularly made the more "sensible" decision in favor of a Wartburg or Trabant. This attitude persevered on the one hand because of a strong emotional bond between people and domestically produced cars and on the other because of the convenience of more repair shops, easier access to spare parts, and in general more knowledge about the car's flaws and what kind of remedy it needed.[25] Although in theory the second-generation foreign cars were more advanced technologically, the chronic lack of spare parts constituted a tremendous shortcoming. Besides, a thorough inspection revealed that these more modern cars were not always what they promised to be. Quite a few of the new owners complained that their recent acquisitions suffered from irremediable flaws.[26] As investigations confirmed, the GDR regularly received whole deliveries of defective cars.[27] Thus not long after the Ladas, Dacias, and Polski Fiats had conquered the East German market, their reputation sank. They caused far too much distress to their owners, many of whom wanted their cars exchanged for domestic models.[28] In the end they chose time-proven products instead of unreliable innovations.

Western cars rarely appeared on Eastern Bloc roads. A moralizing finger was pointed at the big caravans of foreign cars accompanying Ceausescu during his "working visits" through Romania.[29] In the same vein, the neighborhood for the nomenklatura in the northern part of East Berlin was ironically called Volvograd.[30] But it was not only the nomenklatura who had access to foreign cars. Citizens from Eastern Bloc countries who worked in the West were allowed to bring an automobile home, and in the case of Romania, even without paying taxes.[31] Moreover, after the failure of a joint venture between the GDR and Czechoslovakia to develop a new passenger vehicle at the end of the 1970s, both countries' governments stepped up importation of Western cars to improve the overall quality of the car stock.[32] As a consequence, the older cars of the high Party officials came to be replaced with the French Peugeot 305.³³ In addition, a limited number of VW Golfs and Mazdas could be purchased in the capital city of Berlin.³⁴ This trend toward introducing Western cars on a larger scale remained singular among socialist countries, however, and even in the GDR it was restricted to a niche phenomenon: a statistic from 1988 shows only an absolute number of 36,500 Western cars out of a total of almost 3.5 million registered cars.³⁵

All in all, from the late 1960s onward, automobile fantasies and car ownership more and more reflected a desire to free oneself from the constraints of the dictated automobile hierarchies. The given hierarchies of the previous years started fading away and were replaced by a more personalized relationship toward cars. Buying a car turned into a very complicated matter that involved a lot of decisions about details. Price, efficiency, engine power, and fuel consumption became relevant factors. This attests to a delayed normalization of the socialist automobile market and to a certain extent an adaptation to the capitalist model of consumption. On the one hand we can see tendencies similar to those in the West, where the tradition of Sloanism (the mass marketing of "cars for every purse and purpose," discussed in chapter 9) made producers diversify and personalize their products; on the other hand, some striking peculiarities lingered in the socialist part of Europe. Although access to cars had increased and the products had diversified considerably, widespread shortages hindered a genuinely personalized choice with regard to new cars. Still, the changes that occurred despite their limitations proved that socialist citizens did benefit from increased consumption opportunities. Making the decision to buy a car had become a very complex matter, a situation that had consequences for retail practices.

Car Ownership

Cars never ceased to be a highly valued privilege in socialist countries. Before mass motorization, automobiles were the exclusive accessory of the new socialist elite. Heroes of socialist labor and members of the nomenklatura had at their disposal a personal automobile with a chauffeur during work and free time.³⁶ The rise of mass motorization undercut their status as more and more social and professional groups hoped to call an automobile their own. As car ownership spread within society, the nomenklatura feared losing its privileges altogether. Surprisingly, this was not what happened because not enough cars were produced to fill the ever-growing demand. But the democratization of cars also transformed the nomenklatura's relationship to automobiles. As in Hungary (see chapter 3), the Romanian case provides good evidence. Immediately after the Dacia motorization plan got under way, the Central Committee issued a resolution that handed the responsibility for official cars over to users. Romanian authorities tried to get rid of the troublesome task of providing high-ranking officials with cars, chauffeurs, fuel, and spare parts, aiming to reduce costs by encouraging each state employee to buy a new private car that he would also use during working hours. They promised free access to cars without waiting and special repair shops. The catch was that the all-around service package meant new forms of personal responsibility. Yet, like every reform, it was only partially implemented; the lower echelons of power adapted to the new system while the high Party officials kept to their old privileges.[37] This policy was also intended to reduce state expenditures by replacing the old, broken-down, and fuel-consuming Volgas and Pobedas that belonged to state companies and ministries in Romania (and in the USSR for that matter) with the more compact Dacias (and Ladas).[38] And as all too often happened in the socialist part of the world, modernization was initiated from above per official decree.

In time, the exclusivity associated with the nomenklatura's cars faded as new social and professional groups claimed their rights to get an automobile without having to wait in line. A striking example in the Eastern Bloc is that of the World War II veterans of the Soviet Union who regularly received cars because of their importance within the Soviet social body.[39] But during the 1970s workers at big construction sites and specialists willing to accept positions in far-off provinces shared the privilege.[40] In the GDR the entitlement groups were more fragmented—for example, large families, disabled people, and chronically ill persons could claim a car outside the waiting lists, but so could doctors and engineers.[41] Socialist citizens could also turn to their relatives abroad to send them either the needed hard currency or the desired car.[42] More exceptional were the cases in the Soviet Union where several organizations, institutes, or firms requested personal cars in the names of their members and employees. It was well known that in socialist societies the most effective incentives were not financial remunerations but consumer goods, the most prominent of them being the car.[43]

To sum up these preliminary findings, one can say that starting in the 1960s socialist societies witnessed more cars, a greater variety of models, more diversified ways of acquiring them, and a broader range of privileges, as well as greater public acceptance of their private ownership. The changes that took place were threefold: the wishes of the population became more personal, the car supply became more diversified, and access to cars was democratized. The ensuing mass motorization in all three countries offered the chance of leaving the ghosts of the past behind. But after the splendid takeoff, motorization plans were trapped in unsolvable dilemmas. Production figures that lagged behind demand necessitated the retention of preferential retailing. Imports from the neighboring socialist countries were hindered by lack of transport fluency. Western imports were banned because of ideological constraints, although the population fancied these cars. Socialist authorities were trapped between their own ideological standards and economic shortages. Nevertheless, from the 1960s onward, national car markets were dynamic spheres where a lot more than cars was exchanged between the state and its subjects.

The Imaginary West in the Socialist Car Culture

In all Socialist Car narratives the West is the silent point of reference, the invisible other.[44] The personal automobile as an artifact is so deeply inscribed in American and more broadly Western culture that any other appropriation of its meanings still has to contend with its widespread symbolism of freedom, flexibility, and privacy.[45] As the vehicle of the American way of life, it could not be entirely transformed into the vehicle of socialism. The way in which ordinary citizens dealt with the omnipresent traces of capitalism in the socialist car culture presents an opportunity to go beyond the usual commonplaces of a one-sided transfer process from the West to the Eastern camp in the form of a delayed emulation of the Western model. It has to be acknowledged nevertheless that the West provided ideas, technology, and techniques and that the political elite and normal citizens were more than willing to learn and borrow from the Cold War enemy. In an ambiguous amalgam of socialist superiority and the painful awareness of backwardness, best expressed in the "catching up and overtaking the West" discourse, Western products and technologies were welcomed on socialist soil. And it goes without saying that their absorption led also to a series of malfunctions and unexpected idiosyncrasies. But the story of these transfers of know-how has been told more than once.[46]

The following discussion focuses on popular images of the West in socialist narratives. As a starting point I chose Alexei Yurchak's concept of the "imaginary West," referring to a predisposition among the Soviet population to fetishize objects and leftovers of Western provenance, one that grew even more intense during the last decades before the dissolution of the bloc. Yurchak emphasizes the West as an imagined realm that had to be understood as part of socialism and most often had little in common with the authentic West. It was not only the lack of information about the real West that led to certain misperceptions but also the function that the West occupied in this discourse as the forbidden, exotic, subversive, and dangerous counterpart of socialism.[47] On a personal level the West, as a place out of reach for most inhabitants, was equally cherished and demonized.

This approach is especially fruitful in analyzing socialist blockbuster movies. The following examples are exclusively from Romania, but similar illustrations can easily be found for the other two countries. As we are dealing with official movies, a certain moralizing stance toward the decadent West is unavoidable. In the movie *Accident* (*The Accident*, 1976), three teenagers are driving under the influence of alcohol at high speed along a highway. We can see two guys and a girl inside the car, listening to loud pop music, smoking while striking what they believe to be very cool poses, and extravagantly dressed. All in all, it is a quite shabby imitation of gangster road movies, with the protagonists wearing old-fashioned clothes and driving an old car with no car radio but with a huge tape recorder on the backseat instead. As they pass a police patrol, they are signaled to stop. As a result of the ensuing chase, the teenage driver crashes the car into the woods, fatally injuring the girl. He then leaves the scene of the crime. The car passengers' embodiment of the young and fashionable outlaws in Western movies is hilarious. They belong to the so-called *stiliagi*, groups of young people who were infatuated with what they thought Western style might be and for whom in the 1970s the automobile became their most prestigious appendage.[48]

At first glance the West stood for crime and luxury in these types of entertaining movies. Two movies which were set at the Romanian Black Sea Riviera— *Nea Marin Miliaradar* (*Uncle Martin, the Billionaire*, 1979) and *Brigada Diverse la munte și la mare* (*Miscellaneous Brigade in the Mountains and at Sea*, 1971) display the whole range of dubious associations with the West. The Westerners are of course millionaires driving Mercedes; they use cars to smuggle drugs across the border or transport kidnapped persons. Everything is performed as a caricature; the Romanian actors chosen to play the foreign villains speak a horrible version of English with a strong accent. Generally a Western car is used as a vehicle for crime while the Romanian Dacias and ARO off-road vehicles of the local police represent law and order. Subtle ironies inflect this Manichaean master narrative. A beautiful girl is constantly flirting with foreigners in the hotel lobby. When Giorgio, the handsome though diminutive Italian, offers her a ride in his car, she is more than glad to accept. But her joy lasts only until she sees his tiny Fiat Cinquento. Outraged, she slaps him and leaves. She obviously has imagined the West differently.

On an everyday basis, a much more mythical image of the West presented itself to the population. Western goods were ranked higher than their socialist equivalents. Wrappings, lids, and empty boxes of Western products were not thrown away but used for decoration or storage because of their higher symbolic and aesthetic value.[49] The equivalent in car culture would be the fetishization of the first Romanian Dacias with "original" French components. They fetched a higher price than newer cars with Romanian spare parts. And as the story went, French Dacias broke down less often than their indigenous relatives.[50] The East German archives document the case of a car fanatic who gathered one by one the spare parts for a Volkswagen Golf, receiving several components by mail from his West German relatives, and then assembled the entire car on his own.[51] Likewise, the Soviet citizen Zhdanov fought for several years with the Soviet authorities to receive permission to buy a wrecked Chevrolet Bel Air at a moderate price.[52]

Joys and Hardships for Socialist Drivers

The dark side of socialism tells the story of long waiting lists, insufficient cars and spare parts, poor manufacturing quality, and transactions on the side. And the list could go on. The bright side recounts the merry seaside vacations, the pride and joy of finally bringing the car home, the modest (in some cases more than modest) gains from using the car to transport people and goods, and the regular rides to the dacha or the village that made everyday hardships more bearable. They stand for the two sides of the same coin. Thus the last decades of socialism can be understood as a bizarre combination of everyday bliss and suffering. By focusing on the personal automobile one can get precious insights into both sides.[53]

Cars as scarce goods in socialist countries represented not only objects of consumption but also a clever financial investment. According to the East German Opinion Research Institute, saving up for a car was ranked at the top of consumer goals. Additionally, workers earning low wages were inclined to give up certain daily pleasures in order to save enough to buy a car.[54] It has to be mentioned here that car prices were kept artificially high, roughly the equivalent of a two-room apartment, in order to temper the rising demand, a strategy that obviously did not work.[55] On the black market cars were even more costly.[56] Shortly before the fall of the Berlin Wall the average waiting time was between eight and twelve years. In spite of all the limitations, more people inserted their names on the ever-expanding waiting lists. And when the notification to pick up the car finally arrived, new misfortunes awaited the owner. Bringing the car home was quite an adventure. Often there were no gas stations near the places where future owners picked up the new cars, and thus big canisters of gasoline had to be carried there, in some cases with bare hands.[57] Moreover, in astonishingly many cases the brand-new cars had several flaws that the owner discovered only on the way home.[58] And later on, fuel rationing, insufficient garage space, the lack of spare parts, and harassment by neighbors and the police assailed the motorist. Many more such examples can be found, but what is quite surprising, as Lewis Siegelbaum has remarked, is that citizens of the Eastern Bloc were willing to put up with all these hardships. Receiving and maintaining a car under socialist conditions was a hard job, but it seems that most owners accepted the challenge rather than giving up on the dream of having a car. Car ownership involved not only practical gains but also a social component in the form of (in most cases) male bonding that occurred while owners were mending and cleaning their cars in the presence of their fellow car enthusiasts.[59]

Let us consider the plight of the retired car mechanic Zhdanov, who had the chance to buy an old broken-down Chevrolet Bel Air with no motor at a low price and then was denied this opportunity as soon as the Soviet bureaucracy stepped in. Comrade Zhdanov, a lifelong car enthusiast, was asked by his former boss, himself a mechanic, to buy the wreck that was slowly decaying in the yard of a repair shop. The estimated price was around 690 rubles. Just before he picked up the car, a committee of experts, formed as a commission at the shop, set the sale price at the incredible sum of 6,868 rubles. The logic for the new price was very simple: foreign cars were sold in the Soviet Union by way of comparing them to local brands. The Chevrolet was deemed the equivalent of a Chaika, and from the original price 40 percent was subtracted to account for technical damage and wear and tear. Of course Zhdanov was outraged and refused to pay the new price. Because he considered that the commission had done him wrong, he insisted on paying only the 690 rubles. With his protest he climbed one by one the stairs of the Soviet bureaucratic ladder until his letters reached Premier Kosygin. From the very thick correspondence between Zhdanov and the authorities we also find out that the car had formerly belonged to a Belgian citizen, and when it broke down the Soviet mechanics were not able to repair it (another myth shattered!); thus there was nothing for him to do except remove the motor and leave the rest in the yard. More than two years later, shortly before Zhdanov showed interest in the car, the chassis had almost been discarded as old metal. Unfortunately, the documents contain no reference to the outcome of the conflict.[60]

There are many things to be learned from this apparently unspectacular account. It is first and foremost the story of a true car enthusiast—one might even say a car fanatic—under socialist conditions. The Russian word *avtoliubitel'* (car enthusiast) denominates exactly this combination of an enthusiastic though unprofessional driver.[61] In Zhdanov we find the epitome of such a love for the automobile, for he had spent more than two years of his life trying to convince Soviet authorities to allow him to take home the broken Chevrolet for a moderate sum. During this time he invested all his energy in writing one letter after another, not to report a life-threatening situation or a serious wrongdoing but simply to claim a cheap car. This could also be proof of the last decades of socialism as "normal," an example of an ordinary life in less than extraordinary times.[62] In his letters Zhdanov writes about his ardent desire to spend his retired years mending the old car. What impresses us is the amount of time and patience he invested freely just to prove his case. It becomes clear that writing letters to political authorities had a different function in socialist societies, serving as a very specific way of communication that turned into a surrogate for nonexistent public opinion. The act of writing letters of complaint became an institution under whose auspices right and wrong were negotiated.[63] This incident also demonstrates how many hurdles the state erected in the everyday life of its citizens. A commission had to be formed to deal with each trifle. Every simple decision called for massive bureaucratic effort. But maybe foreign cars (broken or not) weren't trifles after all for Eastern Europeans.

AT the end of this tour, I return to the specific nature of the socialist car culture. In light of the manifold contradictions and dilemmas, transfers, and emulation processes that characterized mass motorization in Eastern Europe, how could a *genuine* socialist car culture have existed? Have my arguments been contaminated by the official Party rhetoric that spoke of a true socialist automotive world in each of the three countries? No. For me, the genuine character of the socialist car culture consists exactly in the paradoxes and complications that mass motorization brought about in the Eastern Bloc countries. At the same time, this culture could never fully emancipate itself from the strong influence exerted by Western car cultures. The early success of the capitalist consumer revolution made the population of the Eastern Bloc yearn for the same benefits. To the general thrust after World War II for a more private and flexible use of time and space, socialism had nothing attractive to offer besides uniformity and collectivism. The decisions in favor of private—or to use the language of the time, "personal"—motorization were from the very beginning a dismissal of socialist principles. Moreover, this socialist path never proved capable of offering a viable alternative to Western models. But to regard it as merely a bad imitation of the latter would be a mistake. It produced far too many idiosyncrasies to simply regard it condescendingly as an inferior copy of Western car culture. It is true that only Western transfers made a socialist car culture possible. Nevertheless, how these foreign elements were adapted to the preexisting local conditions demonstrates the particular, and in a sense peculiar, nature of socialist automobility.

So if automobility functioned according to a different logic in the Eastern Bloc, was it necessarily *socialist*? I agree only to a certain extent with the assertion that everything taking place in a political order that called itself socialist necessarily produced socialist outcomes. Beyond that, car culture in the East drew several of its attributes from the economic system of socialism, as it was first implemented in the USSR after 1917. And although this system underwent many contradictory reforms, even in such a special field as private motorization several striking traits remained some six decades later. First, because of the lack of a market, special retail and distribution patterns filled the gap. Second, the highly protected status of the political elite was at no time seriously threatened. Though the privileges enjoyed by the political elite had their utility during the consolidation stage after the civil war in Russia and the Second World War in the rest of Eastern Europe, they proved to be at least in part a hindrance to broad social emancipation. Third, authorities could never fully control the economy of shortages. These systemic determinants and the Western influences were the two coordinates that determined the path toward mass motorization in the Eastern Bloc. The uneasy relationship with the West was one of its main features. So were shortages, privileges, waiting lists, high prices, a certain type of sociability around the car, and the special role mechanics occupied in this system, to mention but a few examples. In this sense the car culture of the USSR, the GDR, and Romania was both genuine and socialist.

9

AUTOBASTELN

Modifying, Maintaining, and Repairing Private Cars in the GDR, 1970–1990

Kurt Möser

The Framework

The topic of working on automobiles by users in the socialist GDR could be tackled with different methods and perspectives. It could be written as a political and social history of consumers in nonconsumerist economies, as a story of subjective approaches to technology, as a subaspect of socialist economies, and even as the history of media popularizing do-it-yourself. Being a historian of technology with a strong focus on sociotechnical contexts, I prefer an approach that focuses on the relationship of users to technological objects and systems but also brings in other aspects of society and culture.

The role of users has come into increasing focus within the history of technology. This somewhat revisionist perspective, introduced more than a decade ago, takes an object- and producer-centered approach. It forms the larger framework of my chapter. There is a difference between my approach and "traditional" social constructivist views, though: in discussions of user modifications, add-ons, repair, and maintenance of vehicles, the claim of a "coconstruction of technologies by users" is not a mere metaphor but a very material fact.[1] To work with mobility objects is more than just defining, formulating, and putting to work one's ideas or perceptions about what a technological object is or should be. It means to work on it, to form it materially according to one's requirements. Thus, user modifications and other practical, concrete mechanical activities of users are a perfect field for

---

The author thanks Lewis Siegelbaum for revising and correcting this chapter and the participants in the Berlin conference for their ideas in response to my presentation.

research into the question of how users matter—without getting stuck in metaphors and research allegories concerning construction.

The history of user modification of cars, but also of maintenance and repairs by users, has not yet been written, although there are useful contributions.[2] Many remarks of mobility historians point to the relevance of assessing maintenance, repair, and other direct manipulations of vehicles, but an overview or a consistent assessment seems to be lacking. Of course, I will not provide this. My aim is to look into some of the functions and roles of consumer "activation" in socialist car cultures. The discussion is also limited by region and time: my focus is on cars and consumers in the German Democratic Republic (GDR) from the 1970s, when a specific type of "automobile society" was formed. For pragmatic reasons I will date the beginning of a national mass car culture proper from the moment the number of cars exceeded the number of two-wheelers. This happened in West Germany in 1957 and in the East in 1972, forming a typical fifteen-year rift between automobility patterns in both states. The early prevalence of motorcycles is a feature of German motorization before and after the war in the East as well as in the West.

Tinkering, repairing, and modifying have to be studied as part of the story of the car by an interdisciplinary approach, as does mobility history in general. Furthermore, to be done properly it has to be placed in the widespread social movement of do-it-yourself, amateur craftsmanship, bricolage, even modeling and home renovation—which I include here under the term *Autobasteln*. Autobasteln in the GDR should be interpreted by considering politics, the economy, the individual bonding of man and technological artifacts, and aesthetics. Many points of entry are possible. Here I will ask whether automobiles in socialist states had not only technological but also social specifics, whether the social construction of cars was different in different societies, and whether users needed or developed other practices and skills than those used in the West.

Autobasteln as Usage

It is essential to understand maintaining and repairing as another form of usage—not driving proper but working with one's car, spending time with it, caring for it, looking after its needs, and forming a relationship. This means several things. It redefines the car as a technical object that requires technical knowledge but also other skills if one is to operate and understand it. In addition, it requires some concrete technical input not only to repair but also to run. Automobiles thus assume a role quite similar to that of pets: both require emotional as well as practical care to handle them. If driving creates a special man-machine relationship, which can be regarded as an extension of one's body, then maintaining and repairing as a form of usage forms a second type of relationship. This requires a user to socialize with her or his object. An aspect of automobility is creating an understanding and ultimately a form of semipersonal bond with one's mobility machine.

In what follows I will argue (1) that usage has to be seen in a wider perspective, transcending driving; (2) that automobiles with high maintenance requirements had a different social construction than did those that could be driven just as they were, without expecting them to require attention; and (3) that the features of these vehicles, combined with lack of sufficient repair infrastructure, forced users to engage in more technical activity and thus created a different type of knowledge as well as specific bonding between man and technology.

Tinkering in East and West

It is possible to identify the two attitudes toward tinkering—necessity and pleasure—with different stages of specific car cultures. Whereas in the early stages of automobile societies the pressure to reduce running costs is generally high—at this stage many car owners spend a considerable part of their income on their car, and many buy cars even if they cannot afford them—in later stages there tends to be "luxury tinkering." The availability of cars beyond the "cars for the existence-minimum" marks the end of the entry stage.[3] Then automobility moves toward a new stage, becoming more and more widespread and complex in terms of artifacts, usage, and cultural attitudes. This fits into a "Sloanistic" broadening of the automobile spectrum.[4] As soon as the car market expands and more social groups move into car ownership, social distinction—and the location of this distinction in the object, that is, the vehicle—comes into play. At this point the role of tinkering changes.

Now modifications by consumers become important: by modifying cars, owners can enter into the pattern of highly differentiated "cars for every purse and purpose" on the user level, providing distinction and individuality not by buying factory-modified vehicles in keeping with Sloanism but by providing distinction rather cheaply by do-it-yourself modifications.[5] Whereas Sloanism provides the desired qualities of one-off cars from the producer side, tinkering does so by consumer activity. The results of private modifications of serial vehicles for social differentiation could be termed "user Sloanism" as opposed to "producer Sloanism" or "industrial Sloanism." We know more about the last form than about user modifications for distinctions.

These remarks apply more to capitalist automobilism. In socialist car cultures there were marked differences in both the entry and the "abundance" stages of automobility. First, economic restrictions on the buyer's part were not all-important as they were in the West. The limiting factor for buying cars in the GDR was often not the availability of funds from the consumer's side. There was a surplus of spending power in the East despite lower wages and much higher car prices. Moreover, often all members of a family were happy to pool their money to buy a car. Instead of cost, the crucial limitation was the lack of available vehicles due to a severe and increasing shortage on the producer's side. The growth of automobile ownership was mainly restricted by limited production, which in the 1980s dramatically widened the gap between increasing demand and stagnating supply, as Eli Rubin points out in chapter 7.[6] Most other infrastructural elements required to run cars—e.g., repair, service, and refueling facilities—were also limited. Thus there were two forms of restriction in growth in the early stage of automobilism in Western and Eastern economies, consumer- and producer-based. Tinkering in both automobile cultures had different causes and functions.

Types of Modifications

Each issue of the quarterly hobby and do-it-yourself journal *Practic* and the *Motor-Jahr* yearbooks contained articles dealing with tinkering and user modification. A brief survey of these publications provides material for a preliminary categorization of user activities and user modifications. Aside from workshop hints and lessons, there were broadly three main methods of "improving" cars. First, articles made suggestions about how to deal with technical shortcomings of the vehicles, such as widening the trunk opening of the Trabant estate (*Practic*, January 1989), suppressing radio interference (*Practic*, April 1989), and improving solar protection (*Practic*, January 1986). A typical example of tinkering as mechanical improvement was a plan to increase the scale of the heating ("Wärmer im Trabant," *Motor Jahr*, 1978; *Practic*, January 1989). The second category consisted of articles striving to improve the vehicles for practical purposes and to modify them for better usage. For instance, there were articles about transforming Trabants into sleeping cells ("Trabant als Schlafkabine," *Practic*, March 1973), about storage trays to hold coffee in the interior (*Practic*, April 1985; February 1987; February 1982) in order to improve cars for "living in," and suggesting ways to increase the load-carrying capacity by building car roof racks or improving the ubiquitous small trailers (*Practic*, January 1979; February 1987). The third category contained articles devoted to helping motorists improve internal safety—for instance, by refitting safety belts or homemade children's seats ("Autositz für Kleinkinder," *Practic*, April 1979).

These articles were typical of specific social and cultural trends in modifying and tinkering. The first was making GDR cars fit for camping, eating, overnighting, and touring. Such modifications reflected the lust of East German citizens for travel despite restricted availability of hotels, geographical possibilities, and finances.[7] Another main trend, represented by the homemade children's seat, reflected obvious shortcomings of GDR automobilism, in this case internal safety. Whereas in the West newer-generation cars from the 1970s onward put more emphasis on passenger safety, there was hardly any improvement in the crashworthiness of Eastern European cars. Even the addition of passenger restraining devices lagged behind. Here the modifying and do-it-yourself movement had to intrude, providing a certain number of safety features. This is an example in which user activity substituted for industrial innovation.

Modifications and Developed Car Cultures

There seems to have been a significant increase in the number of vehicle-related do-it-yourself articles in popular publications during the 1970s and 1980s. This clearly is an indicator of the broadening of car ownership but also could have been a reaction to increasing obsolescence and to the slowing pace of product development and innovation of Eastern European cars. They had long production cycles without significant changes. "Improvements" were viable only if they didn't necessitate radical layout changes and therefore investments in industrial production hardware.

Insofar as user modifications reflected the increasing gap in the 1970s between the shortening of production cycles in the West and a stepped-up pace of innovation of private cars on one hand and the slow redesigning and developing of consumer products in the East on the other, consumer modifications came into play. Individual activities closed this gap in product design (and user orientation) to a certain extent, relieving the strain on the industrial side. If state-planned industry could not keep up with world market innovations and with what users wanted, then the users themselves had to step in—sometimes quite happily, sometimes out of sheer necessity. In any case, tinkering can be seen as reaction from below to delayed innovation. It has to be analyzed as complementary to top-down industrial innovation. I would hesitate to term this a "reinvention" of automobiles, as Kathleen Franz did in regard to American car culture; rather, I see it as a restructuring according to redefined and changed functions and expectations of users.[8]

We now have to identify some of the tools socialist societies provided for consumer activation regarding private cars. Print media served as a central element. Publications of several types made themselves important in giving access to ideas and resources within the socialist car culture. In addition to professional repair shop manuals, specialized publications aimed at the amateur car mechanic included *Ich fahre einen Trabant 601 (I Drive a Trabant)* from the Transpress publishers and the best-selling book by Franz Meissner (*Wie helfe ich mir selbst—How do I Help Myself?*), which had a third printing in 1974. Gerhard Klausing's *Trabant: Pflegen, warten, reparieren (Trabant: Caring, Maintaining, Repairing)* came on the market after 1990 but also reacted to the maintenance specifics of this version of the Socialist Car. In a way these user-related publications could make up for deficient repair and servicing infrastructures. In any case, it would have been cheaper and more economical to publish plans and suggestions for users to improve cars, taking some of the load off the GDR economy.

Tinkering and the Specifics of Eastern Vehicles

Did the Socialist Car as a technical artifact have specific features? For instance, did the cars themselves have a built-in repair friendliness that responded to limited service facilities? More specifically for our subject of tinkering and maintenance, were these cars geared to cater to the needs of being serviced, repaired, or modified by nonprofessional users? Tentatively I would answer yes. Both GDR main types, the Wartburg and especially the Trabant, did require frequent maintenance, were prone to breakdowns, and had short servicing intervals, but at the same time they were simple enough to work with. The Trabant, for instance, had quite short service intervals, including those for greasing axle points, decoking the exhaust, replacing spark plugs, and resetting ignition breaker gaps. On the other hand, its very mechanical features facilitated these tasks. A rather straightforward and unsophisticated two-stroke engine with fewer parts and simpler layout than the mainstream four-stroke simplified, together with good accessibility, the tasks of maintenance and repair. One could quip about the Trabant as about certain British outboard engines, the Seagulls: "They never work, but they are easy to repair."

Another material substrate of tinkering was extremely comprehensive tool kits, which came with some new cars such as Zhigulis (Ladas) and were tailored to the needs of dealing with running repairs by drivers far removed from infrastructural networks or professional support—indeed, far from any outside help at all. This kit included air pumps, devices setting the gap on breaker points, and even lighting below the hood to ease night repairs. One could argue that this situation represented a throwback to the period of pre-infrastructural automobilism, when users had to cope with unreliable technology without any chance of getting outside help.

Seen from a more general perspective, private automobiles in socialist countries retained much longer than in the West their social construction as emphatically *technical* artifacts that had to be run and maintained by individuals who had at least some mechanical competence. In developed Western automobile cultures the social construction tended to demechanize cars more and more, thus freeing users from the need to enact or develop mechanical competence and to tinker, thus broadening and simplifying usage proper. This meant they were able to drive without having to look into the mechanical black box. This marked an important difference in the user cultures between East and West.

Working on New Vehicles

Another difference between Eastern and Western cars was the condition of a new car when it left the factory. When they received their cars, owners of new Ladas or Wartburgs were allotted tasks that had nothing to do with any distinction among generations: there was still much work they had to do to them When Western new cars were handed over to their owners, they had been checked and rechecked to assure quality and a state of near faultlessness. Newness and perfection, typified by spotlessness and even smell became aesthetic qualities. At the core of Western automobility was an image of a clean, factory-immaculate artifact that one could admire before using. Any mechanical handling by the owner would disturb this perfection. In the East, however, imperfection in new cars was the norm (and was wearily anticipated by buyers, who even joked about it). A certain amount of mechanical activity was expected from new owners, and certain tasks were assigned to them—not arbitrarily but in a planned way. An example was the mounting of windshield wipers, which came loose with new cars. But owners' tasks could entail much more in-depth work—for example, rustproofing the inner body parts. The owner's handbook that came with the Russian Lada 1200 strongly advised new owners to completely dismantle the car body and thoroughly flood all cavities with anticorrosion fluid to extend the life of the sheet metal. Otherwise, the expected rust resistance would last for only six years. The essence of all this was a trend toward consumer activation starting right from the handing over of the car to make up for production and/or design deficiencies in the product itself.

Two diverging trends existed between Western and Eastern automobile cultures: whereas in the West automotive manufacturers increasingly discouraged users from modifying, tinkering, and repairing (and this not only by advice but also by various built-in, mechanical limiting features in the cars themselves, like special screw heads), in the case of Eastern cars it was the other way round. Automobiles manufactured and sold in COMECON states (as opposed to the selected ones sold for hard currency in the West, which generally underwent extensive predelivery work by Western importers) demanded attention and work by the owner from the very beginning to make them usable at all and to ensure the extended longevity and service life. This was essential in the replacement-starved GDR car society.

Tinkering and the Socialist Economy

The quasi-official delegation of tasks from the producer to the consumer gave the latter an increased importance as part of the socialist economy. This held true for other fields of do-it-yourself activities as well. Thus this rather humble leisure occupation was elevated to political-economic importance and, indeed, to an activity relevant for the building of socialism. A popular do-it-yourself book sums up this political function: "May this book contribute in its modest way toward imparting practical experience as well as expanding craftsmanly and polytechnical knowledge, thus serving the ends of technical progress, increasing labor productivity, and building socialism."[9] The Socialist Unity Party (SED) assigned high relevance to consumer activity within the socialist economy and society. This conformed to the policies of activating socialist citizens, transferring tasks from public or industrial enterprises to the more or less voluntary *Eigeninitiative* (self-initiative), and teaching and motivating comrades eager to help build socialism. On a personal level, it aimed to create satisfaction in the accomplishment of a difficult mechanical task. It pointedly transformed the socialist consumer into a producer as well, something that he should like and be proud of because of its political value. For historians of technology interested in intersections of political history, artifact- and user-focused technology, and social questions, a better example would be hard to find.

Within the framework of using and handling consumer products, the main task of consumers was to maintain the usability and value of a product that could not and should not be replaced easily and to prolong the time span of usage by nearly all means—in their own interest and the interest of the economy as a whole. The input of servicing and maintenance thus had to be considerably more important than in the West. One of the consequences was a different quantitative relation between driving and "caring." Compared with those in the West, East German cars had lower annual mileages but nonetheless demanded a high number of hours devoted to maintenance and repair. Moreover, owners imposed pressure on themselves not to use the car they owned, or at least not on a daily basis, in order to save it from wear and tear. The time ratio between actual driving and working on one's car could become quite biased toward working.

The already-mentioned deficiencies in infrastructural networks contributed to this ratio as well. The limited number of garages and professional repair shops coupled with the shortage of spare parts resulted in long waiting lists and extended periods of unavailability of private vehicles awaiting the "official" fitting of parts.

Driving to and handing over one's car to a specialized garage was quite impossible. To keep a car operational, most work had to be done by the owners themselves. Thus there was another macroeconomic role for car users: making up for an inadequate maintenance network. In this way they served an economic purpose within the framework of a planned economy that increasingly exhibited *automobile Mangel* (automobile scarcity) due to the lack of investment in the car industry and in the required infrastructures.[10] This integration of cars into the shadow economy—indeed, the formation of this type of economy by and for automobiles—admirably analyzed by Lewis Siegelbaum for the USSR, had its analogue in the GDR.[11]

The scarcity not only of cars but of a car-related infrastructure was one of the symptoms of socialist economics' disregard for transport in general, relegating it to the status of a less "productive" economic sector.[12] In terms introduced by Albert Hirschman fifty years ago, transport was considered part of essentially unproductive "social overhead cost" (SOC) and not part of the coveted "direct productive activity" (DPA).[13] This framework of economically undervaluing mobility helps to explain the planned disregard for the volume of the infrastructural requirements of individual motorization and for its potential for economic growth and innovation.[14]

Compensation for this shortcoming by user activities created side effects that could not have been welcomed officially, though. Tinkering became integrated into the unofficial private subeconomy of socialist GDR, since spare parts or coveted add-on objects were precious and hard to find. The macroeconomic reason was that in order to fulfill the plan, officials valued completed vehicles more than spares, and thus factories prioritized them. The problem was aggravated by a proportionally higher demand for spares by an increasingly aging and repair-prone stock of vehicles that generally demanded more mechanical attention.[15]

Thus an active scene of acquiring, bartering, and hunting for car-related objects developed. Additionally, if GDR citizens had relatives in the West, they could obtain scarce parts by handing over hard currency. Also possible was buying parts with much-sought-after West German marks, affectionately known as *blaue Kacheln* (blue tiles, referring to the color of the hundred-deutsche mark bills). These procedures for privately compensating for scarcity with whatever resources were necessary to keep consumer goods in operation were not limited to automobility. But they developed fully in the field of cars, forming a subversive culture of automobile economics that was at the forefront of the developing subeconomy and spreading.

Abilities of Consumers and the Tasks Tackled

To discuss the specifics of the socialist car culture one also has to tackle the question of the influence of users' technical qualifications and potential differences with these in the West. It is claimed that in the GDR higher education was much more aimed at compatibility with modern technology and industry than in the West, where cultural values as well as concrete educational practices supposedly clung more to obsolete antitechnical approaches. If this was true, what were the other social consequences of a more technologically oriented education? And did this difference influence the different types of automobile cultures?

The question of traditional values of user groups negatively influencing modern car cultures was put forward in West Germany before 1970. For instance, the high accident rate was blamed on the debasement of technology by middle-class drivers, who at the time still formed the main user group. The West German sociologist Dieter Claessens claimed in 1966 that people with more interest in technology and better mechanical abilities would make better automobilists.[16] This would imply that any improvement of driver skills and decrease in the number of accidents would have to start with better understanding of technology and with elevating its sociocultural status.

According to this line of argument, Eastern drivers and owners would have an advantage. But assuming they had a better mechanical education, did this really make a difference? Did the high esteem of practical technology—as exemplified in the polytechnical concept of *Erweiterte Oberschulen* (EOS), combining secondary education with practical job training—influence the attitude and handling of users towards their vehicles? What about the gender aspect? In theory, men and women alike received this polytechnical type of education and were thus equally prepared for working in an industrialized society. And indeed, official statements pointed out that in the GDR many highly qualified women worked in technical professions regarded formerly as male domains. Did this equality extend to tinkering on cars as well? Did women and men alike work on their cars? I have no figures available, but my impression is that despite efforts to provide technical education equally to both men and women, the actual working on cars was in its majority done by men, as related by many narratives of car owners. My question would have to be tackled in the wider framework of role distribution in GDR families, of the relation of education and everyday activities later on, and on gender-specific usage of automobiles.

The transgender polytechnical education in the GDR certainly was not very useful when it came to the nontechnological elements of driving, notably the development of "road sense" and "machine sensibility," which became regarded as much more important for driving than any mechanical skills. The long-term transformation of cars from mechanical devices to driving machines resulted in less emphasis on the mechanical abilities of users and more on the development and employment of other qualities.[17] Alteration in the schedule of driving schools away from the technology of cars reflected this change. The correlation between technical education and driving ability was apparently quite weak.

On the other hand, it is likely that better technical education improved all other forms of usage apart from driving proper, represented by tinkering and modifying. It prepared car owners for the task of keeping their vehicles roadworthy and indeed usable. Note that the technical tasks set by popular textbooks on car maintenance and repairs were often quite demanding. For instance, they included the do-it-yourself manufacturing of special tools for special tasks. Thus the necessities of tinkering and the educational preparation for the required mechanical tasks were closely related.

Vacation Tinkering

If tinkering had specified tasks within the socialist economy as well as nonsocialist side effects, there was an even more private side to it. As already mentioned, one of the specifics of the GDR's car culture was the reconstruction of cars for leisure transport. As a rule, the amount of gear to be lugged around was comparatively larger than in contemporary Western car societies. In order to save premium interior room for people and to increase the amount of trunk space, owners armed their cars with roof racks and/or trailers. In these add-ons the requisites of the ubiquitous private summer houses (*Datschen*) or of camping had to be transported. In some cases the car itself could be transformed into part of a mobile leisure structure. This was the much sought-after two-person roof tent, which could be erected from a roof-rack box and was accessible by a ladder. Most of the camping modifications, though, had to be done by the user. The specific structure of GDR vacationing—scarcity of hotel or private accommodations and therefore the necessity to camp—helped to shape the specific social construction of East German automobiles as integrated vacation vehicles.

Moreover, tinkering with cars could develop into a vacation-oriented activity. Since cars were often parked close to one's tent, they were part of the vacation environment of beach or forest. Physical closeness, spare time, and the necessity of servicing after and before long-distance drives of often overloaded vehicles combined to create favorable conditions for tinkering during one's vacation. (Of course, "long distance" is relative, but since the average GDR vehicle did not accumulate much mileage per annum and at the same time was prone to breakdowns, even moderate distances taxed its mechanical endurance). Therefore, stories and photographs of dismantling Trabants close to a Baltic beach are abundant.

Equally widespread was the sharing of this activity in the mostly crowded vacation areas. Even when the car's owner undertook the task alone, a small crowd often assembled and joined in, if not for the actual *Schrauben* (screwing) then at least for discussing, advising, valuing, or judging of the mechanical work. Even more than tinkering at home, vacation tinkering was an immensely social activity. But more than socializing was involved: people engaged in various forms of cooperation and, above all, the sharing of knowledge. It could be claimed that campgrounds developed into an informal academy of car technology, distributing competence and concrete mechanical handling as part of a specific recreation culture. If this sounds idyllic, however, the shortcomings were evident. The less mechanically minded users were doing servicing not voluntarily at all, as a pastime, but because they simply had no choice. Even vacation tinkering became one of the many symptoms of automobile Mangel.

Modifications for Distinction?

Up to now I have focused on approved or even sponsored modifications. Many articles in magazines aimed at functional improvement of cars that could be termed "producer-substituting user modifications." But if one looks at the cars themselves, it becomes evident that the actual user modifications often deviated from official suggestions. I distinguish between the do-it-yourself culture that was officially tolerated or encouraged for purely rational reasons and other, tentatively termed "aesthetic" modifications that were made from below and had less official approval. In between was an extensive modification culture where functionality could become an excuse—a typical feature of automobility in nearly all cultures.

Photographs of the Trabants crossing the Berlin border in 1989 show many of them sporting special fog headlights, special wing mirrors, or special color schemes—in fact many more radical consumer modifications than were made to West German vehicles. Most modifications did not aim primarily at better usage but had a common trend: they aimed at emulating the features and silhouettes of Western cars. This can be seen as a consumer reaction against Eastern vehicle design, which had become increasingly obsolete from the 1970s on, opening an aesthetic gap with more modern (at least modern-looking) Western vehicles. Thus another quite important reason for modifications was to superficially Westernize East European cars.

With Western cars, a long trend that enveloped not only sporty vehicles but even staid family sedans was termed "sportization." This process, analyzed in the social framework provided by Norbert Elias and Eric Dunning, resulted in a type of vehicle that has been called *Rennreiselimousine* (racing travel sedan).[18] Its special features from the 1960s onward were not only better road-holding and more engine power but also the acquisition of a sporty look. From the late 1960s the design of ordinary cars, for instance, aimed at the pattern of contemporary rally vehicles. Less radical elements comprised more sporty engine characteristics, wider tires, and a stiffer suspension. In East Germany the industry did not cater to this trend at all. But it was unofficially imported, concentrating not on the technical but on the optical characteristics.

This explains why it was fashionable for Trabant owners to add rally mirrors on the mudguards, additional fog lights, or black hoods to reduce glare, all typical features of the coveted sports and rally car looks. In general, users introduced any seemingly dysfunctional elements of car culture that the planned industry and its political control refused to acknowledge—according to them cars should provide functional individual transport and nothing else. Consumer modifications added seemingly nonessential surplus, stressing unacknowledged secondary functions. This process can be interpreted as in accordance with the long trend toward secondary function dominance, a trend that generally characterized car cultures that had moved away from their early stages where motoring spread, and that in the East was pushed by consumers from below, not by a Sloanistic industry. In this process, tinkering became a user-based tool of change.

Here a question arises concerning the role of individualization of cars in a socialist society. In the West, user modification is part of a complex matrix of distinction within automobile culture, adding yet more fine differences to already highly differentiated mass-produced goods.[19] Did a similar social distinction play a major part in the makeup of the socialist car culture? Was social distinction via automobility an issue at all? I assume it was, rather contrary to official proclamations. First, ownership of a car itself was a socially distinctive feature within GDR society, and, second, what car one owned made a difference as well. There was obviously a prestige spectrum ranging from the ubiquitous smallish Trabants at one end to the hand-crafted Eastern functionary vehicles at the other, the Soviet Ladas and imported Western cars being in between. As in the West, the age and condition of cars formed a social pattern too.

If distinction based on cars was common within socialist automobility as a whole, modifications and rebuilding also had an important place. Adding sports mirrors or modifications of any kind allowed mass-produced goods to be transformed into vehicles with social distinction, a situation that undermined the idea of a nominally equal society moving on its historic path toward true socialism.

To summarize, activation of car users by tinkering was two-pronged: it promoted a close man-machine relationship, but it was also a symptom of some of the insufficiencies of the Eastern Bloc car culture. There was tension between fun and necessity in the handling of automotive technology. Modifying and repairing could be sources of satisfaction and dissatisfaction. It seems plausible that there were different social constructions of cars in socialist and Western societies. But more important, it seems to me, were the sociopolitical consequences of individual modifications by users. The attempts to come to terms with technological artifacts, to own them, work on them, modify them, devote time and energy to keep them running, and integrate them into one's private life were activities in a state that had a rather ambivalent position toward private cars.

10

"LITTLE TSARS OF THE ROAD"
Soviet Truck Drivers and Automobility, 1920s–1980s

Lewis H. Siegelbaum

When Heinz Lathe and Günther Meierling, two German ex-POWs who returned to Soviet Russia in 1958, drove south from Moscow in their diesel-powered Mercedes, they passed long lines of trucks but met their first car only after they had traveled forty-three kilometers (twenty-seven miles). Their experience was not unique. "We met a number of lorries, but saw few cars," wrote the British journalist Patrick Sergeant about his trip along the same route a few years earlier. How could it be otherwise when until 1960 fewer than a third of all four-wheeled vehicles produced annually in the USSR were cars, and few cars ventured much beyond the limits of the major cities? Sergeant confidently asserted on the basis of his lengthy road journey that "most Soviet people travel by train, river in the summer, air and long-distance bus." But his German counterparts noted that "lorries do stop" and that there were people with suitcases in all of them.[1] If the Soviet Union could be said to have entered the automobile age by this time, it did so not in "light" (*legkovye*) automobiles—the standard term for cars—but in their heavier cousins, trucks.

Recently scholars have been employing the term "automobility" to characterize "the principal socio-technical institutions and practices that seek to organize, accelerate and shape the spatial movements and impacts of automobiles." Construed as a "hybrid assemblage" consisting of "humans, machines, roads and other spaces, representations, regulatory institutions and a host of related businesses and infrastructural features," the term seemingly encompasses not only cars and their drivers but the trucks and truckers with whom they share the road. Yet thus far the hybrid has been understood exclusively as "*car*-driver," and in the short span of its scholarly existence automobility has become more or less synonymous with car culture. Though automobility may no longer be "a neglected topic within sociology, cultural studies and related disciplines," as Mike Featherstone complained it was a few years back, within automobility studies, trucking still seems neglected.[2]

The purpose of this chapter is twofold: to insert automobility into our understanding of the experience of human movement in Russia, particularly during the decades when trucks outnumbered cars, and to bring the Soviet experience to bear on scholarly conversations about automobility. I will do so by examining truckers partly from the perspective of labor history—who became truckers, the conditions of their work, relations among them and with other motorists, their social status, and the extent to which and why these elements changed over time—and, to get at the broader cultural significance associated with truck driving, partly in terms of the highly gendered images of truckers in both political discourse and popular imagination. I see these two approaches as complementary and have organized their exposition to work in tandem. The nature of truckers' work, their training, and the internal hierarchies of the occupation, after all, structured their representation in important ways; at the same time, the very categories used to distinguish among truckers and differentiate them from "amateur" (*liubitel'skie*) motorists, to say nothing of truckers' own social behavior, arose out of a particular cultural milieu.

Like Soviet truckers themselves, this inquiry into their automobility covers a lot of ground. Although many informational blank spots remain, the disparate materials at hand—articles in newspapers, trade journals, and automotive magazines; data and correspondence from transport workers' unions deposited in Soviet archives; short stories, novels, and films—are rich and plentiful. Moreover, if we waited for all the blank spots to be filled, we probably would be waiting forever. Better to accommodate the truckers even if only partially than to keep them in the penumbra of history.

The Chuiskii Highway, or the Legend of Kol'ka and Raika

Beginning in 2001, a made-for-television serial called *Truckers* (*Dal'noboishchiki*) ran on NTV. The series featured an old, crusty driver named Feodor Ivanych and his quick-tempered driving companion, Sasha Korovin, as they transported all manner of goods (in the inaugural episode it was "humanitarian goods for the wounded fighters in Chechnia") across the length and breadth of the country. "To survive on Russia's roads is not easy," said NTV's website. "Lurking on the highways are terrorists, slave traders, narco-dealers, and totalitarian sects." The series was sufficiently successful to run for several years and to spawn an online real-time game that as of this writing is in its third version, improbably called *Pokorenie*

Ameriki (*Conquest of America*) with "Rig 'n' Roll" placed in parentheses. Populated by oligarchs, sex-slaves, vagabonds, and "criminals of all stripes," *Truckers* is clearly an example of a post-Soviet action thriller. The "old-regime grumbler Ivanych" represents the only obvious connection to Soviet times.[3]

But 2001 also saw the completion of *Two Drivers* (*Ekhali dva shofera*), Aleksandr Kott's first feature film, which reached back nostalgically to the Soviet past. Set in the Urals just after the Great Patriotic War, the film concerns good-natured Kol′ka Snegirov, the driver of a slightly battered AMO (Avtomobil′noe moskovskoe obshchestvo, or Automobile Society of Moscow) truck, and Raika, who drives a green-colored Ford. Those of a certain age were sure to recognize the pair. They had first appeared in a popular song from the 1930s, "The Chuiskii Highway" ("Chuiskii trakt"). The song told of Raika's dare to Kol′ka ("When the AMO overtakes the Ford/ Then Raechka yours will be"). Smitten, Kol′ka is determined that she will be his, and one day when Raika passes him on the narrow Chuiskii Highway in the Altai Mountains, he floors it, pulls even with the Ford, but then plunges into a ravine and is swallowed "by the waves of the silvery Chuia." In 1965 Mikhail Mikheev, a minor Novosibirsk poet, revealed that he had invented the bittersweet story and set it to an old tune as a lighthearted gesture to an old school friend, Nikolai ("Kol′ka") Kovalev, and Kovalev's girlfriend, Raia. Kovalev, it turns out, did drive an AMO after graduating with Mikheev in 1931 from the Biisk technical school, but Raia (whose real name was Iraida) worked as a conductor on a city bus, and both of them lived to a ripe old age. Sung at their wedding, the song subsequently was spread by truckers up and down the Chuiskii Highway and throughout Siberia.[4]

In both reviving and taking poetic license with the early 1930s legend of Kol′ka and Raia, Aleksandr Kott was following a well-worn path. In his documentary film *The Driver's Ballad* (*Shoferskaia ballada*) from 1986, Valerii Solomin rode with retired drivers in old repaired ZIS (Zavod im. Stalina, factory named after Stalin) trucks along the Chuiskii Highway in search of where Kol′ka Snegirov might have gone off the cliff. The actor, writer, and movie director Vasilii Shukshin—who hailed from those parts and had gone to school during the war at the Biisk automobile technical school—repeatedly drew on the Kol′ka-Raika love story, most notably in his directorial debut, *There Lives This Guy* (*Zhivet takoi paren′*, 1964), which opens with the hero driving his GAZ (Gor′kii Avtomobil′nyi Zavod, Gor′kii Automobile Factory)-51 along the Chuiskii Highway. Nor does this exhaust the adaptations of the legend. In "Ol′shanskii trakt" ("The Ol′shanskii Highway"), a song included in an "encyclopedia of drinking songs, 'slang' and 'street' folklore," the equivalents of Kol′ka and Raia drive ZIL (Zavod im. Likhacheva, factory named after Likhachev, successor to AMO and ZIS) and Studebaker trucks and it is not a curve in the road but a MAZ (Minsk Automobile Factory) truck coming in the other direction that does in the unnamed driver of the ZIL. Finally, a provincial Siberian newspaper reported in August 2008 that the legend of Kol'ka and Raia has spawned a monument allegedly erected by Novosibirsk drivers outside Biisk. The monument includes an actual AMO steering wheel.[5]

The continual reworking of the Kol'ka-Raika legend and its survival well into the post-Soviet era suggest its resonance with generations of people and especially, one imagines, truck drivers. The models of trucks change from one version to another, although it cannot be accidental that the male character is seated in domestically produced trucks that have to catch up to, if not surpass, the foreign-made models. What remained constant was that women drivers distracted men, and, except for Aleksandr Kott's post-Soviet happy ending, enticed them to their deaths. In reality, women did drive trucks, especially during wartime, when they assumed many of the jobs traditionally filled by men. The legend, however, conveyed the message that women drivers upset the natural order; all's right with the world only when men are behind the wheel. Perhaps it was not the job itself but its cultural coding as a masculine endeavor that explains the persistence of the legend.

But as in other societies, masculinity in Russia covered a broad range of associations and forms of behavior among men.[6] Moreover, the Kol'ka-Raika legend is only one of the threads that connect truck drivers to the fabric of Soviet history. To track others we need to look beyond the folkloric to other kinds of sources: the records of institutions that employed truck drivers and the trade unions that represented them; magazines, newspapers, and other publications that reported on truckers; and films, photography, and literature about them. From sources such as these at least four kinds of truckers can be discerned: heroes, professionals, loners, and wheeler-dealers. Sometimes presented as ideal types and sometimes merely as an allusion, these different versions of truckers often appeared simultaneously. Their chronologies in any case overlapped, and thus the order in which they will be presented here is fairly arbitrary.

Heroes

Although numbering no more than a few thousand at most, trucks did exist and found commercial employment in prerevolutionary Russia. During the First World War, the Russian military requisitioned over four thousand vehicles of all types (nearly a third of the total in the empire) and placed orders abroad for over thirty thousand vehicles, of which perhaps a third had arrived by the time of the October Revolution.[7] The militarization of vehicles and their drivers continued through the revolutionary era, in which the vehicles appeared in some of the most vivid images, careening through the streets of Petrograd and Moscow with machine guns mounted on their turrets and rifle-bearing Red Guards spilling out of the sides. The fledgling Soviet state eventually tamed and used them for other purposes. During the summer of 1921 as famine raged throughout large parts of the Russian Soviet Federated Socialist Republic (RSFSR), the Commissariat of Transportation organized an expedition of trucks to remove some 3.4 million poods of grain from collection points to railroad stations in Akmolinsk Oblast. A report filed with the commissariat described this relief effort that covered thousands of kilometers in a remote part of the country as the "first experience in Russia of the planned use of trucks for transport on a large scale." Meanwhile, in Moscow drivers of any vehicle engaged in the service of a state institution were required by a decree of the Council of People's Commissars from June 1920 to record in a log book the times of departure and return and the route taken as well as their signatures.[8] These two extremes of braving the elements in performance of heroic deeds on the one hand and conforming to a regimen of strict discipline on the other would continue to define the demands the state made on truckers throughout much of the Soviet period.

During the 1920s, the entire country's fleet of trucks never exceeded ten thousand, of which somewhat more than half were domiciled in Moscow and Leningrad.[9] The numbers actually dwindled during the first half of the decade as models produced before the war or imported during wartime reached the end of their lives. They would have declined even more steeply had not auto mechanics and drivers (the two were often the same) exercised their improvisatory skills by cannibalizing and recycling parts, experimenting with alternative fuels, and engaging in other often heroic measures at depots. A retrospective report prepared in 1933 claimed that whereas in 1922 the main transport company Avtopromtorg had organized freight and passenger transport along 52 routes totaling 3,326 kilometers, the corresponding figures for 1924 were 265 routes of over 14,000 kilometers in length. Still, reflecting the shrinkage of the motor pool, the number of transport workers within the Union of Transport Workers who handled cars and trucks dropped from just under 20,000 in May 1922 to 13,352 a little more than two years later. As a proportion of all workers in the union, who included loaders, carters, warehouse workers, and others, this meant a decline from 16.5 percent to 9 percent.[10]

Domestic production of trucks began in late 1924 with the AMO factory's 1.5-ton F-15 and expanded two years later when the Iaroslavl Automobile Factory started turning out a 3-ton model.[11] In the meantime, various state institutions and voluntary societies seeking to promote automotive development ("automobilization") undertook the organization of test runs (*avtoprobegy*) to determine which models of trucks, cars, and motorcycles were most appropriate for Russia's notoriously precarious roads. Analogous to rallies that had originated in Europe before World War I, the avtoprobegy could be quite elaborate affairs. In late

September 1923, twelve trucks primarily from abroad endured 750 kilometers of roads through north-central Russia in a test run lasting four days. The organizing committee sent gold watches engraved with "First *Avtoprobeg* USSR" to nine intrepid drivers.[12] Two years later a far more elaborate competition, breathlessly covered on a daily basis in *Pravda* as if it were a sporting event, sent thirty-seven trucks from Leningrad to Moscow, then to Kursk and back to Moscow. Part of the "All-Union Automobile Test Run" that included cars and motorcycles, the truck portion concluded on August 28 when comrades Tsipulin and Rupnevskii crossed the finish line on the Serpukhov Highway in their AMOs, "the pride and glory of the USSR," as *Pravda* put it. "We know that the avtoprobeg is not a race," the AMO drivers said in response to "boisterous cries of 'Hurrah' from the crowd of spectators," "but still, our machines came in first."[13]

Of course, the main point here was to celebrate the qualities of the Soviet-made trucks rather than the acumen of the drivers, but drivers would get plenty of other opportunities to shine. Publicity surrounding avtoprobegy of various kinds (agitational, expeditionary, and scientific-technical) increased with the expansion of the AMO (from 1931, ZIS) and the opening of a new truck and car factory in Nizhni-Novgorod (GAZ) in the early 1930s. It peaked in the summer of 1933 with the Moscow–Kara-Kum–Moscow avtoprobeg, a nearly ten thousand-kilometer jaunt by twenty-three vehicles (six cars and seventeen trucks) through some of the most remote parts of the country. Drivers had several roles to play aside from keeping their vehicles on the road and in good order. Along with the bevy of reporters, photographers, and Party activists, they served as the state's eyes on wheels, reporting on the condition of the roads they traversed and the need for improvement. They also figured as agitators, collectively issuing an open letter on the eve of their return to Moscow "to all automobile transport workers" to learn from their experience. But as evidenced by the appearance of their individual portraits in *Izvestiia* on the day of their departure, flattering accounts of their behavior on and off the road, and reports of popular acclaim both during and after the trip, they clearly were intended to embody Soviet heroes.[14]

Whether Party members or not, the drivers exhibited—in journalists' obliging accounts—those classic Bolshevik and not incidentally male qualities of strength ("Soviet shock absorbers are strong, Soviet cars are strong, but stronger still are their drivers"), vigor, and wisdom. They uncomplainingly put up with temperatures in excess of fifty degrees Celsius, sandstorms that obliterated the way forward, dwindling water supplies, venomous lizards and scorpions scampering around their night camps, and other trials. In freeing vehicles stuck in mud and sand they used ingenuity, relied on each other, and observed strict discipline before their "commander," A.M. Miretskii. Finally, they came from the right class backgrounds: Semen Utkin's "biography is like that of the country"; Mikhail Savitskii, the son of a landless peasant, had joined the Bolsheviks in 1917; Miretskii himself was "a simple and disciplined hereditary Artemovsk proletarian." They were, in short, "the best in the Soviet Union."[15]

No other test run would ever match the hoopla of the Moscow–Kara-Kum–Moscow event. In terms of showcasing the drivers, the Great Women's avtoprobeg of the summer of 1936 came close. Like the famous tractor brigade under the Stakhanovite Pasha Angelina and the crew aboard the *Rodina* airplane, the highly publicized event tested the mettle of its female participants, who demonstrated in the words of an editorial in the newspaper *Trud* "that women can fulfill responsible auto-transport tasks no worse than men." They too came from the right (proletarian) backgrounds, many having worked as domestics and washerwomen before entering auto transport. They too exhibited "braveness, skill, and unyieldingness," and in Anastasia Volkova had a commander who was "as demanding of herself as she was demanding of others."[16]

The Great Patriotic War produced driver-heroes too, none more heroic than the men and women who delivered supplies and evacuated people across Lake Ladoga's "road of life," the ice road that linked Leningrad to unoccupied Soviet territory during the siege. From late November 1941 until mid-April 1942, thousands of GAZ-AA and ZIS-5 trucks, buses, and other vehicles traversed the ice in convoys every day. Each trip took several hours across the twenty-five- to thirty-kilometer stretch. Drivers faced the danger of enemy artillery and air bombardment, blinding snowstorms, frostbite, and sudden cracks in the ice. On a single day—December 6—the army lost 126 vehicles. Nevertheless, in January, 261 drivers averaged two trips per day. By March, 355 did three trips per day and another 100 completed five.[17]

It was a regular Stakhanovite festival, for which drivers received unstinting praise. The writer Aleksandr Fadeev described them continuing to drive their trucks after they had been hit by enemy fire and saving precious cargoes as their trucks sank below the lake's surface. To him "the road of life is a road of heroes, forging among themselves a great union of brotherhood, a brotherhood of thousands of people." In her diary entry for February 23, 1942, the poet Vera Inber wrote that "the labour of the Ladoga lorry drivers is a sacred labour." Another poet, Ol'ga Berggolts, testified to their courage in "Leningrad Poem" (1942): "Forward! How the blisters sting! / The palms to the mittens froze. / But he brings flour, driving / to the bakery before dawn."[18]

This kind of self-sacrificial heroism—*podvig* in Russian—was by no means unique to truck drivers. But because the otherwise mundane activities of delivering supplies and transporting people now had attained life-saving significance while also becoming life-endangering to those performing them, their *podvig* seemed especially poignant. Accounts of the great postwar construction projects, especially those in previously uninhabited territory, often contained truckers exhibiting this quality, but none could evoke the same degree of sympathy.[19] The sacral character of the war surely was part of it, but another reason for the public reaction may have been that self-sacrifice—along with other Bolshevik virtues—was losing its cachet among succeeding generations.

Professionals

"Very little has been written about drivers," wrote Boris Zil'pert in the pages of *Behind the Wheel* (*Za rulem*) in 1929. Zil'pert, who was referring not only to truck drivers but to all drivers with a professional license, offered his analysis of them as "a cross between coachmen and aviators." From the former they had inherited "coarseness" and from the latter technical boldness. "Our driver," he continued, "is in love with his machine, but as a self-taught person [*samouchka*], he still thinks it contains elements of magic."[20] The need for proper professional training, for reliable courses certifying competence, became a constant refrain as the demand for drivers increased and the roads, at least in the major cities, thickened with traffic. In the forefront of this effort and offering its own courses was Avtodor (the Society for Cooperation in the Development of Automobilism and Road Improvement) which published *Behind the Wheel*.

Drivers received pay on a graduated scale that depended on their skill category (first for driver-mechanics, second for "highly skilled" drivers, third for ordinary drivers), the size and weight of the truck they drove, the kind and amount of freight they delivered, and the distance they traveled to make deliveries. Also factored in was the time it took to load and unload freight as well as deliver it and return from deliveries. The system invited all manner of abuse, including shortcutting routes to save time and bribing depot foremen to pad weight totals and adjust time sheets.[21] This was why aside from driver training courses, Avtodor, the various auto transport unions, and their corresponding Party committees put so much effort into popularizing attitudes and behavior appropriate to a professional driver. "I've been driving trucks since 1918," comrade Kaliaga told an All-Union meeting of shock worker-drivers in 1934, "and I don't know what an accident is." Although his Ford had clocked fifty-two thousand kilometers, the inspection commission concluded it could go another thirty thousand before capital repairs. Comrade Shul'pinskii, the best driver at a garage servicing the gold mining industry in Bashkiria, outdid Kaliaga. He drove the ZIS-5 he had received in June 1934 over a hundred thousand kilometers without its needing any repairs. How? "I don't overload the vehicle, I change the oil frequently and the air filter at least three times a month, and I keep the truck clean." Comrade Shul'pinskii had the good fortune to rack up his record during the heyday of the Stakhanovite movement and for his pains received a trip to the union's sanatorium, a watch, and a bonus of a thousand rubles.[22]

Cleanliness applied not only to the truck but to oneself. "Each driver must be dressed neatly," intoned Moscow driver Nik. Viktorov in the pages of *Behind the Wheel.* If it was necessary to crawl under the vehicle, one should wear overalls. Rather than gasoline and oil, use soap and water to wash up, and rather than a rag, use a towel.[23] By such measures, one could learn to work in a professional or "cultured" manner. But the discourse of professionalism and associated demands for cultured behavior in a sense created its opposite. As Viktorov acknowledged, the neatly dressed driver risked being mocked by his fellow drivers and mechanics as a "dandy" (*shchegol'*). Their penchant for risk taking, physical prowess, and disorderliness smacked not of being cultured but of the culture of "auto hooliganism." Auto hooligans drove on the left side of the road, refused to give an inch to another vehicle, didn't allow their vehicle to be passed by another if they could help it, ignored people in distress by the side of the road, loved to intimidate pedestrians, and used foul language.[24]

Alcohol was endemic to this culture too. Although forbidden by law, drinking on the premises of garages and depots nonetheless occurred often enough to be reported and condemned repeatedly by the press—in the garage of the Tula depot for supplies to Moscow; at the Grozneft auto depot, where "to get work one must 'treat' comrade Smirnov or the mechanic Sergetskii"; at the garage of the Syzran Consumers' Society; and in the Moscow Soviet garage, to name just a few.[25] Lurid accounts of crashes, injuries, and deaths caused by truck drivers under the influence and of the death sentences meted out to them may have deterred a few, but the culture itself seemed ineradicable.[26]

Professionalism spoke to a powerful strain in Bolshevism that had to do with the mastery of technique. But as David Priestland has argued, "technicism" among Party ideologues coexisted with and occasionally was overwhelmed by class-struggle revivalism.[27] Aside from any specific behavior on the part of truck drivers, what worried authorities most about trucking in the mid-1930s was its "infiltration ... by former kulaks, the disenfranchised [*lishentsy*], bandits and other alien and hostile elements." The occupation allegedly attracted such shiftless types because of the great need for drivers as well as the fact that it involved "individualized labor lacking in control."[28] It provided, in other words, a good place to hide. To weed out these people, the state's road and highway administration (Tsudortrans) and the drivers' union organized an attestation process patterned on the verification of Party documents that the Party's Central Committee had mandated. Somehow the exercise was supposed to enable authorities to identify those who had not completed the required 122 hours of technical training. The press duly reported the discovery of thieves, criminals, and former tsarist officers ("even a major-general" in Leningrad) as well as instances of licenses obtained from inspectors through bribery.[29] Whatever salutary effects these and other security measures produced in all likelihood were temporary.

The lessons supposedly learned before the war needed reinforcement in the aftermath of victory. In Anatolii Rybakov's Stalin-prize winning novel *Drivers* (*Voditeli,* 1950), the hero, Poliakov, director of a provincial depot, reassigns one of the drivers, Maksimov, to the oldest truck in the garage. Maksimov rejects the assignment, reminding Poliakov that he has a first-class license. "I'm not talking about the class," Poliakov cuts him short. "A first-class driver doesn't put an unwashed vehicle in the garage. I can't leave the best bus on the depot in such slovenly hands. Go take the ZIS 24–26."[30] A first-class driver also shouldn't drink and drive, but some continued to do so. The first postwar congress of auto transport workers listened (probably glumly) to a report by the chief state auto inspector, Kuznetsov, in which he claimed that roughly a quarter of all accidents were caused by intoxicated truck drivers.[31]

During the war, a whole new generation of drivers received training on a new generation of trucks, including Studebakers, Dodges, and other models imported via Lend Lease. After demobilization, many drivers and trucks found work with one or another of the ministries' auto pools, in one of the subsidiaries of the Union-wide state transportation agency Soiuztrans, or with the rural-based Soiuzzagottrans and Sovkhoztrans. In the meantime, the road network began to thicken, and reliance on trucks to deliver produce from farms, raw materials from forests and mines, and finished products from factories to railheads grew.[32] Regular intercity freight deliveries by truck, previously a rarity, commenced in 1958.[33]

In 1960 a new and highly differentiated pay system was introduced for all professional drivers. The system gave truckers access to bonus payments for transporting dangerous materials (e.g., flammable or radioactive materials) and economizing on fuel, tire, and engine wear and tear.[34] But the other side of the coin was that early exhaustion of these items made drivers liable for deductions from their wages, or "fines," as one driver put it.[35] Though a small minority among the more than six hundred thousand members of the Union of Auto Transport Workers (as of 1955), long-distance truckers and their professional needs began to appear in the pages of *Behind the Wheel*. Pointing out that the "road is the workplace of drivers," two of them complained of the paucity of gas stations (in fact, none in the Subcarpathian region), the inappropriate provisioning of rest stops (no mineral water, tea, or milk but plenty of vodka and beer along the Minsk Highway), and other irksome conditions.[36]

Truckers thus shared a common interest with another up-and-coming group—auto tourists—from which similar complaints emanated.[37] More generally (as will be detailed below), car owners would form a symbiotic relationship with truckers. But in the long run, as passenger cars proliferated, something of an antagonistic relationship developed between professional and amateur drivers. Class and associated cultural differences go at least some way toward providing an explanation. Officials and white-collar workers were disproportionally represented among car owners. Theirs was not the culture of rough masculinity. As the number—if not the rate—of road accidents mounted, truckers and other professional drivers were apt to blame these "private people" (*chastniki*). Using this very term, S. Isakovskii, a driver from Vologda, wrote to *Behind the Wheel* that "not everyone who wants to buy a car but only those who can demonstrate energy, quickness of reaction, decisiveness, and concentration should have a license. Private persons," he added, "always have a lot of extraneous thoughts." Iu. Katushev wrote from Saratov Oblast that his ten years of experience as a trucker taught him that "'chastniki' are extremely dangerous people," while V. Gromov of Krasnodar contrasted truckers who "work on the road according to a plan" with these "woodpeckers" (a derogatory term equivalent to "birdbrain") who "don't know which pedal to depress." "Private persons" responded in kind. S. Pimenov of Severomorsk asserted that professionals' greater experience behind the wheel did not give them the right to be "rude and loutish." Others referred to the professionals as acting like "little tsars of the road" and "lacking in elementary politeness."[38]

What is striking about these linguistic fusillades is their gendered nature. Both groups in reality were overwhelmingly male, but whereas car owners portrayed professional drivers as rather rough ("rude and loutish") men ("little tsars"), they were characterized in turn the way male drivers typically denounce female drivers (scatterbrained, lacking in decisiveness, easily distracted). In equating bad driving with femininity, professionals were not only reinforcing the near monopoly men had on trucking but policing its male character. As already noted, many women did drive trucks during the war, though even then it was not unheard of for a woman who had received driver training to be assigned to work as a dispatcher or bookkeeper or in some other role not behind the wheel. Some 15 percent of drivers as late as 1945 were women, but a year later that percentage had dropped to 2.[39] Indeed, as the trucks grew in size, the notion of trusting them to a woman became increasingly inconceivable. The prejudice was reinforced "scientifically" by the head of a physiological laboratory for professional drivers, who blithely asserted in 1979 that "the repair of such machines, [and] the occasional removal of obstacles in the road requires significant physical exertion which is contraindicated [*protivopokazano*] for women."[40]

Loners

Before long-distance trucking became routine, writers, filmmakers, and songsters were imagining it. The dominant image they projected was of freedom. One does not usually associate the late Stalin era with this condition, but if anyone experienced freedom—at least freedom of movement—it might have been long-haulers. This, in any case, is how Rybakov imagined it in his novel *Drivers:*

> A long trip! Only a driver knows the poetry of these words. In them is the noise of wind, intense sun, the evening coolness of endless fields, the smell of the forest, sylvan lakes and rivers, cities and villages, chance night lodgings, new people, new places. Broad and spacious! Neither stoplights nor policemen. Put the pedal to the metal, don't worry—be happy! [*Zhmi na vsiu zhelezku, mchis' tol'ko pesni poi!*][41]

Perhaps this relative freedom afforded by individualized labor lacking in control is what had attracted those alien and hostile elements to trucking in the first place. When Sasha Pankratov, the hero of Rybakov's Arbat triology—which is set mostly in the 1930s—returns from three years of Siberian exile, a prospective employer asks him if he would like to work as a mechanic. "No thanks," he replies. "I don't want to answer to others. I'd rather drive."[42]

Always on the run, the imagined truckers of midcentury Soviet Russia were, as in the case of their Hungarian counterparts described by Ferenc Hammer, a "somewhat marginal, suspicious, and envied agent of change, navigat[ing] the field of interplay between socialist social order and its limits." They thus embodied Victor Turner's "liminal personae, threshold people" who "are neither here nor there ... betwixt and between the positions assigned and arranged by law, custom, and convention."[43] Soviet truckers' liminality consisted of being from the Soviet countryside but no longer of it. At the same time, their lack of formal education and cultural refinement kept them at arm's length from urban sophisticates. Especially before regular bus service became a reality but even thereafter, truckers served collective farmers as an alternative source of transportation and also of news, knowledge, and goods from elsewhere. Their vagueness about their backgrounds and family situation imparted to them a sense of mystery and adventure. Women often found them irresistible.

Two songs from the 1958 film *An Ordinary Trip* (*Ocherednoi reis*) suggest the appeal of truck drivers to those stuck in the backwaters. In the first "The Road, the Road" ("Doroga, doroga"), the driver sings to a woman with sparkling eyes but a "naughty look" who wears a print dress "like a bright field of flowers." Even "blizzards that break down doors" will not keep him from finding the route straight to her "sweet heart" ("*k milomu serdtsu/Naiti potochnee marshrut*") The refrain—"The road, the road/It calls us to distant places. /Perhaps a little happiness is left / Perhaps at the turn of the road"—with its repetition of "perhaps," holds out just enough hope. The second song, "The Driver's Song" ("Shoferskaia pesnia"), performed in the film by an accordion-playing driver surrounded by a bevy of adoring women, contains the following stanza:

In appearance, we're not so attractive,	Na vid my ne tak privlekatel'ny,
Simple, rude folk.	Prostoi, grubovatyi narod.
But who looks carefully	No kto prigliaditsia vnimatel'no
Will a driver's soul understand.	Shoferskuiu dushu poimet.[44]

In stories by Vasilii Shukshin, the drivers, like all his heroes, are "loners by choice."[45] Pavel Kholmanskii, the twenty-six-year-old hero of "The Classy Driver," is "dangerous or handsome, it was hard to say which." When he first meets Nastia Platonova the village librarian and a "local beauty," he tells her he is from Moscow, only to deny it the next day. This pair also figures in his film *There Lives This Guy*.

The freedom that these drivers embodied had its costs, though. Not all of them, it seems, chose to be loners. "Don't believe that drivers are unreliable," the singer pleads with his fellow traveling darling in "The Driver's Song." More resigned to a life of going it alone is the driver who repeats the lines in "The Elegy of the Road" ("Dorozhnaia elegiia"): "The road, the road / What torment / To learn about separation, / Separation so soon."[46] Even when a driver lands a wife, his frequent absence can cause problems. In "Zima Junction" (1956), Evgenii Evtushenko's evocation of his native Siberian village, to which he returns after a nine-year absence, the next-door neighbor tells him that his uncle Andrei "is flirting with a woman, a driver's wife."[47]

In some of these ways, the imagined Soviet truckers of the 1950s and '60s resembled their American counterparts. American songs about truckers are laced with expressions of longing and regret, as in Dave Dudley's "One More Mile" ("I may miss you and I may wish that I have stayed / But I'll be movin' it one more mile"), or his "Two Six Packs Away" ("Now Sunday rolls around that's my cigarette day / And my baby's still a waitin' just two six packs away").[48] Many combine profligacy and deprivation. Of course, unlike U.S. truckers, Soviet drivers did not own the trucks they drove. Elegant interiors, new paint jobs, chroming, detailing, and other customized touches and treatments do not appear in evocations of their lives. Nor do trucker bars, road cafés, CB radio communication, and other features familiar to viewers of *White Line Fever* (1975) or the *Smokey and the Bandit* movies (1977, 1980, 1983). But the following observation by the sociologist Lawrence Oullet about the United States rings true for Soviet truckers as well:

> The trucker's subculture itself excites a certain romanticized public interest because it is somewhat mysterious and deviant. The members of this subculture . . . do much

of their work at night, which can be understood as a frontier where one finds greater solitude and tranquility, a camaraderie with fellow night workers, the loosening of social rules and more danger and outlawry.[49]

Wheeler-Dealers

Addressing the drivers' union congress in 1947, chief state auto inspector Kuznetsov, whom we have met already, informed the delegates that the "number of accidents is intensified by the fact that some drivers consider it possible to improve their financial situation by using state vehicles for personal purposes." His audience might have assumed that Kuznetsov was claiming that more time on the road for state vehicles meant more accidents, but his explanation proved more complicated: "Giving lifts to people provides drivers with additional income which means more drinking among drivers."[50] In the 1930s, class—especially of the "alien" variety—explained all mishaps, including traffic accidents. But by the late 1940s it was sufficient to cite enhanced opportunities for on-the-side earnings and drivers' notorious fondness for drink.

It turns out that when drivers gave lifts to people, some were acting not out of altruism or the desire for company but to earn a little additional cash. Kirill Voronov, the hero of *An Ordinary Trip*, was one such driver. As if enacting the scenario described by Kuznetsov in 1947, albeit without the alcohol, he picks up a passenger for money, crashes the new truck he is driving, and destroys its engine. Stripped of his license and reassigned to the job of a fitter, he redeems himself when an emergency requires his outstanding driving skills. This actually was the second film in which a truck driver picks up a passenger with unfortunate results. In *The Rumiantsev Affair* (*Delo Rumiantseva*, 1955), the eponymous hero also crashes his truck with a passenger (Klava) in the cabin. But even more troubles await him when he unknowingly presents a false invoice for the goods he is carrying.[51]

To learn about the experiences of a real-live truck driver and his procurement and distribution of goods, we turn to Gershon (Grisha) Goldshteyn. Nineteen forty-seven, the year of the first postwar truckers' union congress, also happened to be when Grisha, who was born in 1926, left the army and returned to his native Kiev. There he signed on as a truck driver at a prosthetics factory, whose products were much in demand thanks to the war. Thus began his forty-two-year peripatetic career that lasted until retirement in 1990 and subsequent emigration to the United States. Grisha's account of his experiences driving throughout Ukraine reveals a complex web of relations among drivers, dispatchers, warehouse foremen, loaders, store managers, and police that belies the image of truckers' freedom or independence. He depended on "good relations" with management so that assignment to such "dirty" (*chernaia*) work as hauling coal or soot alternated with "clean" (*belaia*) jobs connected with food. Good relations crucially depended on trust. Store managers who trusted him with delivering what they ordered would request his services; if trust was lacking among the police and security guards, they were apt to "weigh everything all over" and otherwise harass him.

Grisha claimed that he stayed strictly within the limits of "natural loss" (the percentage of goods written off by the state to account for breakage and spoilage) and did not resell goods to which he had access, but he did spend a week in prison in the mid-1950s in connection with an investigation into the appearance of large quantities of yeast on the black market. He nevertheless managed to make a decent living, and after the introduction of containers in the early 1960s took home a "salary ... three times as high as that of any engineer." This was only fair given the "very hard physical labor" and the amount of unpaid overtime. Grisha's contention that he did not engage in lawbreaking himself ("we only watched those people who did something—stealing, etc.") may be true even though the environment in which he worked was filled with temptations. As the only Jew (after "the boss forced out ten" others) in a column of three hundred truck drivers and a shock worker who had to go to human resources to collect his medal and thank-you letter rather than receiving them with others at the awards ceremony, perhaps he felt he had to be especially careful.[52]

With the proliferation of cars in the 1970s and '80s, truck drivers assumed a new function that also involved skirting—or in this case, violating—the law. In the absence of sufficient supplies of fuel for ordinary motorists, truckers became the most important providers of "on the side" gasoline. The ease with which they could inflate their distance and haulage reports—not incidentally producing higher wages and eligibility for bonuses—left them with coupons to purchase gas or unused gas itself. Drivers sold the coupons either to gas station attendants (who then would collect cash from car owners) or to car owners. They also sold their unused gas directly to needy motorists. According to a Western economist writing in 1987, at least 75 percent and as much as 87 percent of the gas used by private car owners in 1982 was obtained through these means. The same source also estimated that "the average state driver illegally sold 250–600 liters of gasoline in 1977 and 750–1,000 liters in 1984." Average incomes from illicit sales of gasoline in the latter year may have amounted to seventy-five to one hundred rubles.[53]

FERENC Hammer notes in his reconstruction of the "figure of the trucker" in socialist Hungary that trucking was one of only two nonelite professions that afforded men the privilege of travel to the capitalist West (the other being sleeping car conductors).[54] As far as Soviet truckers are concerned, Grisha Goldshteyn contends that "they did not let them [regular guys] go abroad." Only "special drivers,

Party members" would go, one to Czechoslovakia, another to Hungary, yet another to Germany. "They picked special Communists for that."[55]

Nevertheless, even ordinary Soviet truckers enjoyed unusual access to goods that placed them favorably within what Elena Osokina called the "hierarchy of consumption."[56] And unlike tradespeople, who generally were held in contempt because "they produced nothing but had everything," truckers, as workers, earned the public's respect.[57]

The respect for, even admiration of, truckers derived as well from qualities imputed to them from early on. These included not only the skills associated with taming and periodically reviving the mechanical beasts but also the courage to confront treacherous roads (or their absence), bad weather, and in the extraordinary circumstances of war, enemy bombardment. More fancifully—as reflected in the songs, movies, and stories of the 1950s and '60s—truckers' mobility seemed to capture the imagination of more rooted folk who perhaps understandably mistook the individualized nature of much of their labor for the lack of control. Truckers thus embodied automobility in two senses: first as being somewhere between coachmen and aviators, just as the automobile itself was compared to coaches and airplanes in terms of range and speed; and second, as being more self-directed than most other workers—in other words, little tsars of the road.

In reality, the schedules, weight checks, investigations, and penalties imposed on Soviet truck drivers circumscribed their freedom much as these factors restricted truckers' freedom in the West. The physical demands and emotional stress of frequent separation from home sometimes for months could take its toll. If at first, to cite Grisha again, "there was nature, romanticism," then after years behind the wheel it became "no longer romantic, but regular labor" that one "wouldn't wish . . . on an enemy." Notwithstanding the romanticized version of the lives of long-haul truckers presented in the NTV serial by that name and the fact that real truckers now publicly acknowledge carrying icons in their cabins, Soviet truckers' automobility and the hard work associated with it do not appear to have changed very much.[58]

11

WOMEN AND CARS IN SOVIET AND RUSSIAN SOCIETY

Corinna Kuhr-Korolev

What is the goal in studying marginalia such as Russian women and their relationship to cars? What insight can it offer us, given the fact that cars remained a minority phenomenon in the Soviet Union and that women so rarely sat behind the wheel that they were practically an endangered species? What is the result of thinking about cars in connection with women and society—that is, when questions of automobility, gender relations, and women's emancipation, daily life, and consumption are all brought together?

For different reasons it is unusual to look at social developments in the last two decades of the Soviet Union and in Russia since 1990 through the lens of either cars or women. There has been only one attempt to approach the history of the Soviet Union through the back door by researching cars.[1] Scholars examining the social roles of Soviet and Russian women have tended to confine themselves to typically feminine fields. Perhaps combining these two can produce unexpected insights into the assumptions we have been making about each, and more specifically about those dimensions of consumption and everyday life from which women traditionally have been excluded.

The argument of this chapter is that cars had meaning not just for Soviet men but for women too and that they continued to do so into the post-Soviet era. The meanings sometimes coincided but often did not. This applies to both the concrete and easily described, such as the role of the car in daily life, and the more difficult to grasp: the car as an article of consumption, as an expression of social prestige and individual feminine independence. We are also concerned about the extent to which these meanings have changed over time and especially in recent years, when the number of women drivers has risen dramatically.

11.1 Interviewee Nina P. behind the wheel of her father's car at the age of 5, 1960s.

In comparison with other formerly socialist countries, it can be assumed that Russia is different as far as women behind the wheel are concerned, though whether we are talking about degrees in kind or qualitatively different cultural standards is a question that will require further research. Surely the relative scarcity of cars in the USSR is one variable, but we would also have to assess whether Soviet gender roles were more strictly defined and enforced than elsewhere in the Eastern Bloc, something that has yet to be demonstrated with any degree of persuasiveness.

The topic of automobiles in Russia has hardly been researched from the perspective of gender. The only exception is an article by Rostislav Konenko, who describes the image of women behind the wheel in Soviet propaganda.[2] Lewis Siegelbaum discusses male bonding in Soviet car culture while also acknowledging the role of women.[3] In women's studies there are numerous works on the image, roles, and daily life of Soviet women.[4] For the period since 1990, research has emphasized women's political participation and their part in establishing democracy and civil society.[5] Historians have barely begun to study the daily lives of women since 1990.[6] There are a number of informative sociological studies, however, of which those on the new middle class, its changing values, and changed consumption habits are most important.[7]

My own study of women and cars began with the current situation. There are a variety of easily accessible sources, many of which are on the Internet: pages for women who drive, taxi companies of women for women,[8] women's car clubs,[9] driving schools that specialize in teaching women,[10] and discussion forums in which men can vent their annoyance with women drivers. The printed journal *Zhenshchina za rulem (Women behind the Wheel)* was available throughout the first years of this century, and even the more traditional *Za rulem (Behind the Wheel)* contains a column entitled "Women's Club."[11]

Sources for the Soviet period are far more difficult to come by. In this case one must comb through women's magazines such as *Rabotnitsa (Woman Worker)* or look into *Za rulem* for clues to women behind the wheel. It is therefore necessary to rely on oral sources also. This chapter draws on in-depth interviews with six women and countless conversations with women and men about driving in Russia and in the Soviet Union.[12]

Since this is not just about women at the wheel but also about the relationship of women to cars, we begin with these questions: Under what conditions did Soviet women have access to or use cars, and what meaning did the car have for them? Did they, like men, cherish the Soviet dream of consumption, owning a car of one's own? Did possession of a car evoke pride, given the prestige it indicated, or was it outweighed by the trouble it caused? Did they make the usual connection between driving and freedom or independence? Is there a relationship between women's driving and women's emancipation? The last question brings us to the present. Does the high number of women drivers in contemporary Russia point to a larger shift in their role? Can we see this as a visible step in the direction of equal rights for women, or would that be a superficial conclusion? How do women conduct themselves on the road, and what image do they have of themselves? What do they use cars for, and how do they behave as consumers? Finally, it is interesting to consider how women talk about cars and driving. How do they tell their autobiographies, and how can such oral history be used to tell the story of Soviet life? What attitudes about state and society, about changes in values and lifestyles, are expressed in conversations about cars?

Passenger and Co-owner

In order to understand car culture from a feminine perspective, it is helpful to separate it into the different relationships that women have to cars, as passengers, co-owners, and drivers. These distinctions are more important for women than for men because when men in the Soviet Union owned cars, they drove them. Men took others along; women were taken along. This alone makes a gender differentiation clear: men took an active role and women a passive one. A glance at driving couples (even today) shows that—whether in Russia, Poland, or Germany—the man probably sits behind the wheel 90 percent of the time. It would be wrong to conclude that men have the final say, but the situation corresponded and corresponds to the usual notions of gender roles in both East and West.

A sampling of issues of the magazine *Za rulem* confirms this rule for the Soviet Union in the seventies and eighties. Photos of women at the steering wheel are very rare. The March edition of the magazine is a regular exception; there, every year on the occasion of International Women's Day (March 8), female readers are congratulated and female drivers presented. These portraits correspond to the military-athletic orientation of the magazine.[13] The women's biographies shown there reflect the range of typical Soviet woman-worker careers: they start in the 1930s with training as a truck driver, followed by work in a *kolkhoz* or a factory. The life stories receive a heroic slant during the war years, when the women served in the Red Army, sometimes as the personal chauffeurs of high officers or else as truck drivers. After the war, they would return to civilian life as drivers of small trucks—for example, to deliver bread.[14] In addition to this professional driving activity, there are some references to women engaging in motor sports.[15] Everyday driving by women is not mentioned, however, except occasionally in cartoons or readers' jokes. The lack of such topics was due to the greatly delayed mass motorization of the USSR, compared with other countries of Western and even Eastern Europe.[16]

During the Soviet period, when car ownership was not common and made the higher social position of the owner evident, being a passenger meant more than getting from point A to point B. The prestige of driving extended to those who could ride along. It amounted to a distinction; it offered the possibility of doing things that were denied to others and offered some relief from routine. By virtue of being a mere passenger, one belonged to the class of the better-off. This attitude began with children, who knew that they were in a special position thanks to the car in the family. Moreover, to be taken for a ride or picked up was an aspect of male-female relationships. For women and their friends, having a car owner as an admirer meant the possibility of getting a "good catch" or, in illicit relationships, an acceptable affair, given the benefit that the woman could draw from her connection. Even when it was purely a matter of politeness or inconsequential advances, to get picked up by car was still prestigious, comparable to an invitation to dinner or a bouquet of roses. For example, one of my subjects related that her department supervisor regularly picked her up in the morning, brought her to work, and took her home again in the evening. She was unmarried and childless. Even in retrospect, it meant to her that she had good prospects with the opposite sex and had a special status in the collective and that being single was a result of her own choice.[17]

Alongside the passive "being given a ride" is the active "to have somebody drive you," which today still carries more prestige than driving oneself. The wives of the Soviet nomenklatura were driven to their dachas, could use the official cars of their husbands, and saw it as a part of their lifestyle.[18] Similarly, in Russia today it is common to hire a car and driver. This is paid for either privately or by the passenger's company and is not only for the nouveau riche but also for members of the middle classes.

Co-ownership of a car applied and applies mainly to wives. The prestige that was associated with acquiring a car during the Soviet period profited wives just as much as their husbands/drivers. The money to buy a car came out of the family's budget, to which the wives (who usually worked) had contributed a large part. All the factors involved in the purchase—the decision to buy, the difficulties of acquiring a car, the waiting list, borrowing money from friends and relatives, postponing other purchases—applied equally to wives and husbands.[19] Whether the wives complained later that their husbands spent a lot of time with the car or whether they praised it and found ownership advantageous are questions of secondary importance. It is more important that the car played a large role in and changed the daily life of the family.

One subject described the period during which she and her late husband owned a car as the happiest time of her life.[20] Born in the region of Voronezh in 1940 and raised fatherless under difficult circumstances, she saw her husband's work ("He even had business trips abroad!"), the apartment they were allotted in Moscow, and the ownership of a car as proof of her social ascent and successful life. Considering her husband's early death and social difficulties that have marked her life since the 1990s, her association of the car with her previous happiness is not surprising.

As a childless young couple they had already owned a motorcycle with a sidecar and used it to travel. Then in the 1970s the family acquired a Moskvich and later various models of the Zhiguli. The car was the centerpiece of their leisure time, as their many photographs show. Weekend getaways with friends, picnics in the forest, relatives' visits, camping at the Black Sea: all were made possible by the car. But the photos also make clear that the car was more than a means of transport. It was the backdrop to family photographs. This seems to be not only because the husband and owner was a passionate amateur photographer and wanted to capture his pride on celluloid. There is also the impression that the car was a piece of home on four wheels and had the power to keep the family together. In its shadow the family could set up camp either for a short picnic—*nakryvat' luzhaiku* (to cover the grass), as it was called—or on a longer-term basis as a summer camp. Then the car would be covered for protection and served as extra storage space.[21]

In photographs my subject complies with her given role as wife and mother. She can be seen in a bikini or relaxing on a folding chair but is more often the active housewife who cares for children and is busy with the makeshift household. In commenting on the pictures, she stays in this role. She points out her activity and emphasizes that she was always practical, ready to pull food out of a hat in the middle of nowhere. To this day she fills the role of a person who feeds others. In this she is a typical representative of the older generation of women who often find their life's significance and success in providing for others. Asked whether she wouldn't have wanted to drive the car herself, she answers that she would very much have liked to, but her husband would never have allowed it. She was too much of a "hyper, reckless woman" (*zavodnaia baba*), and he would have seen that as too big a risk. Confirming his opinion, she tells the story of how at the beginning of their marriage she held his eyes shut while he was driving a motorcycle. He promptly dropped her at the gutter and let her cry and stew there for a while before picking her up again. This episode, others like it that come out when looking at the photos, and the photos themselves provide an intimate look into the family's life. The roles that they assigned themselves become as clear as the vital importance of the car for this family.

Women Drivers

Women at the wheel were a rarity in the Soviet period. To this day the idea still has a hold on men (but also on many women) that women are psychologically and physically incapable of driving a car. "A woman at the wheel is like a monkey with a hand grenade" is one famous saying about the subject. This is especially astonishing when considered against the background of the formal equality of the sexes in the Soviet Union. Women worked as builders, bus and streetcar drivers; propaganda celebrated female tractor operators, pilots, and astronauts; but they supposedly couldn't drive a car. It was said that driving was unfeminine and that a driver needed too much physical strength and technical know-how. The second point is moot in view of modern cars. Still, male drivers explain that women cannot concentrate, cannot survey traffic well, and lose their cool in difficult situations. They are, however, credited with driving more carefully and considerately.[22]

It can be assumed that the debate on women drivers has only become more heated since women actually began to drive in sizable numbers. But why did women in the USSR so seldom drive? It was probably due partly to people's notions of women's roles but even more to the division of labor within the family and material circumstances. Even owning a car was unusual and took a lot of work.

11.2–11.5 Interviewee Nadezhda Ia. at different periods of her life.

Everything else that came along with it (contact with the police, repairs, getting spare parts and gas) belonged to the masculine sphere, and thus the driving did as well.[23]

Among the women I interviewed who had driven during the Soviet era, several took over driving duties in the family despite conventional attitudes about proper roles and the division of labor in the family; rarely, however, were they responsible for servicing the car. In two cases, the man of the house—in one household the father, in the other the husband—had obtained his driver's license only at an advanced age and felt uncertain behind the wheel. In other cases, the acquisition

of a dacha and the necessary drives to it were the decisive factors for the women driving. In typical woman-driver careers, moreover, a father often played the determinant role: for want of a son, he got his daughter to accompany him as he took a wrench to the family car, and he also taught her to drive.[24]

One of my interview subjects, a teacher who was born at the end of the 1950s and got a driver's license at age twenty-three at the beginning of the 1980s, provides a good example of a woman driver.[25] The impetus for learning to drive came from her older brother, who had the connections to get her into driving school. Except for a famous actress from the Lenkom Theater, she was the only woman.

Her brother had suggested that she get a driver's license to distract her from the death of their father. It was entirely impossible at the time for them to own a car. She was a graduate of Moscow State University and says she was a Russian teacher at a "completely normal Russian school," but it must have been an especially good one. It was attended not only by the children of the district but also by those whose parents used connections to send them. Her father-in-law owned a dacha in Istra,[26] and she mentions that he was already well-off during the Soviet period. She also tells of a trip to the Baltic in the official car of her best friend's father, who for a while held the position of an assistant minister. Her husband served as an officer in military intelligence. So even though she did not have special status and did not earn much as a teacher, her network of connections and her family made a privileged lifestyle possible.

Only thanks to this situation could she get a driver's license and purchase a used Zhiguli. It was her brother, again, who heard of the possibility of buying a car from a secondhand shop (*komissiony*) in the countryside. She describes, using the passive voice, that it was too much money and they didn't really have it, but the opportunity could not be missed. She describes her own attitude equally passively, when she speaks of repairs and getting spare parts. These tasks were done by her brother and later her husband, who briefly enjoyed driving and fixing the car. She herself added water to the radiator, changed the sparkplugs, and otherwise hammered around a bit on the off chance that she could bring the car back to life after a breakdown.

She uses the active voice only to tell the history of her own driving. She considers herself a good, experienced driver and describes various situations to support that. That includes dealing with men, whether they are other drivers or the police. Her formula has always been friendliness and femininity. In her experience, a smile and a flirtatious comment always get you farther than abuse or rudeness.[27]

In the course of the conversation it becomes possible to see how she dealt with the doubly unusual situation of owning and driving a car. One can see an effort to normalize her unusual position. She plays down the importance of her ownership of the car: it was old; they did not look for it for long; it was found and purchased by chance. For her it was never a status symbol but an object of utility. Although she as a woman driver did not conform to the usual woman's role, she tried to live up to the feminine image by not provoking anybody. She describes her driving as considerate. It seemed important to her to emphasize that the privilege of driving was something she used not "egoistically" for herself but for the good of the family, her acquaintances, and the work collective. Accordingly, she never took longer trips or excursions with it but reserved it chiefly for getting to work, running errands for the family, and going to the dacha. She tells of end-of-year celebrations at school and how she and her friends, laden down with flowers, drove to a café to celebrate; of trips to the dacha with her husband, grandmother, two children, and a large dog; of a blind garage owner, her neighbor, whom she sometimes drove to the doctor and whose garage she purchased from him for a token payment.

It does not occur to her to see her driving as an expression of women's emancipation. She holds back even though she is an enthusiastic driver, played an active and prominent role in the family and in the collective, and was out of line with traditional feminine passivity. In this way she conformed to the unspoken rules that governed Soviet gender relations. Women had a great deal on their shoulders, both professionally and in the family, but this position of being preeminent or stronger than their husbands was not exploited or verbalized (except among women) and was never demonstrated. The methods of women's emancipation focused on cooperation more than confrontation, more on the silent changing of real circumstances than on vocal demands for ideal conditions.

Kul'turnost' on the Road—Gender and Norms of Behavior of Car Drivers and Car Owners

In the descriptions of their own traffic behavior, an attitude becomes apparent that is virtually universal among older female drivers interviewed and that points to general Soviet socialization and an internalization of the socialist system of values and standards. With astonishing mutual conformity, right up to the choice of words, interviewees describe their own behavior in traffic as *kul'turno* (cultured) and thus dissociate themselves both from masculine behavior patterns and from the driving style of the social strata below them. Some typical statements are "I can't imagine myself behind the wheel cursing somebody's mother *[rugat'sia matom]*"[28] "I just couldn't bring myself to bribe a traffic cop";[29] "It would be unthinkable for me to fail to stop and let a woman with a baby carriage cross the road."[30]

These statements are affected by the experience of the past decade or so during which the traffic situation has gotten much more stressful because of the enormous increase in the number of cars, which has had a direct effect on the behavior of drivers. In the larger Russian cities, drivers are caught in virtually permanent gridlock, and their driving habits are characterized by irritation, aggressiveness, and lack of consideration. The combination of a large number of inexperienced drivers, new, fast cars, and bad roads has led to frighteningly high accident rates.[31] That is true in comparison with the 1990s, and all the more in comparison with the 1970s and '80s. On the other hand, the self-descriptions of the female drivers also indicate that the *kul'turnost'* campaigns held at regular intervals starting in the 1920s could boast positive results even in the road-traffic sector.[32]

One educational campaign that was exemplary in this respect was carried out by the editorial staff of the magazine *Za rulem* throughout the year 1984; it involved behavior in traffic, the general attitude toward the car as property, and the topic of women behind the wheel. According to the editorial staff, the readers took great interest in the discussion about appropriate road behavior for socialist citizens. The starting point—as was frequently the case for such campaigns—was a letter to the editor from a reader published in the first issue of the year, titled "We and the Car." With great emotion, the author described her marriage problems, which the purchase of a family car had caused. After one failed marriage each, she and her husband had found happiness for a second time at an advanced age, had married, and lived in perfect harmony up to the time when they had bought their car. Since her childhood days, she had always dreamed of owning a car and had purchased it from her savings. She drove with the greatest enthusiasm and even took care of repairing the car herself. However, her husband, who was otherwise the very embodiment of kindness and helpfulness, spoiled her pleasure in every possible way. Whenever they traveled in the car together, they always argued over who should drive. If she drove, he would make her life hell with rude comments denigrating her well-practiced driving. If he drove, he would become a completely different person, complaining about everything and everybody and acting inconsiderate and aggressive. They would have arguments over the car almost every evening. After a year and a half of this torment, she no longer knew any way out and asked her readers for an answer to the question, "Should I sell the car, or get a divorce?"

In issue nine of that year, an editorial appeared that referred to the topic and placed it in the context of emerging mass motorization. Some ten million Soviet families already owned a car, which meant that about thirty to forty million people had access to a car. Since other consumer desires had now been met, the automobile, which not only served as a means of transportation but was also a consumer item, was the issue that remained. The editorial staff expressed the hope that the car owners would know how to handle this commodity correctly. Without explicitly saying so, the staff appealed for two different things: first, the car should not be raised to the rank of a cult object, and second, people should behave responsibly and politely in traffic.

The letters to the editor printed in the tenth issue indicated that this message had reached its addressees. A selection of letters, which was certainly carefully selected by the editorial staff, displayed a broad range of opinions. They did contain some extreme viewpoints, but these were neutralized by "correct" statements that promoted the desired behavior. The extreme remarks included a letter from a man who expressed his sympathy for the husband in the above case and reported that he had divorced his wife after six years of car ownership. Another wrote tersely, "Women should shut up in cars!" However, the other comments, some written by women, contained well-considered advice: one should train oneself in kul'turnost' and shouldn't make a cult of the car; human relations were more important than cars. The editorial staff and its readers, both male and female, agreed that all discussions about the automobile always concerned society as a whole and that the car was only a catalyst for such discussions.[33]

The thematic and argumentative agreement between the 1984 discussion by the readers on the one hand and the views expressed in interviews with women twenty-five years later on the other is conspicuous. It could be argued that annoyance over inconsiderate drivers is as old as traffic itself. On closer consideration, however, one can discern some specific leitmotifs connected with experiences peculiar to women and social developments in the Soviet Union and post-Soviet Russia. According to my observations, Russian women complain about different negative aspects of road traffic more than men do. As a rule, the latter criticize the unprofessionalism of other road users. This may be due to the fact that although private cars were none too plentiful in the Soviet Union, driving was a common profession; moreover, many men today earn their living as independent taxi drivers. Competition on the road and fast and aggressive driving are legitimate for them—but only if you know what you're doing. Typically, Russian male drivers like to talk about their own vehicles, and they complain about the cars produced in Russia, the quality of which lags far behind that of foreign models. These facts symbolize the weakness of their once-powerful country and hurt their patriotic pride.[34]

Russian women tend to discuss their own choices in favor of a domestic or a foreign car but rarely raise the overall issue of the Russian auto industry. Their main complaint is aimed at aggressive, pushy, and inconsiderate behavior on the part of other drivers, especially men. The women I questioned saw a direct connection between the chaos on the road and the decline in values in today's Russian society. What they call for is consideration, helpfulness, and no overestimation of material value—which corresponds exactly to the kul'turnost' demands of the 1970s and '80s. This observation is informative in the following respect: it shows that an understanding of ku'lturnost' was firmly rooted among the privileged Soviet elite, to which the car-owning and driving women belonged and that it had become part of upper-class culture. In this context, the campaign by the magazine *Za rulem* in 1984 not only appears to be an attempt by the state and Party to educate their own society but also reflects the urgent desire on the part of the upper strata to convey their own moral concepts to the lower classes, which were in the process of becoming motorized. This intellectual separation between "us" (cultured and educated people) and "them" (the uncivilized and intellectually limited masses) resounds like an echo from Soviet times in all complaints about today's traffic behavior.

This demarcation includes the explicit denigration of the car as a piece of property, although in this respect the statements reveal inconsistencies. Thus, two women from the nomenklatura said that it had not been any problem at all to get a car. They quickly got places on the waiting lists at the workplaces of their relatives—in one case the husband, a general, and in the other the father, an army prosecuting attorney. Shortly thereafter, they had their cars. For them, therefore, the cars were far from representing the longed-for, virtually unobtainable consumer dreams that they represented for the mass of Soviet citizens; they were simply ordinary consumer items. In the upper strata to which these women belonged, conspicuous consumption was not the norm. On the one hand it was not seen as "proper" and was considered a sign of being uneducated; on the other, this attitude was a shield against social envy. This behavior seems to have been strongly internalized. Unlike the passenger introduced above who could show a huge number of photos of herself, her family, and their car, these drivers have hardly any photos of their cars or of themselves behind the wheel. To pose in front of the car and to have themselves photographed would have seemed strange to them. Although they consciously did not fetishize their cars in words or deeds, the conversations nevertheless revealed that they were very conscious of the social prestige that the cars carried. One, for instance, raved about her first Volga; the other told about how her son's friends considered her a *krutaia mama*, a "cool mom," because she drove a car. And this car, she explained, was no ordinary car: it was one of the first Zhigulis produced in Togliatti, and those were of considerably better quality than the later models.[35]

New Russia—New Women?

Thus far I have reconstructed the attitudes of women toward the car in Soviet times, although many references to today's situation have appeared in the process. In the following discussion I explicitly address the changes of the past two decades and the question of whether the growing number of woman drivers is proof of more emancipation and a changed set of ideal roles or whether there is continuity. It must be said at the outset that the collapse of the Soviet Union is important to the topic of cars and automobility, but the shift from a Soviet car culture to modern mass car ownership happened much later, at the end of the 1990s and the beginning of the 2000s.[36] Thus there were strong continuities after 1991. The Soviet car culture continued and continues to survive in many regions of Russia. This applies to the low percentage of women behind the wheel and popular opinion of them as drivers. When I speak of mass car ownership and the rapidly rising number of women drivers, this applies mainly to Moscow. Development in other large cities is several years behind.[37]

When we speak of women driving cars, we are generally speaking of women in the Russian middle and upper class. Despite the enormous increase in the number of cars, circa 10 percent per year, we cannot forget that in the Russian provinces especially, car ownership is still a dream for most of the population. Yet in the middle class, cars now belong to the group of possessions that one obviously must have. Most expenses are generated by other things that cost even more: purchase and upkeep of real estate, children's educations, health care costs, and vacations. The middle class, which is now the subject of a vast number of studies, includes people of varied backgrounds and various levels of education. In comparison with the middle classes in other European countries, the Russian middle classes are poor. A family's monthly income can be as low as five hundred dollars or as high as several thousand.[38] Now as ever, a person's official monthly income is not the only important one; supplementary incomes and discounts of all kinds are equally important.

Given the diversity of the Russian middle class, it would be wrong to speak of "the new Russian woman driver." It is rather more appropriate to describe a few types. There is the small group of women around age fifty who were driving during the Soviet period. Today, depending on their financial circumstances, they continue to drive—either small Ladas or, more frequently, foreign small or midsized cars. Their conduct in traffic is superior. The largest group contains women between the ages of twenty-five and fifty. According to the statistics, they buy compact cars priced in the range of eight to twelve thousand euros. Their favorites are the Ford Focus, Hyundai Matrix, and Chevrolet Aveo.[39] On average they have three to five years of driving experience.[40] The smallest but most attention-getting group is made up of young and not-so-young women at the wheels of expensive foreign cars.

There is not enough space here to discuss today's women drivers, their self-image, purchasing habits, or driving habits. In general one can assume that these women have made cars and driving a normal part of their everyday lives. They use them to make their daily lives and errands easier: driving to work, chauffeuring their children, shopping, driving to the dacha. Their purchasing decisions are based on practical and financial considerations more than on lifestyle, taste, or particular wishes regarding furnishings or technical features.

But there are also women for whom the car is more than a utilitarian object. They are especially typical of the new Russia and represent certain tendencies concerning a different feminine self-image. These are often career women or financially independent women whose work is connected to driving in various ways. Two of these women will be introduced here as examples. One earns her living as a taxi driver for the company Women-Taxi, while the other works as an independent real estate agent.⁴¹ Both have received higher education and worked previously in other jobs. The taxi driver worked as an accountant for six years before it got too monotonous for her. She began driving a taxi mostly out of coincidence, and now she values the independence associated with it, the possibility of communicating with many different people, and the driving itself. She tells of a phase when she drove only the night shift and got accustomed to an entirely different daily (or nightly) rhythm. As the speeding tickets piled up and she realized that night driving was like an addiction, she consciously rejected this lifestyle. The real estate agent also describes the romanticism of night driving. "There was a time in my life when I sat in front of the television until eleven at night and then drove off in the car. Till about three in the morning. I did that for one or two years. It was an unusual time, I was in love and it's somehow romantic to be driving at night."

Both women are unmarried; the real estate agent lives with her twenty-year-old daughter. They are on their own and are proud of it. Both have chosen careers that demand constant activity. They cannot afford long breaks, vacations, or illness. They have no state social security or guaranteed monthly income, and they pay no taxes. In exchange, they feel independent, and both emphasize that they cannot imagine returning to a normal work routine. Driving is, for them, a part of their chosen lifestyle. They spend a large portion of every day in the car and feel at home in it, in their element. Even in the worst traffic jam they would not leave the car and walk. Their ability to navigate the chaotic traffic of Moscow without losing their cool confirms their self-confidence and serves as proof that that they can manage their unpredictable lives in Moscow. Instead of "I think, therefore I am," it's "I drive, therefore I survive."⁴² The real estate agent puts it in a nutshell: "I think I can always judge immediately whether a person drives well or poorly. It has nothing to do with being a man or a woman. Character is most important. People who are active and nimble in life can also handle a car well."

In many cases, women in the Soviet Union and Russia secured and secure their own existence and that of their families. Even with a man in the house they often shoulder(ed) the real burden. This strange contrast between the survival of traditional ideal roles and the factual equality of the sexes in many areas has been mentioned in all research on gender in the Soviet Union.⁴³ Soviet women despised men for their weaknesses but were at the same time prepared to put them on a pedestal, take care of them, and forgive their missteps. Women put up with men in their households because they found it important for their social positions. According to traditional values, a happy family was a woman's real career.

Independent women of the new generation, like the taxi driver and the real estate agent, have a somewhat different attitude toward life. They prefer their independence as long as they haven't found the right partner. The conversation about how they deal with male drivers makes clear their basic attitudes toward men in Russia today. They express regret that there are so few "real" men left. The virtues that they miss are chivalry, helpfulness, gallantry (*galantnost'*) and generosity. In agreement with the teacher, who belongs to a different generation, the real estate agent believes that men were more polite in Soviet times, complimented women on their driving while waiting for the light to change, and in case of doubt, gave them the right of way. Breakdowns were no problem because a few drivers would immediately stop and help.[44] The Russian teacher tells how gas could be had out of the tank of a truck for a smile. Every truck driver would have been embarrassed to take money for it. Today, she says, men behave neutrally or indifferently toward women in traffic. But all women can tell of cases when men swore at them as insultingly as possible.

What these women miss is not the equality of the sexes or the elimination of gender differences. They clearly prefer a social order in which they recognize the strengths of men, can demand support from their own position of feminine weakness, and receive recognition of their femininity and beauty. This means that women in Russia are not breaking with traditional gender roles but quite the opposite: they are aiding their rebirth. The difference between this attitude and the one they held during the Soviet period is that they do so self-confidently and are not prepared to pay any price for it—for example, by putting up with a drunken or cheating husband.

There are of course exceptions to this general trend. For example, one of the interviewees who, as the wife of a general, has driven since 1980 and has always worked herself, said that she did not understand the issue "woman at the wheel" at all. As far as she was concerned, there were only drivers. Gender, age, skin color, and sexual preference were immaterial to her. From this point of view, she did not claim any special position for herself but relied only on her own abilities, possibilities, and priorities.[45]

Aggressive Antiemancipation

The way that women demand to get their feminine roles back can sometimes look aggressive and presents the inverse of emancipation. The type of woman who represents it, or is at least accused of it, is the Jeep driver. The young, rich, attractive woman at the wheel of an oversized Jeep, talking on her mobile while taking the right of way and then indifferently sitting at a red light and reapplying her lipstick, is for most people the ultimate negative image of the new Russian woman at the wheel. Social envy is a factor because how could a young woman get the means that are required to purchase that kind of car? Even if it was earned, that is barely possible, and if not earned, then it wasn't legal. Thus people arrive at the conclusion that she is either the offspring of the hated "nouveau riche" or has a rich "patron," which approaches prostitution. Her inadequate capability as a driver is then explained by the fact that she bought or was given her driver's license along with the car. This is the image usually conveyed by men when asked for their opinions on women drivers. Women are more ambivalent about the Jeep driver, with opinions ranging from admiration to rejection.[46]

The image of a self-confident woman with high sex appeal sitting behind the wheel of a big, fast car is one that has been promoted. For example, the magazine *Zhenshchina za rulem* presents an ideal image of the contemporary driver, her attitude toward life, and her lifestyle in a series of portraits and interviews. The protagonists are actresses, singers, and television stars—that is, representatives of Russian glamour and Moscow high society. When asked about their experiences as drivers, these princesses of the road tell stories about prevented assaults, difficult maneuvers in and out of parking spots, flat tires, and how they solved the problem. They represent their own driving as considerate, obedient of traffic laws, and defensive. They value their cars as they do their favorite handbags or dresses and usually choose them according to similar criteria. Color, design, comfort, and safety are most important. In some cases the car is the gift of a husband. In addition, these women offer advice to readers. The message is usually believe in your strength and beauty and you will be successful at work and happy in your family. All consider femininity the ideal. As one television presenter puts it, "I wish you—all women who drive and all those who don't—the chance to arrange your life such that you can remain a woman in all situations." "Remaining a woman" carries certain expectations. It means having the right to be carried along, to receive help and deference, compliments and gifts. All of this is not requested; it is consciously demanded. A man who cannot or will not comply loses his right to recognition, care, and sex. These women are proponents of what can be called "antiemancipation" because despite conventional gender roles and feminine affectations, it would not be appropriate to describe them as objectified or victimized.

"Auto"-Biographies and "Auto"-Discourse

Numerous conversations with men as well as with women confirmed the statement made by the editorial staff of the magazine *Za rulem* in 1984: the issue of automobiles served and serves as a catalyst for a variety of other issues. One asks about a car and gets an entire history. Conversations about the car are small talk but are also conversations about everything: life, society, preferences, gender relations, and living conditions. I point to two aspects gleaned from the interviews I conducted.

The first is the connection between life story and car. For the women I interviewed, the purchase of a car and the experiences with it are connected with central moments in their biographies. These start with childhood memories. For the real estate agent, it was when her estranged father came to visit the family in his Volga. For another interviewee, the wild early years of her marriage are associated with the motorcycle and sidecar. This connection between car and biography is especially clear in the story of the Russian teacher who got her driver's license after her father's death. She was able to afford a Western car straight from the factory after the early death of her husband. Her almost-grown daughters had convinced her to put the money from his life insurance into a car. The taxi driver began driving for hire after an upheaval in her life, the breakup of her marriage and the end of her solid job as an accountant. In the case of the real estate agent, we can follow her way out of the 1990s crises according to her cars: from a Lada that was a gift to a used Lada to a used foreign car and finally to a new foreign car. Thus the study of "auto"-biographies offers a surprisingly productive grasp of daily life and practices, changing values and family life, habits of consumption, and material culture in the Soviet Union and Russia since the 1970s.

The second point is that a conversation about cars and driving is in itself a reflection of the transformations of the last two decades. There are the "haves" with their new prosperity and possibilities of consumption, a gain in personal freedom, and automobility. The flip side is the loss of time, quiet, socializing, and mutual assistance and, in the broadest sense, the loss of kul'turnost'. Aggressive driving is seen as the symptom of a society in which every man (or woman) fights for himself or herself and inconsiderately pursues his or her own interest. The strong contrast between old domestic cars and brand-new Western luxury items is a synecdoche for the inequality in Russian society, and police are seen as the ultimate embodiment of corruption. All in all, complaints about the lawlessness and chaos of traffic match a current description of Russian government and society. As one driver says, "Where is the real difference between our streets and our lives? Only in that you feel it more explicitly on the street: everyone is against you. There are no laws here, either."[47]

NOTES

Introduction

1. Henry Kamm, "Noj Journal; Just Smashing Communism (Got Carried Away)," *New York Times,* April 1, 1992, http://query.nytimes.com/search/sitesearch?query=Noj+Journal&srchst=cse; Jane Perlez, "Albania's Auto Industry: Dealing in Stolen Cars," *New York Times,* August 16, 1997, http://www.nytimes.com/1997/08/16/world/albania-s-auto-industry-dealing-in-stolen-cars.htm (accessed January 20, 2011).

2. With its ever-dwindling stock of vintage American cars sharing road and garage space with Soviet-built Ladas, Cuba deserves—and has received—special treatment elsewhere. See Richard Schweid, *Che's Chevrolet, Fidel's Oldsmobile: On the Road in Cuba* (Chapel Hill: University of North Carolina Press, 2004). The People's Republic of China, where as late as 1990 only one in two hundred people owned a car, also falls outside our purview. For data see National Statistics Bureau, *A Statistical Survey of China, 1996* (Beijing: China Statistics Press, 1996); for an analysis, see Li Gan, "Globalization of the Automobile Industry in China: Dynamics and Barriers in the Greening of Road Transportation" (CICERO Working Paper 9, 2001), http://www.cicero.uio.no/media/1381.pdf (accessed January 10, 2009).

3. Catherine Cooke, preface to *Style and Socialism: Modernity and Material Culture in Post-War Eastern Europe,* ed. Susan E. Reid and David Crowley (Oxford: Berg, 2000), vii.

4. Arjun Appadurai, ed., *The Social Life of Things: Commodities in Cultural Perspective* (Cambridge: Cambridge University Press, 1986). See also Stephen Edgell, Kevin Hetherington, and Alan Warde, eds., *Consumption Matters: The Production and Experience of Consumption* (Oxford: Blackwell, 1996); John Storey, *Cultural Consumption and Everyday Life* (London: Arnold, 1999); Martyn J. Lee, ed., *The Consumer Society Reader* (Malden, MA: Blackwell, 2000).

5. For the most sophisticated of such state-centered analyses, see Ferenc Fehér, Ágnes Heller, and György Márkus, *Dictatorship over Needs: An Analysis of Soviet Societies* (Oxford: Basil Blackwell, 1983).

6. Roberta Sassatelli, *Consumer Culture: History, Theory and Politics* (London: Sage, 2007); Lizabeth Cohen, *A Consumer's Republic: The Politics of Mass Consumption in Postwar America* (New York: Vintage Books, 2003).

7. E. A. Osokina, *Ierarkhiia potrebleniia: O zhizni liudei v usloviiakh stalinskogo snabzheniia, 1928–1935 gg.* (Moscow: Izd-vo MGOU, 1993); Osokina, *Za fasadom "stalinskogo izobiliia": Raspredelenie i rynok v snabzhenii naseleniia v gody industrializatsii, 1927–1941* (Moscow: ROSSPEN, 1998); Julie Hessler, "Cultured Trade: The Stalinist Turn towards Consumerism," in *Stalinism: New Directions,* ed.

Sheila Fitzpatrick (London: Routledge, 2000), 182–209; Jukka Gronow, *Caviar with Champagne: Common Luxury and the Ideals of the Good Life in Stalin's Russia* (Oxford: Berg, 2003); Vera Dunham, *In Stalin's Time: Middleclass Values in Soviet Fiction* (Durham, NC: Duke University Press, 1990).

8. See Mary Neuberger, "Inhaling Luxury: Lighting up in Socialist Bulgaria" (paper presented at the American Association for the Advancement of Slavic Studies, New Orleans, November 15–18, 2007); and György Majtényi, "Socialist Luxury: Lifestyles of the Elite in Hungary during the 1950s and 1960s" (paper presented at conference on "Social Transformations and Social Identities in East-Central and Southeastern Europe under Socialism," Central European University, Budapest, September 28–30, 2007).

9. Mark Edele, "Strange Young Men in Stalin's Moscow: The Birth and Life of the Stiliagi, 1945–1953," *Jahrbücher für Geschichte Osteuropas* 50 (2002): 37–61; Juliane Fürst, "The Importance of Being Stylish: Youth, Culture and Identity in Late Stalinism," in *Late Stalinist Russia: Society between Reconstruction and Reinvention*, ed. Juliane Fürst (London: Routledge, 2006), 209–30; Roger P. Potocki, "The Life and Times of Poland's 'Bikini Boys,'" *Polish Review* 39, no. 3 (1994): 259–90.

10. David Crowley and Susan E. Reid, "Style and Socialism: Modernity and Material Culture in Post-War Eastern Europe," in Reid and Crowley, *Style and Socialism*, 10–14.

11. James Millar, "The Little Deal: Brezhnev's Contribution to Acquisitive Socialism," *Slavic Review* 44, no. 4 (1985): 694–706. For varying use of the "social contract" metaphor, see Linda Cook, *The Soviet Social Contract and Why It Failed: Welfare Policy and Workers' Politics from Brezhnev to Yeltsin* (Cambridge, MA: Harvard University Press, 1993), and with reference to "Soviet-style societies," James R. Millar and Sharon L. Wolchik, "Introduction: The Social Legacies and the Aftermath of Communism," in *The Social Legacy of Communism*, ed. James R. Millar and Sharon L. Wolchik (Washington, DC: Woodrow Wilson Center Press, 1994), 2–10.

12. The literature was inaugurated by Gregory Grossman, "The Second Economy of the Soviet Union," *Problems of Communism* 26, no. 4 (1977): 25–40. For a bibliography, see Gregory Grossman, "The Second Economy in the USSR and Eastern Europe: A Bibliography," in *Berkeley-Duke Occasional Papers on the Second Economy in the USSR* (Washington, DC: WEFA Group, Special Projects, 1990). See also Anna Seleny, *Political Economy of State-Society Relations in Hungary and Poland* (New York: Cambridge University Press, 2006), 161–80.

13. Svetlana Boym, *Common Places: Mythologies of Everyday Life in Russia* (Cambridge, MA: Harvard University Press, 1994), 150.

14. Susan E. Reid, "The Meaning of Home: 'The Only Bit of the World You Can Have to Yourself,'" in *Borders of Socialism: Private Spheres of Soviet Russia*, ed. Lewis H. Siegelbaum (New York: Palgrave Macmillan, 2006), 157–64.

15. Alena V. Ledeneva, *Russia's Economy of Favours: Blat, Networking and Informal Exchange* (Cambridge: Cambridge University Press, 1998); and Ina Merkel, *Utopie und Bedürfnis: Die Geschichte der Konsumkultur in der DDR* (Cologne: Böhlau, 1999). See also I. Merkel, "Consumer Culture in the GDR, or How the Struggle for Antimodernity Was Lost on the Battleground of Consumer Culture," in *Getting and Spending: European and American Consumer Societies in the Twentieth Century*, ed. Susan Strasser, Charles McGovern, and Matthias Judt (Washington, DC: Publications of the German Historical Institute, 1998), 281–300.

16. In addition to previous citations, see Sandrine Kott, *Le communism au quotidien: Les entreprises d'état dans la societé est-allemande* (Paris: Belin, 2001); Philipp Heldmann, "Negotiating Consumption in a Dictatorship: Consumer Politics in the GDR in the 1950s and 1960s," in *The Politics of Consumption: Material Culture and Citizenship in Europe and America*, ed. Martin Daunton and Matthew Hilton (Oxford: Berg, 2002), 185–202; David Crowley and Susan E. Reid, eds., *Socialist Spaces: Sites of Everyday Life in the Eastern Bloc* (Oxford: Berg, 2002); Judd Stitziel, *Fashioning Socialism: Clothing, Politics, and Consumer Culture in East Germany* (Oxford: Berg, 2005); Eli Rubin, "East German Plastics: Technology, Gender and Teleological Structures of Everyday Life," *German History* 25, no. 4 (2007): 596–624; Eli Rubin, *Synthetic Socialism: Plastics and Dictatorship in the German Democratic Republic* (Chapel Hill: University of North Carolina Press, 2008); Ferenc Hammer, "Sartorial Manoeuvres in the Dusk: Blue Jeans in Socialist Hungary," in *Citizenship and Consumption*, ed. Kate Soper and Frank Trentmann (Basingstoke, UK: Palgrave Macmillan, 2008), 51–68; Katherine Pence and Paul Betts, eds., *Socialist Modern: East German Everyday Culture and Politics* (Ann Arbor: University of Michigan Press, 2008).

17. See, for example, Rubin, *Synthetic Socialism*, 225: "Plastics . . . formed a major middle ground where the needs of the regime and the needs of the population could meet." For a more extensive use of this framework, see Alexei Yurchak, *Everything Was Forever, Until It Was No More: The Last Soviet Generation* (Princeton: Princeton University Press, 2006).

18. See György Péteri, ed., *Imagining the West in Eastern Europe and the Soviet Union* (Pittsburgh: University of Pittsburgh Press, 2010); and David Crowley and Susan E. Reid, eds., *Pleasures in Socialism: Leisure and Luxury in the Eastern Bloc* (Evanston, IL: Northwestern University Press, 2010).

19. For a recent exception see Jukka Gronow and Sergei Zhuravlev, "Soviet Luxuries from Champagne to Private Cars," in Crowley and Reid, *Pleasures in Socialism*, 121–46. On the Trabant see Jonathan Zatlin, "The Vehicle of Desire: The Trabant, the Wartburg, and the End of the GDR," *German History* 15, no. 3 (1997): 358–80; Raymond G. Stokes, "Plastics and the New Society: The German Democratic Republic in the 1950s and 1960s," in Crowley and Reid, *Style and Socialism*, 65–80. The afterlife of the Trabant has inspired a good deal of analysis. See, for example, Ina Merkel, "From Stigma to Cult: Changing Meanings in East German Consumer Culture," in *The Making of the Consumer: Knowledge, Power and Identity in the Modern World*, ed. Frank Trentmann (Oxford: Berg, 2006), 252–57; Daphne Berdahl, "Re-Presenting the Socialist Modern: Museums and Memory in the Former GDR," in Pence and Betts, *Socialist Modern*, 348–51.

20. See also Lewis H. Siegelbaum, *Cars for Comrades: The Life of the Soviet Automobile* (Ithaca: Cornell University Press, 2008).

21. Gijs Mom, "Writing the History of Automobilism as a History of Consumption: Some Thoughts on the Future of Mobility History" (paper presented to the Socialist Car Conference, Berlin, June 12–14, 2008).

22. See, respectively, Rolf Torstendahl, *Bureaucratisation in Northwestern Europe, 1880–1985: Domination and Governance* (London: Routledge, 1991), 100–104; Mary Nolan, *Visions of Modernity: American Business and the Modernization of Germany* (New York: Oxford University Press, 1994), 30–57, 131–53; Greg Grandin, *Fordlandia: The Rise and Fall of Henry Ford's Forgotten Jungle City* (New York: Metropolitan Books, 2009), 11–15; Gérard Bordenave, "Ford of Europe, 1967–2003," in *Ford, 1903–2003: The European History*, ed. Hubert Bonin, Yannick Lung, and Steven Tolliday (Paris: PLAGE, 2003), 1:243–317; Paul Thomas, "Searching for Identity: Ford Motor Company in the German Market (1903–2003)," in Bonin, Lung, and Tolliday, *Ford*, 2:151–95; and Yves Cohen, "The Soviet Fordson: Between the Politics of Stalin and the Philosophy of Ford," in *Ford*, 2:531–58.

23. Pence and Betts, introduction to *Socialist Modern*, 11–15; Péteri, introduction to *Imagining the West*, 4–10.

24. Michael David-Fox, "Multiple Modernities vs. Neo-Traditionalism: On Recent Debates in Russian and Soviet History," *Jahrbücher für Geschichte Osteuropas* 55, no. 4 (2006): 535–55 (quotation on 550). See also Michael Werner and Bénédictine Zimmerman, "Beyond Comparison: *Histoire Croisée* and the Challenge of Reflexivity," *History and Theory* 45 (February 2006): 30–50, and Michael Geyer and Sheila Fitzpatrick, eds., *Beyond Totalitarianism: Stalinism and Nazism Compared* (Cambridge: Cambridge University Press, 2009), 35: "To be sure, the image of the other is by now rather well explored, but the monstrous imbrications and entanglements of Nazism and Stalinism have yet to be fully recognized. For however we turn them, the past, present, and future of both regimes and what came of them are inseparable from their *histoire croisée*."

25. For a fascinating study of failed attempts (largely involving the GDR and Czechoslovakia) to produce a "COMECON car," see Burghard Ciesla, "Difficult Relations: German Automobile Construction and the Economic Alliance in Eastern Europe (1945–1990)," unpublished paper, n.d.

26. John Bushnell, "The 'New Soviet Man' Turns Pessimist," in *The Soviet Union since Stalin*, ed. Stephen F. Cohen, Alexander Rabinowitch, and Robert Sharlet (Bloomington: Indiana University Press, 1980), 191–94.

27. Wendy Bracewell, "Adventures in the Marketplace: Yugoslav Travel Writing and Tourism in the 1950s–1960s," in *Turizm: The Russian and East European Tourist under Capitalism and Socialism*, ed. Anne E. Gorsuch and Diane P. Koenker (Ithaca: Cornell University Press, 2006), 264. Cf. Bushnell, "The 'New Soviet Man,'" 191: "For Soviet citizens, to arrive in East Berlin, Warsaw, Prague, or Budapest is to visit their own version of the West, prosperous but prosaic."

28. Mike Featherstone, "Automobilities, an Introduction," *Theory, Culture and Society* 21, no. 4–5 (2004): 2. This is a summary of Urry's understanding. See also John Urry, "The 'System' of Automobility," *Theory, Culture & Society* 21, nos. 4–5 (2004): 25–39.

29. Robert Argenbright, "*Avtomobilshchina:* Driven to the Brink in Moscow," *Urban Geography* 29, no. 7 (2008): 683–84.

30. Steffen Böhm et al., "Part One: Conceptualizing Automobility," *Sociological Review* 54, no. 1 (2006): 1–3.

31. Rolf Hellebust, *Flesh to Metal: Soviet Literature and the Alchemy of Revolution* (Ithaca: Cornell University Press, 2003).

32. Tim Edensor, "Automobility and National Identity: Representation, Geography and Driving Practice," *Theory, Culture & Society* 21, nos. 4–5 (2004): 102–3 (emphasis in original).

33. See also the remark of a Soviet sociologist—that "car owners involuntarily are compelled to raise their own technical culture which can be considered a positive development"—in V. T. Efimov and G. I. Mikerin, "Avtomobilizatsiia v razvitom sotsialicheskom obshchestve," *Sotsiologicheskie issledovaniia*, no. 1 (1976): 134.

34. Jukka Gronow, "Vzlet i padenie Lada ('Zhiguli') v Finliandii. Prodazhi, imidzh i otnoshenie k sovetskim avtomobiliam v Finliandii v 1970–1990-kh gg.," in *Istoriia OAO "AVTOVAZ": Uroki, problemy, sovremennost', Materialy II Vserossiiskoi nauchnoi konferentsii, 26–27 oktiabria 2005 g.*, ed. R. G. Pikhoia (Togliatti: OAO "AVTOVAZ," 2005), 268–70.

35. S. V. Zhuravlev et al., *AVTOVAZ mezhdu proshlym i budushchim: Istoriia volzhskogo avtomobil'nogo zavoda 1966–2005* (Moscow: RAGS, 2006), 172–81; Peter Hamilton, "The Lada: A Cultural Icon," in *Autopia: Cars and Culture*, ed. Peter Wollen and Joe Kerr (London: Reaktion Books, 2002), 191–98.

36. Cf. Kristin Ross, *Fast Cars, Clean Bodies: Decolonization and the Reordering of French Culture* (Cambridge: MIT Press, 1996), 19: "The car *is* the commodity form as such of the twentieth century."

37. Urry, "The 'System' of Automobility," 25–26.

38. Edensor, "Automobility and National Identity," 108.

39. Merkel, "From Stigma to Cult," 254–55.

40. Ivan Dykhovichnyi, director. In 2000, more than eighty thousand readers of the Russian car magazine *Za rulem* voted for Russia's "best automobile of the twentieth century." The Lada 2101 received one quarter of all the votes, more than any other car. See Elena Varshavskaia, "Vy vybrali VAZ-2101," *Za rulem*, no. 1 (2000): 4–6.

1 The Elusive People's Car

1. Jonathan Zeitlin and Gary Herrigel, eds., *Americanization and Its Limits: Reworking US Technology and Management in Post-War Europe and Japan* (Oxford: Oxford University Press, 2000), 2–3. By the American model of mass production the authors mean "high volume manufacture of standardized goods using special purpose machinery and predominantly unskilled labour—together with the host of systematic management techniques, organizational structures and research and marketing services developed for its efficient administration and effective exploitation." On the relevance of "practices" in the Americanization debate see Yves Cohen, "Administration, Politique et Techniques. Réflections sur la Matérialité des Pratiques Administratives dans la Russie Stalinienne, 1922–1940," *Cahiers du Monde Russe* 44, nos. 2–3 (2002): 269–307.

2. Tim Edensor, "Automobility and National Identity. Representation, Geography and Driving Practice," *Theory, Culture & Society* 21, nos. 4–5 (2004): 101–20, and John Urry, "The 'System' of Automobility," *Theory, Culture & Society* 21, nos. 4–5 (2004): 25–39. For a contribution to the issue of Czech national identity see Ladislav Holy, *The Little Czech and the Great Czech Nation: National Identity and the Post-Communist Social Transformation* (Cambridge: Cambridge University Press, 1996).

3. Sandrine Kott, "Pour une Histoire Sociale du Pouvoir en Europe Communiste: Introduction Thématique," *Revue d'Histoire Moderne et Contemporaine* 49, no. 2 (2002), 5–24, and Kott, *Le communisme au quotidien. Les entreprises d'état dans la societé est-allemande* (Paris: Belin 2001).

4. *Auto. Officielní orgán autoklubu RČS* was the monthly official magazine of the Czechoslovak Autoclub. In 1949 it was renamed *Motorista*.

5. Raymond Stokes, *Constructing Socialism: Technology and Change in East Germany 1945–1990* (Baltimore: Johns Hopkins University Press, 2000), 112–13, and Stokes, "In Search of the Socialist Artefact. Technology and Ideology in East Germany, 1945–1962," *German History* 15 (1997): 221–39; see also Radovan Richta, *La Via Cecoslovacca. Civiltà al Bivio: Le Proposte di Praga per un Nuovo Socialismo* (Milan: Franco Angeli 1968).

6. Alice Teichová, "Czechoslovakia: The Halting Pace to Scope and Scale," in *Big Business and the Wealth of Nations*, ed. Alfred Chandler, Franco Amatori, and Takashi Hikino (Cambridge: Cambridge University Press, 1997), 447–61, and Teichova, *The Czechoslovak Economy 1918–1980* (London: Routledge, 1984), 150.

7. Jaroslav Frei, "Jaký bude osud našho automobilového průmyslu" [What will be the future of our motor vehicle industry], *Auto*, no. A1 (1946): 1–6; Jaroslav Frei directed Jawa Motor, one of the main producers of cars and motorcycles in the interwar period that from 1946 specialized in the production of motorcycles.

8. Ibid.

9. František Kec, "Vyroba automobilu v nové republice" [The production of motor vehicles in the new Republic], *Auto*, no. A1 (1946): 6–7.

10. Karel Zámečnik, "Význam znárodnení Československého automobilového průmyslu" [The significance of nationalization of the motor vehicle industry], *Auto*, nos. A7–A8 (1946): 104–5.

11. Frei, "Jaký bude osud," and also Karel Výška, "Ještě k výrobě automobilů v nové republice" [Again concerning the production of automobiles in the new republic], *Auto*, no. B3 (1946): 50–51.

12. This was announced in the liberated city of Košice in East Slovakia on April 5, 1945. The programs had been agreed on by the government in exile in London with the Communists and had been heavily conditioned by them. For some contextualization, see Bradley F. Abrams, *The Struggle for the Soul of the Nation: Czech Culture and the Rise of Communism* (Lanham, MD: Rowman & Littlefield, 2004); Teichova, "Czechoslovakia: The Halting Pace to Scope and Scale," 447–61; and Teichova, "For and against the Marshall Plan in Czechoslovakia," in *Le Plan Marshall et le Relèvement Economique de l'Europe. Colloque tenu à Bercy les 21, 22, 23 mars 1991*, ed. René Girault and Maurice Lévy-Leboyer (Paris: L'Imprimerie Nationale, 1993), 840.

13. Alexander Taub, responsible for engine construction at General Motors, was invited by the General Direction of the Mechanical and Steel Industry (Generální Ředitelství Kovodělného a Strojírenského Průmyslu, KOVO). His reports were translated from English to Czech by Frei.

14. Alexander Taub, "A People's Technology," report to Dr. Ing. F. Fabinger, general director of KOVO, Prague, September 1946, Historical Archives Škoda Auto (AŠA), records of Automobilové Závody, Národní Podnik/p (AZNP/p), b. 4, 6; see also František Herbert Žalud, *Přežili jsme. Zkušenosti z Mého Života 1919–1993, Popsané pro Má Vnoučata a Jejich Generaci* [We have survived. My life experience written for my grandchildren and their generation] (Prague: Trilabit, 1998), and V. Fava, "Tecnici, ingegneri e fordismo. Škoda e Fiat nelle relazioni di viaggio in America," *Imprese e Storia* 22 (2000): 201–49.

15. Taub, "A People's Technology," 8.

16. "Soubor přednášek o poznatcích získaných v USA Přednášeno v AKRCs dne 2.února 1948" [File of lessons on experiences in the U.S. Presented on February 2, 1948, at the Czechoslovak Automobile Club], AŠA, AZNP/p, 4: the file includes the texts of the lessons of František Fabinger, Vladimír Matouš, Václav Křêmár, Richard Kneschik, Zdeněk Kejval. See also the complete reports: Vladimír Matouš, *Cestovní zprávy z USA, Výtah z cestovních zpráv od 31. srpna do 12. listopadu 1947* [Extract of the report of the trip to the U.S., from August 31, 1947, to November 12, 1947]; Václav Křêmár, *Automobilové továrny v USA, Zpráva z cesty konané v červenci-září 1947* [Automobile factories in the U.S. Report of the July–September 1947 trip], AŠA, AZNP/p, 4.

17. The debate about the future of automobile production emerges from the minutes of the meeting of the technical board of the AKRCs Czechoslovak Automobile Club published in *Svět Motorů* between 1949 and 1950: see in particular "Nemístní luxus" [a senseless luxury], *Svět Motorů*, no. 76 (1950): 164.

18. The War Production Board was established as a government agency in January 1942 by Franklin D. Roosevelt. Its purpose was to regulate the production and allocation of materials and fuel during World War II; Rudolf Slánsky was secretary general of the Communist Party until 1951 and was sentenced to death in 1952. See Karel Kaplan and Pavel Paleček, *Komunistický Režim a Politické Procesy v Československu* [The Communist regime and the political trials in Czechoslovakia] (Brno: Barrister and Principal, 2001).

19. Valentina Fava, "Between American Fordism and 'Soviet Fordism': The Czechoslovak Way towards Mass Production," in *The Sovietization of Eastern Europe: New Perspectives on the Post-War Period*, ed. Balázs Apor, Péter Apor, and Eduard Arfon Rees (Washington, DC: New Academia Publishing, 2008), 47–64.

20. "Zvýšíme brannost našeho národa" [Let us improve our country's defensive capacity], *Svět Motorů*, no. 116 (1951): 1443, and "Poslání a úkoly Československych motoristů" [Functions and tasks of Czech motorists], *Svět Motorů*, no. 130, 1952, 6.

21. Adolf Tůma, "Rozvoj motorové doprava" [Development of transport on two wheels], *Svět Motorů*, no. 83 (1950): 387. The author was president of the Autoclub. For the Soviet precedent see Lewis H. Siegelbaum, *Cars for Comrades: The Life of the Soviet Automobile* (Ithaca: Cornell University Press, 2008), 141–42, 210.

22. Tůma, "Rozvoj motorové doprava."

23. Joseph Neufus, "Reorganisace Autoklubu RČS a jeho příští úkoly" [Reorganization of the Czech Autoclub and its future tasks], *Svět Motorů*, no. 74 (1950): 99. The author was a member of the board of the Autoclub: "Driving is no longer the privilege of people who exploit the workers, as in the time of the First Republic. The figures show that our cars now finish up directly in the hands of workers. Even if now this isn't evident because of the lack of cars, it can be seen from the fate of motorcycles.... The impetuous access of the working class to motoring forces us to prepare our drivers for various responsibilities connected to the nation's defense."

24. Reorganisace Mototechny [The reorganization of the Mototechna], *Svět Motorů*, no. 122 (1952): 97. The Mototechna was the enterprise responsible for distribution in the domestic market, while Motokov was the distributor for the foreign market.

25. "Cars signify national identity as familiar, iconic, manufactured objects emerging out of historic systems of production and expertise." Edensor, "Automobility and National Identity," 103.

26. "Pryč s Masarykovskými legendami" [Let us eliminate the legends about Masaryk], *Svět Motorů*, no. 148 (1953): 358.

27. The author of "Nemístní luxus" goes on to say, "We know from the complaints that arrive to our editors how many people want to drive a vehicle, how many wish a people's car were produced, how many ask for car prices to be reduced, as they do in the West. That they do it is true. But the question is, who they do it for and who benefits!"

28. I have treated this question in V. Fava, "The Automobile Industry and CMEA Integration: Evidence from the Czechoslovak Case and Reflections on an Unexpected Failure," *Jahrbuch für Wirtschaftsgeschichte/Economic History Yearbook*, no. 2 (2008): 93–115.

29. Fava, "Between American Fordism and 'Soviet Fordism,'" 56–61.

30. Cf. Stručné rozbory změn výrobního program Automobilových Závodů n.p. Ml Boleslav od roku 1946 [Brief synthesis of the changes in the production program of the AZNP from 1946], 26 March 1954, Státní Ustřední Archiv (State Archives of the Czech Republic) (SÚA), records of Československé Závody Automobilové a Letecké národní podnik (Czechoslovak Automobile and Aviation Works, national enterprise) (ČZAL), b. 86.

31. Fava, "Between American Fordism and 'Soviet Fordism.'"

32. Data supporting this hypothesis can be found in Valentina Fava, "Motor Vehicles vs. Dollars: Selling Socialist Cars in Neutral Markets. Some Evidence from the ŠKODA Auto Case," in *A Gap in the Iron Curtain: Economic Relations between Neutral and Socialist Countries in Cold War Europe*, ed. Alice Teichova, Gertrude Burcel Enderle, and Petr Franaszek (Warsaw: Jagiellonian University Press, 2009), 251–69.

33. Program vývojového oddělení pro vozidla [Program for a development department for motor vehicles], document signed by eng. Karel Výška, 22 June 1949, SÚA,ČZAL, b. 64.

34. "Naše cesta k lidovému vozu" [Our journey toward a People's Car], *Svět Motorů*, no. 164 (1954): 4–5, continued in issue 165 (1954): 38–39. The author was an engineer of the AZNP; an article titled "Malý automobil—velký problém" [Small car—big problem] had already appeared in nos. 161–62 (1953): 800.

35. On Czech attitudes in 1956 see Muriel Blaive, *Une déstalinisation manquée: Tchécoslovaquie 1956* (Paris: Editions Complexe, 2005).

36. Stokes, *Constructing Socialism*, 112–13.

37. *Návrh perspektivního plánu oboru osobní automobily od roku 1956 do roku 1975* [Ideas for the future plan concerning automobile production from 1956 to 1975], SÚA, records of Ministerstvo Automobilového Průmyslu a Zemědělských Strojů (Ministry of Automobile Industry and Agricultural Machinery) (MAP), b. 200.

38. *Návrh perspektivního plánu oboru osobní automobily od roku 1956 do roku 1975*.

39. Oborová Konference pro osobní automobily [Sectoral conference concerning automobile production], 30–31 March 1956, AŠA, records of AZNP, b. 8.

40. Oborová Konference pro osobní automobily.

41. III etapa plánu royvoje a specialisace pro osobní automobily 1955–1960 [Third stage of the development and specialization plan for automobiles], AŠA, AZNP, b. 26. For technical and construction details of models, see Jan Kožíšek and Jan Králík, *L&K-Škoda* (Prague: Motor Press, 1997); for an exhaustive description of the models produced and productive methods, see Marius R. Cedrých and Lukaš Nachtmann, *Škoda. Auta známá i neznámá. Prototypy i seriové automobily vyráběné od roku 1934* (Prague: Grada, 2003), 141–55.

42. "Rozvoj automobilového průmyslu v ČSR" [Development of the automobile industry in Czechoslovakia] (document produced by Český Statistický Úřad), 1970, AŠA, AZNP, b. 34, and "Podnikatelský záměr na výrobu osob. aut. v ČSSR do roku 1980" [Company's esteem for the production of automobiles in Czechoslovakia until 1980], April 1968, AZNP, b. 65. According to available data, in 1965 production reached 77,000 units and in 1968 125,000 units, with a growth of 95 percent between 1962 and 1968. This is even more noteworthy if compared with 1957, when the lines of Mladá Boleslav produced only 35,000 cars. However, these are still tiny numbers if compared with foreign production figures (in 1968, in West Germany 2,900,000 pieces were produced, and in Italy 1,500,000). For a comparison with the Italian case, see Duccio Bigazzi, *La grande fabbrica* (Milan: Feltrinelli, 2000), 179, and with the world industry, Jean Paul Bardou, Jean Jacques Chanaron, Patrick Fridenson, and James Laux, *The Automobile Revolution* (Chapel Hill: University of North Carolina Press, 1982).

43. Rozvoj automobilového průmyslu v ČSR, AŠA, AZNP, b. 34. In the same period, according to the same source, car density in West Germany increased from one car for every 20 inhabitants to one for every 5.1; in 1967, in Great Britain from one vehicle for every 11 to one for every 5; and in France from one for every 12 to one for every 4.5.

44. "Spartak—Mezityp lidového automobilu" [Spartak: A popular auto means], *Svět Motorů*, no. 189 (1954): 756–57; V. Janírek, "Ještě něco o Spartaku" [Another remark about the Spartak], *Svět Motorů*, no. 190 (1954): 53. "Deset let vývoje a výroby automobilů" [Ten years of motor vehicle development and production], *Svět Motorů*, no. 198 (1954): 298–99; "Lépe využívat zahraničních technických poznatků a zintensivnit propagaci nové techniky" [Better to use foreign technology and intensify propaganda], *Svět Motorů*, no. 209 (1955): 1.

45. "Prodej osobních automobilů v roce 1957" [Auto sales in 1957], *Svět Motorů*, no. 240 (1956): 823; "Prodej osobních automobilů obyvatelskvu v roce 1956" [Auto sales to the population in 1956], *Svět Motorů*, no. 218 (1956): 122; "Kdy a jak si budeme moci koupit automobil" [When and how we will be able to buy a car], *Svět Motorů*, no. 244 (1957): 107–108.

46. Karel Hruska, "Motoristé před volbami" [Motorists facing the elections], *Svět Motorů*, no. 250 (1957), and also "V Italii a u nás, na pomoc předvolebním besedám" [In Italy and at home. Helping the electoral campaign], *Svět Motorů*, no. 195 (1956): 742.

47. "K některým otázkám daně z motorových vozidel" [Concerning some questions on motor vehicle taxes], *Svět Motorů*, no. 266 (1957): 1; Karel Šimon, "Strana a vláda pečují o rozvoj motorismu" [The government and the party deal with motorization development], *Svět Motorů*, no. 261 (1957): 1; Václav Jirout, "Více, lépe a levněji" [More, better and cheaper], *Svět Motorů*, no. 262 (1957):1.

48. *Návrh perspektivního plánu oboru osobní automobily od roku 1956 do roku 1975.*
49. Janos Kornai, *The Socialist System: The Political Economy of Communism* (Princeton: Princeton University Press: 1992).
50. 14 September 1953 SÚA, Úřad předsednictva vlády—tajná spisovna (Office of the President of the Government—secret documents) (ÚPV-T), b. 48.
51. Zápis z aktivu s delegáty Motokovu ze zahraničí a zastupci Motokovu se zástupci [Minutes of the meeting of the Motokov foreign delegates with the representatives of AZNP], AŠA, AZNP, b. 8a. Cf. Zápis z konference techniků zahraničních zástupců o voze Škoda 1000 MB pořádané v AZNP Mladá Boleslav [Minutes of the foreign technical members' meeting concerning the Škoda 1000 MB vehicle], 14–15 March 1966, AZNP, b. 8; and Zpráva o opatřeních k zavedení prodeje vozu Škoda 1000 MB na vybraných kapitalistických trzích [Report on the conditions for the launch of the Škoda 1000 MB on selected capitalist markets], 8 April 1964, AZNP, b. 8a.
52. V. Fava, "Motor Vehicles vs. Dollars," and Fava, "The Automobile Industry and CMEA Integration."
53. See Porady Ředitelů [Meetings of the managers], 1952–68, AŠA, AZNP, b. 8.
54. Zpráva o plnění usnesení politického byra UV KSČ ze dne 16-4 a 9–10–1957 o opatřeních k zajištění kvality nákladních automobilů Š706 a osobních automobilů Š440 [Report on the implementation of the resolution of the political committee of the Czechoslovak Communist Party concerning the improvement of the quality of the Š706 truck and of the Š440 automobile] December 14, 1957, SÚA, MAP, b. 30; Zpráva pro segretariát ministra o organizaci, technologii a efektivnosti výroby, o výzkumu, kvalitě výrobků, 1955–1958 [Report to the secretary of the minister concerning the organization, technology, and efficiency of the production, research, and quality of products], SÚA, MAP, 94; and Specialisace a kooperace jako jeden z vázných činitelů ovlivnujících dálší rozvoj vyroby [Specialization and cooperation as one of the most important aspects influencing the further development of production], September 1957, AŠA, AZNP b. 48.
55. Zpráva pro segretariát ministra o organizaci.
56. Jiri Jirasek, *Organizační řízení. Vývoj teorie podnikového řízení* (Prague: Institut řízení, 1987), 131–63, and Gerard McDermott, *Embedded Politics: Industrial Networks and Institutional Change* (Ann Arbor: University of Michigan Press, 2002), 28–63.
57. Teichova, *Czechoslovakia*, 447–61 and Teichova, *The Czechoslovak Economy*, 150.
58. Problematika trhu a cenová politika v novych podmínkách řízení, 6 June 1967 [Problems concerning market and prices definition according to the new management methods], AŠA, AZNP, b. 8.
59. Výtah z přednášky o marketingu a jeho aplikaci v AZNP Mladá Boleslav [Synthesis of the lectures on marketing and its implementation in AZNP], AŠA, AZNP, b. 20.
60. "Marketing is a total system of interacting business activity designed to plan, price, promote and distribute want-satisfying products and services to present to potential customers." The definition is found in G. Volpato, "Evoluzione delle strategie di marketing nell'industria automobilistica internazionale," *Annali di Storia dell'impresa*, 1986, 126n6. For studies on marketing in the GDR cf. Marcello Anselmo, "Der werktatige Verbraucher: Defining the Socialist consumer. Market research in GDR 1960s/ '70s," in B. Apor, P. Apor, Rees, *The Sovietization of Eastern Europe*, 77–91.
61. ŠA, AZNP, b. 65, p. 5.
62. Yves Cohen, "The Soviet Fordson. Between the Politics of Stalin and the Philosophy of Ford, 1924–1932," and Boris Shpotov, "Ford in Russia from 1909 to World War II," in *Ford 1903–2003: The European History*, ed. H. Bonin et al. (Paris: 2003), 531–58 and 525–29, respectively.
63. Ina Merkel, "Consumer Culture in the GDR, or How the Struggle for Antimodernity was Lost on the Battleground of Consumer Culture," in *Getting and Spending: European and American Consumer Societies in the Twentieth Century*, ed. Susan Strasser, Charles McGovern, and Matthias Judt (Washington, DC: Publications of the German Historical Institute, 1998), 281–300. I thank Brigitte Le Normand for pointing out this literature to me.
64. André Steiner, "Dissolution of the Dictatorship over Needs? Consumer Behaviour and Economic Reform in East Germany in the 1960s," in Strasser, McGovern, and Matthias, *Getting and Spending*, 167–85.
65. April 1968, AŠA, AZNP, b. 65.

66. Transcription of a long television interview with the director of the AZNP in 1967 on the future of automobility in Czechoslovakia, AŠA, AZNP, b. 20. Compared with other documents, this seems the most significant and ironic.

67. This was part of the strategy of "normalization" as discussed by Paulina Bren, "Weekend Getaways: The Chata, the Tramp and the Politics of Private Life in Post-1968 Czechoslovakia," in *Socialist Spaces: Sites of Everyday Life in the Eastern Bloc*, ed. David Crowley and Susan E. Reid (Oxford: Berg, 2002). See also Paulina Bren, "Mirror, Mirror, on the Wall . . . Is the West the Fairest of Them All? Czechoslovak Normalization and Its (Dis)contents," in *Imagining the West in Eastern Europe and the Soviet Union*, ed. György Péteri (Pittsburgh: University of Pittsburgh Press, 2010), 172–93.

2 Cars as Favors in People's Poland

1. For a review of the literature on the Soviet Union see Paul Gregory and Mark Harrison, "Allocation under Dictatorship: Research in Stalin's Archives," *Journal of Economic Literature* 43, no. 3 (2005): 721–61.

2. Julie Hessler, "Cultured Trade: The Stalinist Turn towards Consumerism," in *Stalinism: New Directions*, ed. Sheila Fitzpatrick (London: Routledge, 2000), 182–209. See also Jukka Gronow, *Caviar with Champagne: Common Luxury and the Ideals of the Good Life in Stalin's Russia* (New York: Berg, 2004).

3. Ferenc Fehér, Agnes Heller, and György Márkus, *Dictatorship over Needs* (Oxford: Palgrave Macmillan 1986); Ferenc Fehér, "Paternalism as Mode of Legitimation in Soviet-Type Societies," in *Political Legitimation in Communist States*, ed. Thomas H. Rigby and Ferenc Fehér (New York: Palgrave Macmillan, 1982).

4. *Bigosowy socjalizm* is the Polish equivalent of Hungarian "goulash communism." Marcin Zaremba, "'Bigosowy socjalizm.' Dekada Gierka," in *Polacy wobec PRL. Strategie przystosowawcze*, ed. Grzegorz Miernik (Kielce: Kieleckie Towarzystwo Naukowe, 2003).

5. On the agency problem in car distribution see Valery Lazarev and Paul R. Gregory, "The Wheels of a Command Economy," *Economic History Review* 55, no. 2 (May 2002): 324–48.

6. On clientelism in various historical settings see Antoni Mączak, *Klientela* (Warsaw: Semper, 1994).

7. Krzysztof Jasiewicz, "Transport i Łączność," in *Problemy gospodarcze Drugiej Rzeczypospolitej*, ed. Irena Kostrowicka (Warsaw: Państwowe Wydawnictwo Ekonomiczne, 1989), 207.

8. Mirosław Chrzanowski, *Motoryzacja Wojska Polskiego 1921–1939* (Warsaw: Bellona, 2007), 133–58.

9. On PZInż see Jan Tarczyński, Krzysztof Barbarski, and Adam Jońca, *Pojazdy w Wojsku Polskim* (Pruszków: Ajaks, 1995), 86–87; Kazimierz Groniowski, *Technika motoryzacyjna w Polsce w okresie międzywojennym* (Wroclaw: Zakład Narodowy im. Ossolińskich, 1965), 106–12.

10. Józef Makłowicz, *Zmotoryzujmy Polskę* (Warsaw: 1939), 23.

11. Aleksander Rostocki, *Rozwój motoryzacji w planie 6-letnim* (Warsaw: Ministerstwo Obrony Narodowej(Ministry of National Defense), 1951), 51.

12. Karol Jerzy Mórawski, *Syrena. Samochód PRL* (Warsaw: Trio, 2005).

13. *Prace Rady Motoryzacyjnej 1958–1964* (Warsaw: Wydawnictwa Komunikacji i Łączności, 1965), 67–68.

14. Ibid., 69–70.

15. Opinion of the Motorization Council on regulating, through the customs system, imports of cars by private individuals, June 1967, Archiwum Akt Nowych (Archive of Modern Records) (AAN), Główny Urząd Ceł (Central Directorate of Customs) (GUC), 12/37, not paginated.

16. Andrzej Tymowski, "Cztery kółka a budżet domowy," *Życie Gospodarcze*, January 9, 1966, 3.

17. Zbigniew Boniecki, ed., *Jest u nas fabryka w Warszawie. Opowieść o FSO* (Warsaw: Daewoo-FSO, 1999), 75–80.

18. "Polityka cen zgodna z interesami niżej zarabiających grup ludności," *Motor*, no. 22 (1969): 2.

19. "Dlaczego Polski Fiat 125 p kosztuje 180 000 złotych?" *Motor*, nos. 51–52(1969): 7.

20. Andrzej Wróblewski, "Czekając na wehikuł," *Życie Warszawy,* January 29, 1966; Wróblewski, "Hamulce i demokratyzacja," *Życie Warszawy,* February 2, 1966.

21. The first 126p's that had left the factory in the summer of 1973 went to, among others, the construction workers building the Katowice steelworks, the biggest industrial enterprise of the Gierek era. Cf. "Pierwsze PF 126 p w rękach właścicieli," *Motor,* no. 36 (1973): 1.

22. Andrzej Krzysztof Wróblewski, "Samochody dla każdego," *świat,* September 24, 1967.

23. Zdzisław Krasiński, ed., *Rynek motoryzacyjny* (Warsaw: Wydawnictwa Komunikacji i Łączności 1980), 112–13.

24. In 1969, the liberal weekly *Polityka* published an article by Józef Pajestka, a prominent economist, deputy chairman of the governmental Planning Commission and future member of the Party Central Committee. The text was entitled "For a Social Dimension of Motorization" and recommended starting production of a popular car. As Andrzej Krzysztof Wróblewski, a *Polityka* journalist, writing extensively about cars and the car industry, recalls, after the article appeared, the journal received an enormous number of letters from its readers, nearly all in favor of the idea. The top leadership decided, however, that it was too early for an open discussion of Pajestka's ideas. Władysław Gomułka was afraid to awake consumer desires. Wróblewski, *Polska na kółkach* (Warsaw: Iskry 1989), 28–29.

25. Public opinion poll: Social Attitude toward Motorization, Ośrodek Badania Opinii Publicznej (Public Opinion Research Center), March 1977, Archiwum TNS OBOP (Archive of TNS OBOP), 06.114.77.

26. *Rocznik Statystyczny 1980* (Warsaw: Główny Urząd Statystyczny, 1981), 294.

27. *Motor,* no. 7 (1973): 1.

28. Andrzej Klominek, *Życie w "Przekroju"* (Warsaw: Oficyna Wydawnicza Most), 185.

29. AAN, Urząd Rady Ministrów (Office of the Council of Ministers) (URM) 3.1/2, 3.1/3.

30. Tadeusz Mołdawa, *Ludzie władzy* (Warsaw: Wydawnictwo Naukowe PWN, 1991), 178, 328.

31. Jerzy Stembowicz, *Struktura organizacyjna i tryb funkcjonowania rządu PRL* (Warsaw: Centralny Ośrodek Metodyczny Studiów Nauk Politycznych, 1974), 17–21.

32. Włodzimierz P. to the URM, September 27, 1977, AAN, URM 3.1/2, f. 3.

33. Roman Ł. to the URM, January 3, 1978, AAN, URM 3.1/2, f. 22.

34. The Communist Party of Poland was treated as an illegal organization by Polish authorities before the war. In 1938 the party was dissolved by the Communist International. Its leaders were summoned to Moscow and murdered.

35. Janusz S. to the URM, April 12, 1978, AAN, URM 3.1/2, f. 25.

36. Jan K. to the URM, January 4, 1980, AAN, URM 3.1/2, f. 66.

37. Czesław P. to the URM, July 18, 1980, AAN, URM 3.1/3, f. 29.

38. Krysyna K.–T. to the URM, March 25, 1978, AAN, URM 3.1/2, f. 23. See also Note of the Audit Division of the URM on the allotment of coupon for a Wartburg to Krystyna K.-T., April 3, 1978, AAN, URM 3.1/2, f. 17–18.

39. Stanisława R. to the URM, August 18, 1978, AAN, URM 3.1/2, f. 30.

40. Jan M. to the URM, August 12, 1980, AAN, URM 3.1/3, f. 32.

41. Stefan H. to the URM, July 3, 1980, AAN, URM 3.1/3, f. 27.

42. Marian T. to the Office of Veterans, March 13, 1978, AAN, URM 3.1/2, f. 20.

43. Hubert D. to the URM, March 1, 1980, AAN, URM 3.1/3, f. 7.

44. Bożena Z. to the URM, March 11, 1980, AAN, URM 3.1/2, f. 14–15.

45. Piotr D. to the URM, January 8, 1979, AAN, URM 3.1/3, f. 37.

46. AAN, URM 34/60, 34/61.

47. Zofia P., explanatory note, June 28, 1984, AAN, URM 34/60, f. 20–21.

48. Ibid., f. 90.

49. See, for example, the case of Józef P., an official at the Commission for the Management of Trade Union Assets, who requested a car on December 9, 1983, finally receiving it on June 14, 1985. AAN, URM 34/60, f. 256–57.

50. See, for example, Antoni C. to Piotr Karpiuk, August 1983, AAN, URM 34/61, f. 19.

51. A typical example: AAN, URM 34/60, f. 189.

52. Czesław G. to Piotr Karpiuk, February 20, 1984, AAN, URM 34/61, f. 10–11.

53. Marcin Kula et al., *Supliki do najwyższej władzy* (Warsaw: Instytut Studiów Politycznych PAN, 1996). On supplications in the Soviet Union under Stalinism see Lewis H. Siegelbaum, "'Dear Comrade, You Ask What We Need.' Socialist Paternalism and Soviet Rural 'Notables' in the Mid-1930s," *Slavic Review* 57, no. 1 (1998): 107–32.

3 Alternative Modernity?

1. I also raised this issue in an earlier publication. See György Péteri, "Streetcars of Desire: Cars and Automobilism in Communist Hungary (1958–70)," *Social History* 34, no. 1 (2009): 1–28.
2. Cf. ibid., 8.
3. One of these was A. J. Koseljov, *Személyi tulajdon a szocializmusban* [Personal ownership under socialism] (Budapest: Kossuth Könyvkiadó, 1964), the Russian original of which is Aleksandr Iakovlevich Koshelev, *Lichnaia sobstvennost' v sotsialisticheskom obshchestve* (Moscow: Izdatel'stvo sotsialno-ekonomicheskoi literatury, 1963).
4. Artúr Kiss, "A szocialista típusú fogyasztási mód és változásainak egyes kérdései (Elméleti módszertani vázlat) [Selected issues related to the socialist-type mode of consumption and its changes. A theoretical and methodological outline]," *Tájékoztató. Filozófia, Politikai gazdaságtan, Tudományos szocializmus* [Information. Philosophy, political economy, scientific socialism], no. 4 (1973): 42–63.
5. Cf. § 5. on p. 50 of A. Kiss, "A szocialista típusú."
6. Péteri, "Streetcars of Desire," 3.
7. "Lakossági személygépkocsi kereslet 1980-ig" [Private demand for cars until 1980], Budapest, 1974, III/2/16. sz. Melléklet (Appendix nr. 16), by Országos Piackutató Intézet (National Institute for Market Research), in MERKUR Személygépkocsi Értékesítö Vállalat iratai (Papers of the MERKUR Personal Car Retailing Company), XXIX-G-149, box 46, Magyar Országos Levéltár (Hungarian National Archives) (MOL).
8. "Resolution of the HSWP Central Committee Secretariat on Some Problems of Party-Economic and Administrative Management," Budapest, 29 August 1957, Papers of the Department of Party-Economic (*pártgazdasági*) and Administrative Management (PGO) of the HSWP Central Committee, MOL 288. f. 37/1957. 2. öe., fol. 189.
9. MOL 288. f. 37/1957. 1. öe., fol. 80.
10. MOL 288. f. 37/1957. 2. öe., fol. 139.
11. These included such perks as holidays free of charge at resorts owned and maintained by the state, personal use of cars, the establishment and use of telephone lines in the homes of functionaries free of charge, and longer periods of paid holidays than prescribed in the country's labor legislation.
12. Introductory speech by PGO chief, Pálné Laczkó, to the national meeting of economic department leaders of the Budapest and county Party committees, 24 May 1957, MOL 288. f. 37/1957, 5. öe., fols. 28–29.
13. Ibid., fol. 32.
14. Minutes of the PGO meeting of 14 October, 1957. MOL 288. f. 37/1957. 1. öe., fols. 18–29.
15. Minutes of the 8–9 September 1958 meeting with the county economic department chiefs, MOL 288. f. 37/1958. 1. öe., fols. 17–18.
16. Ibid., fol. 18.
17. MOL 288. f. 37/1958. 1. öe., fol. 186.
18. MOL 288. f. 37/1958. 1. öe., fol. 255.
19. MOL 288. f. 37/1960. 6. öe., fols. 246–253.
20. MOL 288. f. 37/1960. 6. öe., fol. 245.
21. MOL 288. f. 37/1967. 4. öe., fol. 149.
22. For reports on dubious practices with waybills prevalent in various county organizations, consult MOL 288. f. 37/1960. 6. öe., fol. 262; MOL 288. f. 37/1960. 6. öe., fol. 259; MOL 288. f. 37/1960. 6. öe., fol. 263; MOL 288. f. 37/1960. 6. öe., fol. 264; MOL 288. f. 37/1961. 1. öe., fol. 221; MOL 288. f. 37/1962. 5. öe., fol. 263; MOL 288. f. 37/1962. 6. öe., fol. 9; MOL 288. f. 37/1962. 6. öe., fols. 65–66; MOL 288. f. 37/1964. 7. öe., fol. 33; MOL 288. f. 37/1965. 6. öe., fol. 98; MOL 288. f. 37/1965. 7. öe., fols.

58 ff; MOL 288. f. 37/1965. 7. öe., fols. 123 ff; MOL 288. f. 37/1965. 8. öe., fol. 79; MOL 288. f. 37/1966. 3. öe., fol. 125; MOL 288. f. 37/1966. 3. öe., fol. 152; MOL 288. f. 37/1966. 4. öe., fol. 32; MOL 288. f. 37/1966. 5. öe., fol. 12; MOL 288. f. 37/1966. 5. öe., fol. 71; MOL 288. f. 37/1966. 6. öe., fol. 344; MOL 288. f. 37/1967. 3. öe., fol. 48; MOL 288. f. 37/1967. 4. öe., fol. 87; MOL 288. f. 37/1967. 4. öe., fol. 82; MOL 288. f. 37/1968. 3. öe., fol. 79; MOL 288. f. 37/1968. 3. öe., fol. 229; MOL 288. f. 37/1968. 5. öe., fol. 60; MOL 288. f. 37/1972. 6. öe., fol. 166; MOL 288. f. 37/1973. 4. öe., fol. 60; MOL 288. f. 37/1974. 3. öe., fols. 214–215; MOL 288. f. 37/1976. 6. öe., fol. 92; MOL 288. f. 37/1977. 3. öe., fol. 140; MOL 288. f. 37/1977. 3. öe., fol. 190; MOL 288. f. 37/1977. 4. öe., fol. 70; MOL 288. f. 37/1977. 6. öe., fol. 115.; MOL 288. f. 37/1980. 13. öe., fol. 84. For documents commenting on malpractice with regard to waybill administration prevalent in the country as a whole and in groups of counties see MOL 288. f. 37/1961. 2. öe., fol. 216; in the Communist Youth Organization: MOL 288. f. 37/1963. 6. öe., fol. 98; MOL 288. f. 37/1964. 1. öe., fol. 46; MOL 288. f. 37/1967. 4. öe., fol. 149; MOL 288. f. 37/1960. 6. öe., fol. 262; MOL 288. f. 37/1973. 1. öe., fol. 107. On dubious practices of waybill administration in the case of the Central Committee apparatus, consult MOL 288. f. 37/1960. 14. öe., fols. 57 ff. and fols. 96 ff.

23. "The relationship between county political leaders and chauffeurs is not always appropriate," PGO chief Laczkó commented in 1958. "They would often spend hours together in revelries, but don't have enough time for political work. In one case, nine cars appeared at one particular place [in connection with a drinking party] from eleven districts." (MOL 288. f. 37/1958. 1. öe., fol. 7.) For other comments on the "unprincipled" [*elvtelen*] relationship between political employees of the party and chauffeurs see MOL 288. f. 37/1958. 1. öe., fol. 186; MOL 288. f. 37/1959. 1. öe., fol. 22; MOL 288. f. 37/1960. 14. öe., fol. 59; MOL 288. f. 37/1967. 4. öe., fol. 143.

24. MOL 288. f. 37/1969. 1. öe., fols. 148 ff.

25. MOL 288. f. 7/1972. 407. öe., fol. 23.

26. MOL 288. f. 37/1971. 2. öe., fol. 30.

27. MOL 288. f. 37/1973. 2. öe., fol. 10.

28. Investigating their waybills, the PGO found in one county in 1958 that over a ten-month period the apparatus used, without entitlements or permissions, more than 5,000 car-kilometers for private purposes (MOL 288. f. 37/1958. 1. öe., fol. 186). Assuming that this applied to all the eighteen counties and Budapest and extending the hypothetical period to a whole year, we get close to 120,000 kilometers of irregular car use. But this was in 1958, when the apparatus was half as big as in 1971. Therefore, it is not implausible to believe that the extent of irregular car use was close to the total of legitimate entitlements for private use in the early 1970s.

29. MOL 288. f. 37/1957. 1. öe., fols. 102–105.

30. MOL 288. f. 37/1964. 3. öe., fols. 20–21.

31. MOL 288. f. 37/1964. 5. öe., fol. 12.

32. MOL 288. f. 37/1965. 2. öe., fol. 26.

33. For documents concerning preparatory investigations, background, and even interdepartmental conflicts over the decree, see the papers of the Central Commission of People's Control, MOL XVII-2-a 13. t.-424. tsz—a–1976, box 210.

34. MOL 288. f. 7/1972. 407. öe. fols. 1–38.

35. Indeed, the economic and technical management of the cars belonging to top Party and government officials had been taken care of, ever since the early 1960s, by the security services [*Kormányörség*] under the Ministry of Interior and not by the so-called Party garage supervised by the PGO.

36. MOL 288. f. 37/1973. 1. öe., fols. 106–107.

37. MOL 288 f. 7/1978. 541. öe., fol. 9.

38. MOL 288. f. 37/1958. 1. öe., fols. 184–85.

39. MOL 288. f. 37/1959. 1. öe., fol. 3.

40. MOL 288. f. 37/1960. 14. öe., fols. 57–58.

41. MOL 288. f. 37/1961. 1. öe., fol. 26.

42. For a few of the many cases, consult MOL 288. f. 37/1960. 3. öe. fol. 47; MOL 288. f. 37/1960. 3. öe., fol. 136; MOL 288. f. 37/1961. 4. öe., fol. 151.

43. MOL 288. f. 37/1963. 6. öe., fol. 98–99.

44. MOL 288. f. 37/1964. 3. öe., fols. 57–58.

45. MOL 288. f. 37/1965. 2. öe., fols. 26–28.
46. MOL 288. f. 37/1967. 4. öe., fols. 145–146.
47. MOL 288. f. 37/1977. 8. öe., fol. 79.
48. MOL 288. f. 37/1958. 1. öe., fol. 144.
49. MOL 288. f. 37/1958. 1. öe., fols. 413–414.
50. MOL 288. f. 37/1957. 1. öe., fols. 251–253.
51. The PGO put forward a proposal to increase the number of cars available for district Party committees with the argument that "besides cars, other means of transport either because of their timetables or because of the health hazards involved in their use, can be resorted to only under specific conditions" (MOL 288. f. 37/1960. 14. öe., fol. 51). Indeed, riding motorbikes in the winter was not good for anyone's health; and it is also quite probable that collective transport outside county centers and other cities was hardly comparable to that in the networks binding Budapest and the county centers together.
52. MOL 288. f. 37/1959. 2. öe., fol. 94.
53. MOL 288. f. 37/1977. 4. öe., fol. 102.
54. For revealing proportions between the tiny sums (budgeted and) used for collective transports and the enormous amounts going into the use of cars, see MOL 288. f. 37/1960. 14. öe., fol. 58; MOL 288. f. 37/1960. 14. öe., fol. 96; MOL 288. f. 37/1965. 2. öe., fol. 26; MOL 288. f. 37/1968. 2. öe., fols. 41–42; MOL 288. f. 37/1969. 2. öe., fols. 50–51; MOL 288. f. 37/1970. 3. öe., fol. 106; MOL 288. f. 37/1974. 2. öe., fol. 63; MOL 288. f. 37/1978. 7. öe., fols. 51–52.
55. MOL 288. f. 37/1971. 2. öe., fol. 30.
56. MOL 288. f. 37/1971. 3. öe., fol. 1. This measure was then confirmed by the resolutions of the Central Committee Secretariat of December 20, 1971, in connection with its discussions about the budget of 1972. MOL 288. f. 37/1971. 2. öe., fols. 138–141.
57. MOL 288. f. 7/1972. 407. öe., fol. 27.
58. In 1972, 1.2 million car-kilometers were accumulated in chauffeurless Party cars—which corresponded approximately to the annual workload of forty to fifty professional chauffeurs. This brought with it an economy of 1.3 million Fts. MOL 288. f. 37/1973. 1. öe., fol. 108.
59. Ibid.
60. MOL 288. f. 37/1977. 3. öe., fol. 7.
61. MOL 288. f. 37/1977. 10. öe., fol. 125.
62. MOL 288. f. 371958. 1. öe., fols. 359ff.
63. MOL 288. f. 37/1959. 11. öe., fols. 43–44.
64. See, for example, MOL 288. f. 37/1961. 2. öe., fols. 208 ff. and MOL 288. f. 37/1962. 1. öe., fols. 137–138.
65. For a detailed instruction for the implementation of the resolution of June 11, 1963, see MOL 288. f. 37/1963. 7. öe., fol. 18. New additional regulations, in accordance with the norms obtaining in state administration, were issued in 1965. MOL 288. f. 37/1965. 3. öe., fol. 69.
66. On these concerns see MOL 288. f. 37/1965. 2. öe., fols. 106–107.
67. MOL 288. f. 37/1966. 6. öe., fols. 149–151.
68. MOL 288. f. 37/1973 [1971]. 1. öe., fol. 63.
69. MOL 288. f. 37/1971. 2. öe., fol. 30.
70. MOL 288. f. 37/1973. 4. öe., fol. 70.
71. MOL 288. f. 37/1973. 1. öe., fols. 100–101.
72. MOL 288. f. 37/1974. 1. öe., fol. 93.
73. MOL 288. f. 37/1974. 4. öe., fol. 133.
74. MOL 288. f. 37/1974. 4. öe., fols. 100–111.
75. MOL 288. f. 37/1974. 4. öe., fols. 66–68.
76. MOL 288. f. 37/1974. 3. öe., fols. 158–159.
77. MOL 288. f. 37/1977 1. öe., fol. 73.
78. MOL 288. f. 37/1977. 1. öe., fols. 73–75. See also MOL 288. f. 37/1978. 10. öe., fols. 99–109. For the details of a car sales campaign, see the PGO's reports for 1978 (MOL 288. f. 37/1979. 1. öe., fols. 36–38) and for 1979 (MOL 288. f. 37/1979. 3. öe., fols. 248–249).

79. MOL 288. f. 37/1978. 1. öe., fols. 82–83.
80. MOL 288. f. 37/1981. 6. öe., fol. 30 (emphasis added).

4 Planning for Mobility

1. Barbara Schmucki, *Der Traum vom Verkehrsfluss. Städtische Verkehrsplanung seit 1945 im deutsch-deutschen Vergleich* (Frankfurt: Campus, 2001), 117.
2. Mike Featherstone, "Automobilities: An introduction," *Theory, Culture & Society* 21, nos. 4–5 (2004): 1–24; John Urry, "The 'System' of Automobility," *Theory, Culture & Society* 21, nos. 4–5 (2004): 25–39.
3. Russian: *obshchestvennyi tsentr*; German: *Mittelpunkt des gesellschaftlichen Lebens*.
4. See, for example, Andrei Ivanov's chapter on the development of Togliatti between planning and self-organization, "The City of Tolyatti as a Socio-Urban Phenomenon," in *New Towns for the 21st Century: The Planned vs. The Unplanned City*, ed. Michelle Provoost (Amsterdam: SUN, 2010), 116–35. I thank the author for his helpful comments on this chapter.
5. Deutsche Bauakademie, ed., "Grundsätze der Planung und Gestaltung sozialistischer Stadtzentren," *Deutsche Architektur*, no. 8 (1960), special supplement.
6. Frank Betker, "Der öffentliche Raum in der 'sozialistischen Stadt': Städtebau in der DDR zwischen Utopie und Alltag," in *Geschichte der Planung des öffentlichen Raums*, ed. Christoph Bernhardt (Dortmund: IRPUD, 2005), 153–63, 155.
7. On the constructivist heritage and the orientation toward international architectural models, cf. Stephen V. Bittner, *The Many Lives of Khrushchev's Thaw: Experience and Memory in Moscow's Arbat* (Ithaca: Cornell University Press, 2008), 105–40, and Anna Bronovickaja, "Dreams of Something Distant: Soviet Architecture and the West from Thaw to Perestroika," *Project Russia* 34 (2004): 89–104.
8. See Angelus Eisinger, *Die Stadt der Architekten. Anatomie einer Selbstdemontage* (Basel: Birkhäuser, 2006), for an analytical approach to urbanism as a sociopolitical practice.
9. For the purposes of this chapter, production of space is understood as defined by Henri Lefebvre, encompassing the conception, representation, and lived experience of space. Henri Lefebvre, *The Production of Space* (Oxford: Blackwell, 1991 [1974]).
10. V.A. Lavrov, "Arkhitektura gorodskogo tsentra," *Arkhitektura SSSR*, no. 3 (1960): 38–44.
11. For the USSR, see R. Khametskii, "Nekotorye strukturnye osobennosti tsentra sovremennogo goroda," *Arkhitektura SSSR*, 1964, no. 9, 11–15, and Lewis Siegelbaum, *Cars for Comrades: The Life of the Soviet Automobile* (Ithaca: Cornell University Press, 2008), 84–87; for the GDR, see Schmucki, *Der Traum vom Verkehrsfluss*, 140, and Wolfgang Weigel, *Verkehr in der modernen Stadt* (Berlin: VEB Transpress, 1962), 85–88.
12. At least for some important segments of society, such as skilled workers in the new industries and higher cadres in politics, engineering, or research, this mobility also became a real-life experience. In one case engineers of the automobile plant at Togliatti were flown to Moscow by company plane and chauffeured along the capital's new highways in limousines. See Nordica Nettleton, "Driving towards Consumerism: AvtoVAZ," *Cahiers du monde russe* 47 (2006): 131–51.
13. Preparations for this restructuring date back to the late 1940s, when promising architects like Mikhail Posokhin, who was to become city architect of Moscow in 1960 and a top figure in the State Committee for Civilian Construction (Gosgrazhdanstroi), were developing experimental methods and designs for cost-efficient building based on industrial production of standard elements. Bittner's remark, in *Many Lives of Khrushchev's Thaw*, 110, that this happened "apparently on a lark" seems not very convincing.
14. Cf. Khametskii, "Nekotorye strukturnye osobennosti"; V.A. Lavrov, *Gorod i ego obshchestvennyi tsentr* (Moscow: Stroiizdat, 1964); N.V. Baranov, *Kompozitsiia tsentra goroda* (Moscow: Stroiizdat, 1964); Hans Schmidt et al., *Funktion und Komposition der Stadtzentren. Untersuchungen am Beispiel der Stadtzentren Berlin, Leipzig, Dresden und Karl-Marx-Stadt* (Berlin: Deutsche Bauinformation, 1967), Klaus Andrä, "Umgestaltung von Stadtzentren," *Architektur der DDR*, no. 10 (1967): 584–87; Bruno

Flierl, "Der Zentrale Ort in Berlin. Zur räumlichen Inszenierung sozialistischer Zentralität," in *Kunstdokumentation SBZ/DDR 1945–1990*, ed. G. Feist et al. (Cologne: DuMont, 1996), 320–57.

15. *Vsesoiuznoe soveshchanie po transportnomu stroitel'stvu, 17–18 apr. 1959 g. Sbornik trudov* (Moscow: Gosstroiizdat, 1960); *Vsesoiuznoe soveshchanie po gradostroitel'stvu; 7–10 iiunia 1960 g. Sokrashchennyi stenograficheskii otchet* (Moscow: Gosstroiizdat, 1960).

16. V. A. Kucherenko, "Über den Stand und die Maßnahmen zur Verbesserung des Städtebaus in der UdSSR," in *Städtebau in der Sowjetunion. Materialien der Allunionskonferenz zu Fragen des Städtebaus, Moskau, Juni 1960*, ed. Deutsche Bauakademie (Berlin: Deutsche Bauinformation 1960), 9–27, 15.

17. Peter Doehler, "Rekonstruktion der Stadtzentren," in *Kolloquium für Städtebau*, vol. 1 (Weimar: Hochschule für Architektur und Bauwesen Weimar, 1960), 11–13.

18. These institutions included the Central Research and Planning Institute for Urban Planning (CNIIP Gradostroitel'stva); the Research Institute for History, Theory and Prospective Problems of Soviet Architecture in Moscow; and their GDR equivalents, the Institute for Regional, Urban and Rural Planning and the Institute of the Theory and History of Architecture, both branches of the Deutsche Bauakademie in Berlin. See Schmucki, *Der Traum vom Verkehrsfluss*, 86, on the development of traffic planning research and literature in the GDR.

19. See, e.g., CNIIP Gradostroitel'stva, ed., *Osnovy sovetskogo gradostroitel'va*, vol. 1–4 (Moscow: Stroiizdat, 1966, 1967, and 1969); V. A. Cherepanov, *Transport v gradostroitel'stve* (Moscow: Stroiizdat, 1964).

20. Lavrov, "Arkhitektura," 42; Weigel, *Verkehr*, 7–8, 42.

21. Kucherenko, "Über den Stand," 17.

22. Weigel, *Verkehr*; Manuel Sanchez-Arcas, *Stadt und Verkehr. Verkehrs- und Stadtplanung in den USA und in Westeuropa* (Berlin: Deutsche Bauakademie, 1968).

23. Interviews with Bruno Flierl, editor of the GDR's most important journal for architecture, *Deutsche Architektur* from 1962–65, Berlin, August 2008; with Il'ia Lezhava and Viacheslav Loktev, today professors and in the early 1960s doctoral students at the Moscow Architectural Institute, Moscow, December 2008; and with Evgenii Ass, who regularly read lectures on foreign architecture at the Moscow House of Architects in the 1960s and 1970s, Moscow, December 2010. See also Bronovickaja, "Dreams of Something Distant."

24. Lavrov, *Gorod*, 136.

25. Nettleton, "Driving towards Consumerism," 132. In interviews, Bruno Flierl and Il'ia Lezhava pointed out how closely publications on architectural theory were supervised by the party organs of the GDR and the USSR during the 1960s. Flierl himself was removed as editor of the journal *Deutsche Architektur* for ideological mistakes in the mid-1960s. His subsequent theoretical publication *Gesellschaft und Architektur in unserer Epoche. Ein Beitrag zur architekturtheoretischen Forschung in der ideologischen Auseinandersetzung zwischen Sozialismus und Kapitalismus* (Berlin: Deutsche Bauakademie, 1973) is an instructive balancing act between an ideological justification and a serious engagement with contemporary urban theory.

26. Thomas Topfstedt, *Städtebau in der DDR 1955–1971* (Leipzig: Seemann, 1988), 49; Betker, "Der öffentliche Raum," 155.

27. Lavrov, "Arkhitektura," 43–44; Khametskii, "Nekotorye strukturnye osobennosti."

28. See Dorothea Tscheschner, "Der Alexanderplatz unter der Hypothek des Verkehrs," in *Das Alexanderhaus. Der Alexanderplatz*, ed. Hans-Joachim Pysall (Berlin: Jovis, 1998), 55–76, 72.

29. N. N. "Tvorcheskie zadachi proektirovaniia gorodskikh tsentrov," *Arkhitektura SSSR*, no. 5 (1968): 1–12; and Orders of the State Committee for Civic Building (Gosgrazhdanstroi), Rossiiskii Gosudarstvennyi Arkhiv Ekonomiki (RGAE), f. 5, op. 1, d. 12, 23, 436, 743, 903.

30. Khametskii, "Nekotorye strukturnye osobennosti"; Weigel, *Verkehr*, 117, argues that arterial roads could generate a new experience of the cityscape "like rivers."

31. Tscheschner, "Der Alexanderplatz," 68. See also Weigel, *Verkehr*, 76. In spring 1964, a delegation of seven GDR planners led by the Berlin city architect, Joachim Näther, spent a week in Moscow to discuss variants of the traffic solution at the CNIIP gradostroitel'stva and the Institute for the General Plan of Moscow, with consultations by leading Soviet planners such as N. Baranov and M. Posokhin. Correspondence in RGAE, f. 5, op. 1, d. 277, 7–8.

32. Gisa Weszkalnys, "Alexanderplatz. An Ethnographic Study of Place and Planning in Contemporary Berlin" (PhD diss., Cambridge University, 2004).

33. I. L. Buseva-Davydova et al., *Moskva: Architekturnyi putevoditel'* (Moscow: Stroiizdat, 1996).

34. See Bittner, *Many Lives of Khrushchev's Thaw*, and the interpretation of Prospekt Kalinina as "Soviet Times Square" by Monica Rüthers, *Moskau bauen von Lenin bis Chrušćev* (Vienna: Böhlau, 2007), 212.

35. A. Baburov, A. Gutnov et al., *Novyi element rasseleniia. Na puti k novomu gorodu* (Moscow: Stroiizdat, 1966), published in English as *The Ideal Communist City* (New York: Braziller, 1971); Zinaida N. Iargina, *Gorod budushchego* (Moscow: Znanie, 1968), published in the GDR as *Die Stadt der Zukunft* (Berlin: Urania, 1969); A. Ikonnikov, "La ville de demain," *Architecture d'aujourd'hui* 147 (1969–70): 5–8; Michel Ragon, "Recherches actuelles en U.R.S.S.," *Urbanisme* 127–28 (1972): 36–40.

36. Jane A. Sharp, "The Personal Visions and Public Spaces of the Movement Group," in *Cold War Modern Design 1945–1970*, ed. David Crowley and Jane Pavitt (London: V&A Publishing, 2008), 234–41.

37. Published in Justus Dahinden, *Stadtstrukturen für morgen* (Stuttgart: Hatje, 1971), 82–83.

38. These parameters for an ideal functional and socialist city reach back to the international urbanist debates of the 1920s and 1930s in the context of the Congrès Internationaux d'Architecture Moderne (International Congresses of Modern Architecture—CIAM) and in the Soviet Union. Cf. Nikolai A. Miliutin, *Sotsgorod* (Moscow: Gosudarstvennoe Izdatel'stvo 1930); Harald Bodenschatz, Christiane Post, eds., *Städtebau im Schatten Stalins, Die internationale Suche nach der sozialistischen Stadt in der Sowjetunion 1929–1935* (Berlin: Verlagshaus Braun, 2004).

39. Mikhail Posokhin, *Gorod dlia cheloveka* (Moscow: Izd. Agentstva Pechati Novosti, 1973); N. N., "Tvorcheskie zadachi," 2–5; Timothy J. Colton, *Moscow: Governing the Socialist Metropolis* (Cambridge, MA: Belknap Press, 1995), 456–75.

40. Given the slow pace of car production, the threat would have been an ultimate overcrowding of public transport rather than unresolvable traffic jams.

41. A. Vedeneev et al., "Zelenograd," *Arkhitektura SSSR*, no. 10 (1969): 4–25; Pierre Merlin, "Urbanisme et villes nouvelles en Union Soviétique," *Cahiers de l'IAURP* 38 (1974): 43.

42. Designing such generic New Towns was a common diploma topic at the Moscow Architecture Institute (MARCHI) from the late 1950s, as the albums kept in the Institute's Archive illustrate. For Siberian New Towns, see Barbara Engel, *Öffentliche Räume in den blauen Städten Russlands. Entwicklungen, Status und Perspektiven* (Tübingen: Wasmuth, 2004).

43. See V. A. Shkvarikov, *Gradostroitel'stvo SSSR 1917–1967* (Moscow: Izd. literatury po stroitel'stvu, 1967), 317.

44. The special role attributed to automobility in this carmaking city has already been highlighted in a comprehensive local history project by AvtoVAZ and by Siegelbaum, *Cars for Comrades*, and Nettleton, "Driving towards Consumerism." See also S. I. Lysova, *Geograficheskie osobennosti formirovaniia goroda Tol'iatti* (Togliatti: Akademiia upravleniia, 2004).

45. Albrecht Wiesener, "Als die Zukunft noch nicht vergangen war—Der Aufbau der Chemiearbeiterstadt Halle-Neustadt 1958–1980," in *Geschichte der Stadt Halle*, vol. 2, ed. Werner Freitag and Katrin Minner (Halle: MDV, 2006), 442–56, 450.

46. See, e.g., "Novye goroda," *Dekorativnoe iskusstvo SSSR*, 1970, 4, 14–22; Evgenii Astakhov, *Tol'iatti—Gorod na Volge. Fotoal'bom* (Moscow: Sovetskaia Rossiia, 1983); Gerald Große and Hans Jürgen Steinmann, *Zwei an der Saale: Halle/Halle-Neustadt* (Leipzig: VEB F.A. Brockhaus, 1979), 10, 24, 28–31, 134–39.

47. Nettleton, "Driving towards Consumerism," 132.

5 Automobility in Yugoslavia between Urban Planner, Market, and Motorist

1. Mike Featherstone, "Automobilities: An introduction," *Theory, Culture & Society* 21, nos. 4–5 (2004): 1–24; John Urry, "The 'System' of Automobility," *Theory, Culture & Society* 21, nos. 4–5 (2004): 25–39.

2. The reverse was also true: the reconstruction of Skopje in 1963 served as a learning experience for urban planners from all over Yugoslavia, including Belgrade. Milica Janković, "Nova prigradska naselja u Skoplju," *Arhitektura Urbanizam* 28 (1964): 36–41.

3. Urban planning at this time was seen as a subcomponent of the architectural profession. Belgrade's Visoka Tehnička Škola did not offer a program in urban planning. Instead, an urban planning course was offered to architecture students. "Referat organizacije narodne omladine arhitektonslog fakultet tehniccke velike škole u Beogradu," *Arhitektura* 1–2 (1950): 63–64.

4. The composition of the planning team can be found in Beograd: *Generalni urbanistički plan 1950* (Belgrade: Izdanje izvršnog odbora N.O. Beograda, 1951), 3.

5. Le Corbusier, *The Athens Charter* (New York: Grossman Publishers, 1973), 79–85; Le Corbusier, *The Radiant City* (New York: Orion Press, 1964 [first published 1933]), 119–21.

6. Le Corbusier, *The Radiant City*, 121–26.

7. Miloš Crvčanin, "Saobraćaj Beograda," in *Beograd: Generalni urbanistički plan 1950* (Belgrade: Izdanje izvršnog odbora N.O. Beograda, 1951), 97–98.

8. Nikola Gavrilović, "Kolovozni saobraćaj," in *Beograd*, 108–12.

9. Vido Vrbanić, "Urbanistički plan Novog Beograda," in *Beograd*, 118–34.

10. The Athens Charter, arts. 65–72.

11. Vrbanić, "Urbanistički plan Novog Beograda," 121, 123.

12. Michel Paileret, "The Rise and Fall of Yugoslav Socialism: A Case Study of the Yugo Automobile Enterprise, 1954–1992," in *Economic Transformations in East and Central Europe*, ed. David F. Good (London: Routledge, 1994), 93–109.

13. "Prednost domaćim automobilima umesto povećanog uvoza," *Borba*, June 15, 1968. Advertisements: "Škoda: Kvalitet sigurnost udobnost i ekonomičnost," *Borba*, May 4, 1968; "Mazda: Drumska lepotica dalekog istoka," *Politika*, May 4, 1968; "Wartburg: Limuzina i karavan," *Politika*, May 4, 1968; "Novo!!! Novi tip—ista cena," *Politika*, May 25, 1968; "Volvo: Brz, siguran, dugotrajan," *Borba*, September 11, 1968.

14. "Do kraja godine 59 novih benzinskih stanica," *Borba*, June 25, 1968.

15. "Na kredit! Bez žiranata! Mini Wash," *Politika*, May 8, 1968.

16. "Iz sadržaja revije auto (br. 4)," *Politika*, May 30, 1968.

17. "Za motorizovane turiste," *Borba*, May 24, 1968.

18. "Neko vikend, neko kuću," *Beogradska Nedelja*, August 28, 1966. On the dacha see Stephen Lovell, *Summerfolk: A History of the Dacha, 1710–2000* (Ithaca: Cornell University Press, 2003); on the chata see Paulina Bren, "Weekend Getaways: The Chata, the Tramp and the Politics of Private Life in Post-1968 Czechoslovakia," in *Socialist Spaces: Sites of Everyday Life in the Eastern Bloc*, ed. David Crowley and Susan E. Reid (Oxford: Berg, 2002).

19. See Auto Moto Savez Serbije (the Automobile Association of Serbia), http://www.yurally.co.rs/ (accessed December 14, 2008).

20. Bratislav Stojanović, "Blok 1 i 2," *Urbanizam Beograda*, no. 30 (1975): 28.

21. Stojanka Stošić, "Mesna zajednica u bloc 29," *Urbanizam Beograda*, no. 25 (1974): 21.

22. *Generalni urbanistički plan Beograda* (Belgrade: Beogradski izdavačko-grafički zavod, 1972), 26.

23. Ibid., 62–64.

24. Radomir Mišić, "Higijenski aspekti urbanističkog planiranja Beograda," *Urbanizam Beograda*, supplement for XV Savetovanje urbanista Jugoslavije, October 16–17, 1969, 41–43.

25. *Generalni urbanistički plan Beograda*, 11–12.

26. Ibid., 26, 94, 96.

27. Miloš Perović, "Procesi urbanog planiranja sedme decenije u Jugoslaviji" (PhD diss., University of Belgrade, 1983).

28. On the topic of urban planners' commitment to collectivist modes of consuming housing, see Brigitte Le Normand, "Make No Little Plan: Modernist Projects and Spontaneous Growth in Belgrade, 1945–1967," *East Central Europe* 33, nos. 1–2 (2006): 241–64.

29. *Generalni urbanistički plan Beograda*, 26.

30. Ibid., 115.

31. Ibid., 114–15.

6 On the Streets of a Truck-Building City

1. At the urging of the local residents, who had never referred to themselves as "brezhnevtsy," the town got its original name back in 1988. "Postanovlenie Tsentral'nogo Komiteta KPSS, Prezidiuma Verkhovnogo Soveta SSSR i Soveta Ministrov SSSR ob uvekovechenii pamiati Leonida Il'icha Brezhneva," *Znamia kommunizma,* November 24, 1982; "S vozvrashcheniem, Naberezhnye Chelny! V TsK KPSS, Prezidiuma Verkhovnogo Soveta SSSR, Soveta Ministrov SSSR," *Znamia kommunizma,* January 8, 1988.
2. In the Soviet context, an apartment of one's own does not mean that people owned their apartments but that they did not share them with other parties (as in a *kommunalka*).
3. *KamAZ, organizatsiia stroitel'stva i proizvodstvo stroitel'nykh rabot,* dlia sluzhebnogo pol'zovaniia, eks. no. 003438 (Moscow: Stroiizdat, 1986), 111–13; Iagfar Garipov, "Molodye goroda: Formirovanie naseleniia, mezhnatsional'nye i mezhkonfessional'nye otnosheniia," *Islam v tatarskom mire, istoriia i sovremennost', materialy mezhdunarodnogo simpoziuma, Kazan' 29 aprelia–1 maia 1996 g., Panorama-forum,* special issue, no. 12 (1997): 266–77.
4. "Dokumenty rasskazyvaiut, dokladnaia zapiska Ministra A. Tarasova v Sovet Ministrov SSSR," in *Prikam'e,* al'manakh no. 8 (Naberezhnye Chelny: KO Nizhniaia Kama, 1989), 7; B. Rubanenko and R. Pateev, "Naberezhnye Chelny. Proektirovanie, stroitel'stvo," *Arkhitektura SSSR,* no. 8 (1976): 5–23.
5. *KamAZ, organizatsiia i proizvodstvo montazhnykh i spetsial'nykh rabot,* dlia sluzhebnogo pol'zovaniia, eks. no. 000767 (Moscow: Stroiizdat, 1986), 4; Rubanenko and Pateev, "Naberezhnye Chelny," 6.
6. "Sekretar' gorkoma KPSS N. Shkatov pervomu sekretariu Tatarskogo obkoma KPSS tov. Tabeevu F.A.," 26 June 1969, Tsentral'nyi Gosudarstvennyi Arkhiv Istoriko-Politicheskoi Dokumentatsii Respubliki Tatarstan (TsGA IPD RT), f. 7403, op. 1, d. 169, l. 1; "Ukaz Prezidiuma Verkhovnogo Soveta RSFSR No. 916 ob utverzhdenii vkliucheniia v sostav goroda Brezhneva Tatarskoi ASSR nekotorykh naselennykh punktov Tukaevskogo raiona," *Vedomosti Verkhovnogo Soveta RSFSR,* no. 28 (1342) (1987): 666 (decree dated July 12, 1987); A. Dubrovskii, ed., *Sosedi Naberezhnykh Chelnov* (Naberezhnye Chelny: KO Nizhniaia Kama, 2000); R. G. Aisin, ed., *V zolotykh ogniakh gidrostantsii*... (Naberezhnye Chelny: Tatarstanskoe otdelenie Soiuza rossiiskikh pisatelei, 2004).
7. Western researchers use the term "social contract" to describe relations between the political leadership and the population in the post-Stalinist Soviet Union. One contracting party provides social security and promotes the production of consumer goods; the other provides its participation at the cost of its civil rights.
8. KamAZ produced and produces for the army as well, however. The trucks were used in the war in Afghanistan.
9. Interview with Nikolai Aleshkov, Naberezhnye Chelny, November 11, 2004.
10. Nikolai Aleshkov, "Vse uzhe krug moikh druzei," in *Lebedi nad Chelnami* (Moscow: Izvestiia, 1981), 43–44.
11. The Village Prose movement began during the Thaw. Its proponents—Valentin Rasputin, Viktor Astaf'ev, Vasilii Bykov, and others—drew a nostalgic picture of traditional, dying villages. In the Brezhnev era, the Village Prose writers played an ambivalent role: they were harshly criticized for idealizing the patriarchal past, yet at the same time they were allowed to publish their works and were among the most popular writers of the time. See Geoffrey Hosking, *Beyond Socialism: Soviet Fiction since Ivan Denisovich* (New York: Holmes and Meier, 1980), 50–83.
12. Monica Rüthers, *Moskau bauen von Lenin bis Chruščev. Öffentliche Räume zwischen Utopie, Terror und Alltag* (Vienna: Böhlau, 2007), 59–72; Rüthers, "Images of a Better Life: Visual Culture and Soviet Consumer Taste during the Thaw" (paper presented at the ICCEES Congress in Berlin, July 26, 2005).
13. Rubanenko and Pateev, "Naberezhnye Chelny," 5–7; Archives of the Architects' Association of Naberezhnye Chelny, general plan, GP 262, l. 32 (I was denied access to the archives of the Architects' Association, but I was allowed to see this file with the information presented here, which, unfortunately, is not precise); "Spravki sel'sko-khoziaistvennogo otdela obkomu KPSS o razvitii sel'skogo khoziaistva v sviazi so stroitel'stvom KamAZa, nachato 13 aprelia 1970 g., okoncheno 5 iiunia 1970 g. R.

Belaiev Ministru sel'skogo khoziaistva TASSR tovarishchu Minushevu, F.Kh.," 24 April 1970, TsGA IPD RT, f. 7403, op. 1, d. 199, l. 3–4.

14. Arturo Soría y Mata, *Tratados de urbanismo y sociedad* (Madrid: Clan Ed, 2004).

15. Frederick S. Starr, "Visionary Town Planning during the Cultural Revolution," in *Cultural Revolution in Russia, 1928–1931,* ed. Sheila Fitzpatrick (Bloomington: Indiana University Press, 1978), 207–40.

16. N. A. Miliutin, *Sotsgorod: The Problem of Building Socialist Cities* (Cambridge, MA: MIT Press, 1974).

17. Barbara Engel, *Öffentliche Räume in den blauen Städten Russlands. Entwicklungen, Status und Perspektiven. Funktionale und räumliche Anforderungen an die Erneuerung öffentlicher Räume in den neuen Industriestädten Sibiriens unter veränderten sozioökonomischen Bedingungen* (Tübingen: Wasmuth, 2004), 58, 83–88.

18. Miliutin, *Sotsgorod,* 65.

19. The implementation of this principle cannot be discussed in detail here. Suffice it to mention that considerable disparities existed in the standard of living among the population of Naberezhnye Chelny during the Brezhnev era, though segregation according to social or ethnic criteria remained largely absent.

20. For the Garden City movement, see Ebenezer Howard, *To-morrow: A Peaceful Path to Real Reform* (1898; repr., London: Routledge, 2003). Howard proposed self-contained urban units for approximately thirty thousand people. Each house should have its own garden.

21. N. V. Gogol', *Mertvye dushi* (Moscow: Eksmo, 2006), 384.

22. A. A. Adamesku and A. G. Dubrovskii, "Naberezhnye Chelny—gorod budushchego," *Geografiia v shkole,* no. 5 (1979): 6.

23. "Zhiloi raion No. I," *Vse o KamAZe,* no. 3 (1973): 59.

24. The oil crises led to a gradual return of the streetcar to the cities of the West.

25. V. Nilov, I. Cherezov, S. Magai, and M. Bibishev, "Tsentr goroda: Byt' ili ne byt'," *Znamia kommunizma,* November 26, 1988. See also the account of a tram driver: Lev Sherstennikov, *Tsvet Chelnov (Avtograd)* (Moscow: Molodaia gvardiia, 1976), 100.

26. "Spravka o rabote partiinogo komiteta i general'noi direktsii Kamskogo ob"edineniia po proizvodstvu bol'shegruznykh avtomobilei po podboru, rasstanovke i zakrepleniiu kadrov," 6 April 1979, TsGA IPD RT, f. 7403, op. 1, d. 435, l. 17; Gumer Nuretdinov, "My mnogoe sokhranili," in *Chelovecheskii faktor* (Naberezhnye Chelny, 1999), 74.

27. Nuretdinov, "My mnogoe sokhranili," 74.

28. M. A. Smirnova-Bukharaeva, "Priznanie v . . . neliubvi. Chelny pod pristal'nym oknom byvshei zhitel'nitsy Kazani," *Kazan',* nos. 1–2 (1994): 60; "Spravki o kriticheskikh zamechaniiakh i predlozheniiakh kommunistov, vyskazannykh na IV gorodskoi partkonferentsii," TsGA IPD RT, f. 7403, op. 1, d. 213, ll. 26, 47; V. Nilov et al., "Tsentr goroda: Byt' ili ne byt'."

29. A. V. Riabushin, *Voprosy formirovaniia novykh tipov zhilishch v sviazi s razvitiem kommunisticheskogo byta,* aftoreferat (Moscow: Nauchno-issledovatel'skii Institut teorii i istorii arkhitektury i stroitel'noi tekhniki ASiA SSSR, 1962), 11–12.

30. Monica Rüthers, "Schneller wohnen in Moskau: Novye Čeremuški Nr. 9, das erste Viertel in industrieller Massenbauweise, 1956–1970," in *Städteplanung—Planungsstädte,* ed. Bruno Fritzsche and Hans-Jörg Stercken (Zurich: Chronos-Verlag, 2006), 159.

31. "Spravki o kriticheskikh zamechaniiakh, l. 47.

32. Miliutin, *Sotsgorod,* 65.

33. Rubanenko and Pateev, "Naberezhnye Chelny," 7.

34. "Spravka stroitel'nogo otdela o khode stroitel'stva goroda za 1970 god," TsGA IPD RT, f. 7403, op. 1, d. 198, l. 2–4; "Plany raboty i spravki stroitel'nogo otdela o stroitel'stve ob"ektov sotskul'tbyta," nachato ianvar' 1971 g., okoncheno dekabr' 1971 g., TsGA IPD RT, f. 7403, op. 1, d. 227, l. 4; "Pis'ma komsomol'tsev i molodezhi, zhelaiushchikh rabotat' na KamAZe za 1971 god," TsGA IPD RT, f. 7467, op. 1, d. 122, l. 4; "Plany raboty i spravki stroitel'nogo otdela o khode stroitel'stva KamAZa i goroda," nachato ianvar' 1972 g., okoncheno dekabr' 1972 g., TsGA IPD RT, f. 7403, op. 1, d. 259, ll. 47–49, 59.

35. Interview with Marat Abdullin, Kazan, November 24, 2004 (name altered).

36. *KamAZ, organizatsiia stroitel'stva i proizvodstvo stroitel'nykh rabot*, 248; TsGA IPD RT, f. 7403, op. 1, d. 334. Johannes Grützmacher considers the car one of the most important material incentives for working on the Baikal-Amur Mainline (BAM), another large-scale project of the Brezhnev era. According to him, those who worked on the BAM received a coupon for a car after three years. That the car was of greater significance as an incentive to mobilization for the BAM than for KamAZ may be explained, presumably, by the fact that, because of its geographical location, Naberezhnye Chelny had more to offer than Siberia. Johannes Grützmacher, "Die Bajkal-Amur-Magistrale. Anspruch und Scheitern eines technischen Großprojekts in der Brežnev-Ära" (master's thesis, University of Tübingen, 2000), 67, http://w210.ub.uni-tuebingen.de/dbt/volltexte/2001/206 (accessed January 29, 2009).

37. *Osnovy zakonodatel'stva Soiuza SSSR i soiuznykh respublik o trude* (Moscow: Izd. Izvestiia sov. deputatov trudiashchikhsia, 1970), 25 (art. 55 of the labor legislation).

38. This statement is based on documents of KamAZ and Kamgesenergostroi, which were responsible for the distribution. Further research would be in order here—for example, an evaluation of the official registration of cars and a systematic comparison with other cities.

39. "Spravki, informatsii o rabote partinykh organizatsii po bor'be s p'ianstvom i alkogolizmom v 1975 godu," TsGA IPD RT, f. 7403, op. 1, d. 334. l. 47.

40. "Spravka o khode vypolneniia postanovleniia TsK KPSS i Soveta Ministrov SSSR ot 23 iiulia 1966 goda: O merakh po usileniiu bor'by s prestupnost'iu," 2 March 1978, TsGA IPD RT, f. 7403, op. 1, d. 442, l. 9.

41. "Spravka o prodelannoi politiko-vospitatel'noi rabote po preduprezhdeniiu narushenii trudovoi i transportnoi distsipliny i v obshchestvennykh mestakh sredi kollektiva Naberezhno-Chelninskogo passazhirskogo avtotransportnogo predpriiatiia 'Tattransupravleniia' za 1975 god," TsGA IPD RT, f. 7403, op. 1, d. 334, ll. 35–38.

42. Barbara Schmucki, *Der Traum vom Verkehrsfluss. Städtische Verkehrsplanung seit 1945 im deutsch-deutschen Vergleich* (Frankfurt am Main: Campus-Verlag, 2001), 96.

43. Wilhelm Kainrath, *Die Bandstadt. Städtebauliche Vision oder reales Modell der Stadtentwicklung?* (Vienna: Picus-Verlag, 1997), http://www.arcosanti.org/today/2005/04/20/1114021985000.html (accessed January 29, 2009).

7 Understanding a Car in the Context of a System

1. The Horch (Audi) factory in Zwickau, which would become the Trabant factory, had 3,800 machines carted away to the USSR, under SMAD (Soviet Military Administration of Germany) order number 44—leaving only about 2 percent of the factory intact. See Peter Kirchberg, *Plaste, Blech und Planwirtschaft: Die Geschichte des Automobilbaus in der DDR* (Berlin: Nicolai, 2000), 35.

2. Theo Steigler, *Der Trabant wird 50!* (Dresden: Edition Sächsische Zeitung, 2007), 20–22.

3. Ibid., 174–75.

4. For the most comprehensive and best work on the history of the Chemical Triangle and the central role of the chemical and synthetics industry in late nineteenth- and twentieth-century German history, see especially the work of Rainer Karlsch and Ray Stokes, including their coauthored *The Chemistry Must Be Right* (Schkopau: Buna Sow Leuna Olefinverbund GmbH, 2001), and *Faktor Öl: Die Mineralwirtschaft in Deutschland, 1859–1974* (Munich: C.H. Beck, 2003), as well as Stokes's "Autarky, Ideology and Technological Lag: The Case of the East German Chemical Industry 1945–1964," *Central European History* 28 (1995): 29–45, and *Constructing Socialism: Technology and Change in East Germany, 1945–1990* (Baltimore: Johns Hopkins University Press, 2000).

5. See Dolores Augustine on the campaign to create cadres of "socialist scientists" in *Red Prometheus: Engineering and Dictatorship in East Germany: 1945–1990* (Cambridge, MA: MIT Press, 2007).

6. Kirchberg, 536; Stiegler, *Der Trabant*, 71.

7. Stiegler, *Der Trabant*, 156–57.

8. Ibid., 157.

9. Ibid., 190.

10. See in particular Martin Roemers, *Trabant: Die letzten Tage der Produktion* (Berlin: Ernst Wasmuth Verlag, 2007), on the final days of the Trabant.
11. Stiegler, *Der Trabant*, 87.
12. Jonathan Zatlin, "The Vehicle of Desire: The Trabant, the Wartburg, and the End of the GDR," *German History* 15, no. 3 (1997): 367.
13. Kirchberg, 724–25.
14. Zatlin, "Vehicle of Desire," 369.
15. Ibid., 373; Kirchberg, 530–31.
16. Zatlin, "Vehicle of Desire," 371.
17. VEB Sachsenring Automobilwerke Zwickau, *Reparaturhandbuch für Personenkraftwagen 'Trabant 601,'* 9th ed. (Leipzig: VEB Fachbuchverlag Leipzig, 1972).
18. Kirchberg, 570–71.
19. VEB Sachsenring Automobilwerke Zwickau, *Reparaturhandbuch*, 68–71.
20. See Alf Lüdtke, "'Helden der Arbeit'—Mühe beim Arbeiten. Zur missmutigen Loyalität von Industriearbeitern in der DDR," in *Sozialgeschichte der DDR,* ed. Hartmut Kaeble, Jürgen Kocka, and Hartmut Zwahr (Stuttgart: Klett-Cota, 1994), 188–213; Lüdtke, "The World of Men's Work, East and West" in *Socialist Modern: East German Everyday Culture and Politics,* ed. Katherine Pence and Paul Betts (Ann Arbor: University of Michigan Press, 2008), 234–52; and his edited volumes *Herrschaft als sozialer Praxis. Historische und sozio-anthropologische Studien* (Göttingen: Vandenhoeck and Ruprecht, 1991), and *The History of Everyday Life: Reconstructing Historical Experiences and Ways of Life,* trans. William Templer (Princeton: Princeton University Press, 1995).
21. Joachim Palutzki, *Architektur in der DDR* (Berlin: Reimer, 2000), 194.
22. Günter Peters, *Historische Stadtplanungen für den Berliner Nordosten* (Berlin: Bezirksamt Marzahn von Berlin, Abt. Jugend, Bildung und Kultur, Kulturamt/Heimatmuseum, 1997), 24–26.
23. Günter Peters, *Hütten, Platten Wohnquartiere. Berlin-Marzahn: Ein junger Bezirk mit altem Namen* (Berlin: MAZZ Verlagsgesellschaft, 1998), 42–44, mentions a number of such plans. One, the *Generealsiedlungsplan für die Reichshauptstadt,* was drawn up by the leader of the Stadtbaurat, Martin Wagner. It resulted in the *Bevölkerungsplan der Stadtgemeinde Berlin (Population Plan for the Municipality of Berlin),* published in 1928 from the Amt für Stadtplanung (Office for Urban Planning), which called for the settlement of 115,000 people in Marzahn-Biesdorf.
24. Peters, *Historische Stadtplanungen,* 12. Between 1871 and 1908 Berlin's population rose from eight hundred thousand to two million, and as a response to the overcrowding, the Berliner Architektenverein (Berlin Architects' Association), which had long been working on a plan to build canals out to the northeast, held a competition for the best plan (*Grundplan fur die Bebauung von Gross-Berlin*—Basic Plan for the Construction of Greater Berlin). First prize was awarded to Hermann Jansen's plan to extend the infrastructure and workers' settlements to Marzahn and northward to Buch.
25. Hermann Zech, *Strassennamen Ortsteil Marzahn* (Berlin: Bezirksamt Marzahn von Berlin, Abt. Jugend, Familie und Kultur, Kulturamt/Heimatmuseum, 1994), 27.
26. "Information über die Beratung am 8.1.1974 zur städtebaulichen Lösung des Stasdtteiles Biesdorf-Marahn," Bundesarchiv-Lichterfeld (BA-L), Planung des neuen Stadtteiles Biesdorf-Marzahn, 1973–1975, DH 21389, p. 1.
27. "Information über die Beratung am 8.1.1974 zur städtebaulichen Lösung des Stasdtteiles Biesdorf-Marahn," 3, and "Grundlagenmaterial für die Bebauungskonzeption des Stadtteils Biesdorf/Marzhan" (Magistrat der Hauptstadt der DDR—Berlin—Abt. Generalplanung Berlin, 15.10.1973), 11, BA-L DH2 21389: Planung des neuen Stadtteiles Bisedorf-Marzahn, 1973–1975.
28. "Information über die Beratung am 8.1.1974 zur städtebaulichen Lösung des Stasdtteiles Biesdorf-Marahn," 3.
29. Verein Kids & Co., ed., *Marzahn-Südspitze: Leben im ersten Wohngebiet der Berliner Grossiedlung* (Berlin: Bezirksamt Marzahn-Hellersdorf Abt. Ökologische Stadtentwicklung, 2002), 36.
30. Ibid., 46.
31. "Kosmoswimpel Ansporn im Wettbewerb," *Berlin-Marzahn Aktuell,* September 28, 1978, 2.

8 The Common Heritage of the Socialist Car Culture

1. Peter Kirchberg, *Plaste, Blech und Planwirtschaft. Die Geschichte des Automobilbaus in der DDR* (Berlin: Nicolai, 2005).
2. Adrian Cioroian, *Pe umerii lui Marx. O indroducere în comunismul românesc* (Bucharest: Curtea veche, 2005), 400–403; Vladimir Tismaneanu, *Stalinism for all Seasons: A Political History of Romanian Communism* (Berkeley: University of California Press, 2003), 167; Mary Fulbrook, *Anatomy of a Dictatorship: Inside the GDR, 1949–1989* (Oxford: Oxford University Press 1995).
3. Susan E. Reid, "Cold War in the Kitchen: Gender and the De-Stalinization of Consumer Taste in the Soviet Union under Khrushchev," *Slavic Review* 61, no. 2 (2002): 212–52.
4. John Urry, "The 'System' of Automobility," *Theory, Culture & Society* 21, nos. 4–5 (2004): 25–39, 26–27.
5. Daniel Miller, "Driven Societies," in *Car Cultures*, ed. Daniel Miller (London: Berg, 2001), 1–33, 15.
6. David Crowley and Susan E. Reid, introduction to *Style and Socialism: Modernity and Material Culture in Post-War Eastern Europe* (Oxford: Berg, 2000), 4.
7. Susan Zimmermann, "Wohlfahrtspolitik und sozialistische Entwicklungsstrategie in den 'anderen' Hälfte Europas im 20. Jahrhundert," in *Sozialpolitik in der Peripherie. Entwicklungsmuster und Wandel in Lateinamerika, Afrika, Asien und Europa*, ed. Johannes Jäger, Georg Melinz, and Susan Zimmermann (Frankfurt am Main: Brandes und Apsel, 2001), 211–37; Christoph Boyer and Peter Skyba, "Sozial- und Konsumpolitik als Stabilisierungsstrategie. Zur Genese der 'Einheit von Wirtschafts- und Sozialpolitik' in der DDR," *Deutschlandarchiv* 32, no. 5 (1999): 577–90.
8. John Urry speaks of a viral dissemination of "automobility," emerging first in North America and then spreading into all corners of the world. Urry, "The 'System' of Automobility," 27.
9. Kurt S. Schultz, "Building the 'Soviet Detroit': Construction of the Nizhnii-Novgorod Automobile Factory, 1927–1933," *Slavic Review* 49, no. 2 (1990): 200–212.
10. Wolfgang Sachs, *For Love of the Automobile: Looking Back into the History of Our Desires* (Berkeley: University of California Press, 1984).
11. Wolfgang König, *Volkswagen, Volksempfänger, Volksgemeinschaft. 'Volksprodukte' im Dritten Reich. Vom Scheitern einer nationalsozialistischen Konsumgesellschaft* (Paderborn: Schöningh, 2004), 151–53.
12. Reinhold Bauer, *Pkw-Bau in der DDR. Zur Innovationsschwäche von Zentralverwaltungswirtschaften* (Frankfurt am Main: Lang, 1999), 137–41.
13. Eli Rubin, "The Order of Substitutes: Plastic Consumer Goods in the *Volkswirtschaft* and Everyday Domestic Life in the GDR," in *Consuming Germany in the Cold War*, ed. David F. Crew (Oxford: Berg, 2003), 87–121; Wolfgang Schröder, *AWO, MZ, Trabant und Wartburg: Die Motorrad und Pkw-Produktion in der DDR* (Bremen: Bogenschutz, 1995), 40; Bauer, *Pkw-Bau*, 71. See also chapter 7 in this book.
14. Kirchberg, *Plaste*, 158–59.
15. Alfred Jante, "Fragen zur Automobilentwicklung im Sozialismus," *Kraftfahrzeugtechnik* 11, no. 4 (1961): 137–39.
16. Luminita Gatejel, "The Wheels of Desire: Automobility Discourses in the Soviet Union," in *Towards Mobility: Varieties of Automobilism in East and West*, ed. Corinna Kuhr-Korolev and Dirk Schlinkert (Hannover: Volkswagen AG, 2009), 31–41.
17. Aleksei N. Kosygin, "Povyshenie nauchnoi obosnovannosti planov—Vazhneishaia zadacha planovykh organov," *Planovoe Khoziaistvo* 42, no. 4 (1965): 3–10.
18. Lewis H. Siegelbaum, *Cars for Comrades: The Life of the Soviet Automobile* (Ithaca: Cornell University Press, 2008), 84–87.
19. Ibid., 99.
20. Ralf Ahrens, *Gegenseitige Wirtschaftshilfe? Die DDR im RGW-Strukturen und handelspolitische Strategien, 1963–1976* (Cologne: Böhlau, 2000), 152–60; Cioroian, *Pe umerii lui Marx*, 364–66; Dan Cătănuş, "Divergenţele româno-sovietice din C.A.E.R. şi consecinţele lor asupra politicii externe a României, 1961–1962," *Archivele Totalitarismului* 48–49, nos. 3–4 (2005): 68–80.

21. Minutes of the Central Executive Committee of the Romanian Communist Party, 16 August 1966, Arhivele Naționale Istorice Centrale (ANIC), fond C.C. al P.C.R., Cancelarie, dosar nr. 105/1966.
22. Vladimir Tismaneanu, *Stalinism*, 170–72; Alina Pavelescu, "Charles de Gaulle și 'marile ambiții' ale comuniștilor români, mai 1968," *Arhivele Totalitarismului* 48–49, nos. 3–4 (2005): 191–98.
23. Rossiiskii Gosudarstvennyi Arkhiv Noveishei Istorii (RGANI), f. 5, op. 30, d. 262, l. 51.
24. Letters dated 14 March 1977 and 26 March 1977, Bundesarchiv Berlin (BArchB), Ministerium für Handel und Versorgung, DL1/22953, o. S.
25. Letters dated 6 June 1977 and 30 April 1977, BArchB, DL1/22953, o. S.
26. RGANI, f. 5, op. 67, d. 369, l. 84; BArchB, DL1/22953, o. S. (13.04.1977; 25.05.1977).
27. RGANI, f. 5, op. 69, d. 1159, l. 15; ANIC, secția Brașov, 2/1975, 124.
28. Letter dated 25 June 1980, BArchB, Ministerium für Allgemeine Maschinen-, Landmaschinen- und Fahrzeugbau, DG7/616, o. S.; letter dated 15 September 1977, DG7/165, o. S.
29. Sanda Stolojan, *Avec de Gaulle en Roumanie* (Paris: Herne, 1991).
30. "Dampf machen. Ost-Berlin erwägt als Gegenleistung für mehr Bonner Wirtschaftshilfe," *Der Spiegel*, October 18, 1976, 56.
31. ANIC, fond C.C. al P.C.R.—Cancelarie, dosar nr. 4/1972, f. 210.
32. BArchB, Stiftung Archiv der Parteien und Massenorganisationen (SAPMO),DY30/ J IV 2/2 1529, 17.7.1973, 45f.; see also Bauer, *Pkw-Bau*, 250.
33. BArchB, SAPMO, DY30/9171 (Büro des Politbüros), 23.10.1979, 22f.
34. BArchB, DL1/22953, o. S., 14.03.1977; SAPMO, DY30/9064, o. S., 21.08.1981.
35. *Private Pkw nach Typen, Statistisches Jahrbuch der DDR* (Berlin: Staatsverlag der DDR,1988), 74.
36. RGANI, f. 5, op. 42, d. 99, ll. 1–6.
37. ANIC, secția Brașov, fond 32, Partidul Comunist Român, Comitetul Județean Brașov, dosar nr. 94/1974, p. 287.
38. ANIC, fond C.C. al P.C.R.—Organizatorica, dosar nr. 35/1974, p. 22; Rossiiskii Gosudarstvennyi Arkhiv Ekonomiki (RGAE), f. 465, op. 1, d. 848, l. 75; d. 1401, l. 74.
39. Mark Edele, "Soviet Veterans as an Entitlement Group, 1945–1955," *Slavic Review* 65, no. 1 (2006): 111–37.
40. RGAE, f. 465, op. 1, d. 1775, l. 89; V. V. Voronov and I. P. Smirnov, "Zakreplenie molodezhi v zone BAMa," *Sotsiologicheskie issledovaniia*, no. 2 (1982), 16; Johannes Grützmacher, "Verkehr. Kraftverkehr," in *Handbuch der Geschichte Rußlands, 1945–1991*, ed. Stefan Plaggenborg, vol. 5 (Stuttgart: Hirsemann 2003), 1130.
41. BArchB, DL1/22952, o. S.
42. ANIC, fond C.C. al P.C.R.—Cancelarie, dosar nr. 4/1972, f. 210; Franka Schneider, "'Jedem nach dem Wohnsitz seiner Tante.' Die GENEX Geschenkdienst GmbH," in *Wunderwirtschaft. DDR-Konsumkultur in der 60er Jahren*, ed. Ina Merkel (Cologne: Böhlau, 1996), 223–32.
43. RGAE, f. 465, op. 1, d. 1579, l. 129; d. 1581, l. 130; d. 842, l. 133; d. 1767, l. 62.
44. See György Péteri, ed., *Imagining the West in Eastern Europe and the Soviet Union* (Pittsburgh: University of Pittsburgh Press, 2010).
45. Urry, "The 'System' of Automobility," 25–26; Miller, "Driven Societies," 10; James Flink, *The Car Culture* (Cambridge: Cambridge University Press, 1975).
46. Jean-Jacques Chanaron, "Lada: Viability of Fordism," in *One Best Way? Trajectories and Industrial Models of the World's Automobile Producers*, ed. Michel Freyssenet (Oxford: Oxford University Press, 1998), 440–50; Robert Boyer, "Hybridization and Models of Production: Geography, History, and Theory," in *Between Imitation and Innovation: The Transfer and Hybridization of Productive Models in the International Automobile Industry*, ed. Robert Boyer (Oxford: Oxford University Press, 1998), 23–57, 41.
47. Alexei Yurchak, *Everything Was Forever, Until It Was No More: The Last Soviet Generation* (Princeton: Princeton University Press, 2006), 158–206.
48. Juliane Fürst, "The Arrival of Spring? Changes and Continuities in Soviet Youth Culture and Policy between Stalin and Khrushchev," in *The Dilemmas of De-Stalinization: Negotiating Cultural and Social Change in the Khrushchev Era*, ed. Polly Jones (London: Routledge, 2006), 135–53.

49. Liviu Chelcea and Puiu Latea, *România profundă în comunism* (Bucharest: Nemira, 2000).
50. Talks with the author's relatives.
51. BArchB, SAPMO, DY30/IVB2/ 215, S. 146.
52. RGAE, f. 465, op. 1, d. 1028, l. 187.
53. Lewis H. Siegelbaum, "The Impact of Motorization on Soviet Society after 1945," in Kuhr-Korolev and Schlinkert, *Towards Mobility*.
54. Annelies Albrecht and Hans Dietrich, "Der Einfluß der wachsenden Ausstattung der Bevölkerungshaushalte mit Personenkraftwagen auf die Verbrauchstsruktur," *Mitteilungen des Instituts für Marktforschung (MIfMF)*, no. 1 (1968): 29–31.
55. BArchB, SAPMO, DY30/IVA2/6.10/190, 5.2.1965.
56. BArchB, DL1/22952, o. S. (25.05.1977).
57. Talks with the author's relatives.
58. RGANI, f. 5, op. 67, d. 369, l. 84; BArchB, DL1/22953, o. S. (13.04.1977; 25.05.1977); "Brief Anton S. an die Redaktion 'Prisma' des Fernsehers der DDR, 14. April 1989," in *DDR-Geschichte in Dokumenten*, ed. Matthias Judt (Berlin: Links, 1998), 142–43.
59. Lewis H. Siegelbaum, "On the Side: Car Culture in the USSR, 1960s–1980s," *Technology and Culture* 50 (January 2009): 1–23.
60. RGAE, f. 465, op. 1, d. 1028, l. 187.
61. Maria R. Zezina, "The Introduction of Motor Vehicles on a Mass Scale in the USSR: From Idea to Implementation," in Kuhr-Korolev and Schlinkert, *Towards Mobility*.
62. Catriona Kelly, "Ordinary Life in Extraordinary Times: Chronicles of the Quotidian in Russia and the Soviet Union," *Kritika: Explorations in Russian and Eurasian History* 3, no. 4 (2002): 631–51.
63. Jonathan B. Zatlin, *The Currency of Socialism: Money and Political Culture in East Germany* (Cambridge: Cambridge University Press, 2007), 286–320.

9 Autobasteln

1. Cf. Wibe Bijker, Thomas P. Hughes, and Trevor Pinch, *The Social Construction of Technological Systems: New Directions in the Sociology and History of Technology* (Cambridge, MA: MIT Press, 1987), 8, and Nelly Oudshoorn and Trevor Pinch, "Introduction: How Users and Non-Users Matter," in *How Users Matter: The Co-Construction of Users and Technologies* (Cambridge, MA: MIT Press, 2003), 1–25.
2. Kathleen Franz, *Tinkering: Consumers Reinvent the Early Automobile* (Philadelphia: University of Pennsylvania Press, 2005); Ronald Kline and Trevor Pinch, "Users as Agents of Technological Change: The Social Construction of the Automobile in the Rural United States," *Technology and Culture* 37, no. 4 (1996): 763–95; Reinhold Reith, "Reparieren—Ein Thema der Technikgeschichte?" in *Kleine Betriebe—Angepasste Technologie?* ed. Reinhold Reith and Dorothea Schmidt (Münster: Waxmann, 2002), 139–61.
3. Joachim Krause, "La deux chevaux—Autos für das Existenzminimum. Vorbereitungen zur Dekmalpflege," in *Zwischen Fahrrad und Fliessband, absolut modern sein* (exhibition catalog of the Neue Gesellschaft für Bildende Kunst, Staatliche Kunsthalle Berlin) (West Berlin: Elefanten Press, 1986).
4. A reference to Alfred P. Sloan, president and CEO of General Motors from 1923 onward and the father of mass marketing of cars based on the principle of periodic upgrades of models.
5. Kurt Möser, *Die Geschichte des Autos* (Frankfurt am Main: New York: Campus, 2002).
6. See Peter Kirchberg, *Plaste, Blech und Planwirtschaft. Die Geschichte des Automobilbaus in der DDR* (Berlin: Nicolai, 2000).
7. See Scott Miranda, "Camping in East Germany: Making 'Rough' Nature More Comfortable," in *Pleasures in Socialism: Leisure and Luxury in the Eastern Bloc*, ed. David Crowley and Susan E. Reid (Evanston, IL: Northwestern University Press, 2010), 197–216.
8. Franz, *Tinkering*, p. 794.
9. Werner Hirte, foreword to his *1000 Dinge selbst gebaut. Das Buch des Bastlers*, 4th ed. (Leipzig: Urania, 1967).

10. Peter Kirchberg, "Der automobile Mangel—Anmerkungen zu den Grundlagen der Autokultur in der DDR," in *Technik und Gesellschaft. Jahrbuch 10: Automobil und Automobilismus,* ed. Gert Schmidt (Frankfurt am Main: Campus Fachbuch, 1999), 237–50; Reinhard Bauer, "PKW-Bau in der DDR. Zur Innovationsschwäche von Zentralverwaltungswirtschaften," Diss. Frankfurt /M., 1999, foreword.

11. Lewis H. Siegelbaum, *Cars for Comrades: The Life of the Soviet Automobile* (Ithaca: Cornell University Press, 2008), 242–47.

12. Kirchberg, "Der automobile Mangel."

13. A. O. Hirschman, *Strategy of Economic Development* (New Haven: Yale University Press, 1958), 4.

14. Kurt Möser, "Prinzipielles zur Transportgeschichte," in *Transportgeschichte,* ed. Rolf Peter Sieferle (Berlin: LIT, 2008), 39–78.

15. Kirchberg, "Der automobile Mangel," 248ff.

16. Dieter Claessens, *Zur Soziologie des Strassen verkehrs. Ders., Angst, Furcht und gesellschaftlicher Druck* (Dortmund: Ruhfus, 1966), 23–31; Dieter Claessens, *Soziologische und sozialpsychologische Aspekte des Fahrens im Verkehrsfluss. Ders., Angst, Furcht und gesellschaftlicher Druck* (Dortmund: Ruhfus, 1966), 38–42.

17. Kurt Möser, "'Der Kampf des Automobilisten mit seiner Maschine'—Eine Skizze der Vermittlung der Autotechnik und des Fahrenlernens im 20. Jahrhundert," in *Technikvermittlung und Technikpopularisierung—Historische und didaktische Perspektiven,* ed. Lars Bluma, Karl Pichol, and Wolfhard Weber (Münster: Waxmann, 2004), 98–102.

18. Andreas Knie, "Die Interpretation des Autos als Rennreiselimousine. Genese, Bedeutungsprägung, Fixierungen und verkehrspolitische Konsequenzen," in *Geschichte der Zukunft des Verkehrs. Verkehrskonzepte von der Krühen Neuzeit vis zum 21. Jahhundert,* ed. Hans-Liudger Dienel and Helmut Trischler (Frankfurt am Main: Campus, 1997), 243–59.

19. Pierre Bourdieu, *Die feinen Unterschiede* (Frankfurt am Main: Suhrkamp Verlag, 1990), 17–27.

10 "Little Tsars of the Road"

1. Heinz Lathe and Günther Meierling, *Return to Russia,* trans. Charlotte Dixon (London: Galley Press, 1961), 55; Patrick Sergeant, *Another Road to Samarkand* (London: Hodder and Staughton, 1955), 24.

2. See the special issue on "Automobilities," *Theory, Culture & Society* 21, nos. 4–5 (2004),2, 25–26 and the special issue on conceptualizing, governing, and representing automobility in *Sociological Review* 54, issue s1 (2006), 1–3. See also the program for "Automobility: A Conference on the 100th Anniversary of the Model T" (Hagley Museum and Library, Wilmington, Delaware, November 6–7, 2008), http://www.hagley.lib.de.us/library/center/conferences/poster/2008autoposter.pdf.

3. All references and quotations are from the "Dal'noboishchiki" home page at http://www.ntvkino.ru/movies/dalnoboy and the World-Art site devoted to the serial at http://www.world-art.ru/cinema/cinema.php?id=4312 (accessed October 22, 2008).

4. For the song's words, see A. Denisenko, ed. *Sirenevyi tuman: Entsyklopediia zastol'nykh pesen, "blatnoi" i "ulichnoi" fol'klor* (Novosibirsk: Mangazeia, 2001), 459–61. See also V. V. Briukhov "K 80-letiiu Chuiskogo trakta," http://www.biusk.secna.ru/jurnal/n_10_2002/kultura/bruhov.doc (accessed October 24, 2008), and V. N. Shipilov, "K 80-letiiu Chuiskogo trakta," http://www.biysk.secna.ru/jurnal/n_10_2002/kultura/shipilov.doc (accessed October 24, 2008).

5. See Denisenko, *Sirenevyi tuman,* 258–59, back cover. There is a "Moscow Highway" variant as well. On Shukshin see Kathleen Parthé, "Shukshin at Large," in *Vasily Shukshin: Stories from a Siberian Village,* trans. Laura Michael and John Givens (DeKalb: Northern Illinois University Press, 1996), ix–xii. For the film script see Vasilii Shukshin, *Kinopovesti,* 2nd ed. (Moscow: Iskusstvo, 1988), 5–47. The opening line ("There is in the Altai a highway—the Chuiskii") echoes that of the song ("There is along the Chuiskii a road"). On the monument, see Tat'iana Alekseevich, "Est' po chuiskomu traktu doroga," *Krasnoiarskii rabochii,* August 21, 2008, http://www.krasrab.com/archive/2008/08/21/14/ (accessed October 19, 2008).

6. For this point with respect to U.S. auto factory workers, see Stephen Meyer, "Work, Play, and Power: Masculine Culture on the Automotive Shop Floor," in *Boys and Their Toys? Masculinity, Technology, and Class in America*, ed. Roger Horowitz (New York: Routledge, 2001), 13–32.

7. "Avtomobil' v okt. 1917 goda," *Za rulem*, no. 8 (1928): 28; "Avtomobil'naia khronika," *Za rulem*, nos. 21–22 (1937): 47.

8. Correspondence of Central Committee with provincial departments on condition of auto transport in 1921, Gosudarstvennyi Arkhiv Rossiiskoi Federatsii (GARF), f. 5454, op. 4, d. 69, ll. 21–22; *Dekrety Sovetskoi vlasti*, 16 vols. (Moscow: Gosizdpolit. Litry, 1957–99), 9:76–80.

9. Tsudortrans, *Avtodorozhnoe khoziaistvo SSSR v tsifrakh, statisticheskii sbornik* (Moscow-Leningrad: Gostransport, 1935), 139. The figures given are 5,550 on January 1, 1925; 5,906 on January 1, 1927; 6,517 on January 1, 1928; and 9,000 on January 9, 1929.

10. Preparatory material for the First All-Union Congress of the Union of Drivers, 1933, GARF, f. 5454, op. 16, d. 1, ll. 29–31; Information of the Central Committee of the union on membership, 1921–1924, GARF, f. 5454, op. 7, d. 151, l. 1.

11. Lev Shugurov, *Avtomobil'naia Moskva: Stoletie 1902–2001* (Moscow: TsDTS, 2004), 25–32, 36–41. Muscovites referred to hybrid vehicles whose parts had been cannibalized from others as "mixed soup" (*sbornaia solianka*).

12. Protocols of sessions of committee of All-Russian Experimental Avtoprobeg), Rossiiskii Gosudarstvennyi Arkhiv Ekonomiki (RGAE), f. 1884, op. 5, ed. kh. 93, ll. 58, 70–71, 114; Rules and conditions of participation in All-Russian Experimental Avtoprobeg), RGAE, f. 1884, op. 5, d. 104, ll. 1–15; *Pravda*, September 28, 1923, 3.

13. *Pravda*, August 22, 1925, 3; August 24, 1925, 3; August 29, 1925, 3. For more on avtoprobegy see Lewis H. Siegelbaum, "Soviet Car Rallies of the 1920s and '30s and the Road to Socialism," *Slavic Review* 64, no. 2 (2005): 247–73.

14. Siegelbaum, "Soviet Car Rallies," 252–53; *Izvestiia*, July 5, 1933, 4; September 30, 1933, 4; S. U., "Moskva vsrechaet geroev karakumskogo avtoprobega," *Za rulem*, no. 20 (1933): 7–8.

15. El'-Registan and L. Brontman, *Moskva–Kara-Kum–Moskva* (Moscow: Sovetskaia literatura, 1934), 62, 94, 97–98, 106, 132, 149, 167, 173. The book is in the form of a "condensed laconic diary" by the correspondents from *Izvestiia* and *Pravda*. At least one report, sent by the political leader (*politrukovod*) whom the Party had assigned, claimed that indiscipline was rife, with drivers greeting orders with "a torrent of bad language." Report of N. A. Grustlivov to chairman of the committee Kuibyshev, August 26, 1933, GARF, f. 4426, op. 1, d. 373, ll.23–32.

16. *Pravda*, July 31, 1936, 6; September 30, 1936, 6; *Trud*, September 30, 1936, 3; October 1, 1936, 1 (editorial); *Izvestiia*, September 30, 1936, 4; *Za rulem*, no. 21 (1936): 6. On Angelina, among the most famous of rural Stakhanovites, see Pasha Angelina, *O samom glavnom* (Moscow, 1948); on the *Rodina*, see L. Brontman and L. Khvat, *Geroicheskii perelet "Rodiny"* (Moscow: Gosizdpollit, 1938).

17. F. Lagunov, "Po l'du Ladogi," *Zvezda*, no. 1 (1964): 162–66; V. M. Koval'chuk, "Kommunikatsii blokirovannogo Leningrada," in *Leningradskaia epopeia: Organizatsiia oborony i naselenie goroda*, ed. V. M. Koval'chuk, N. A. Lomagin, and V. A. Shishkin (St. Petersburg: RAN, 1995), 86; David Glantz, *The Battle for Leningrad, 1941–1944* (Lawrence: University Press of Kansas, 2002), 142–43.

18. A. Fadeev, "Gorod velikikh zodchikh," *Slaviane*, nos. 5–6 (1942): 59–62; Vera Inber, *Leningrad Diary*, trans. Serge M. Wolff and Rachel Grieve (London: Hutchinson, 1971), 66; Berggolts quoted in A.D. Kharitonov, *Legendarnaia ledovaia trassa* (Moscow: Voenizdat, 1965), 61, and translated by me.

19. See, for example, A. A. Nedeshev, F. F. Bybin, and A.M. Kotel'nikov, *BAM i osvoenie Zabaikal'ia* (Novosibirsk: Nauka Sib. otd-nie, 1979); B. S. Starin, *Sotsialisticheskoe sorevnovanie stroitelei BAMa 1974–1984 gg.* (Novosibirsk: Nauka, 1987).

20. Boris Zil'pert,"O russkom shofere," *Za rulem*, no. 2 (1929): 13.

21. F. Korzun, "Novaia sistema zarplaty shoferov," *Za rulem*, no. 5 (1934): 24; "Kodeks povedeniia khoroshego shofera," *Za rulem*, no. 1 (1934): 22. See also a report dated July 16, 1933, "On the condition of auto transport in republic and departmental auto firms" in GARF, f. 5446, op. 14, d. 2012, ll. 11–17. The report claimed that 50–55 percent of vehicles were out of commission as a result of carelessness, swapping of parts, and lack of proper training of drivers.

22. *Za rulem*, no. 1 (1934): 15; no. 9 (1936): 1–6. On the Stakhanovite movement, which rewarded with "accelerated piece-rate wages" workers who overfulfilled their norms, see Lewis H. Siegelbaum, *Stakhanovism and the Politics of Productivity in the USSR, 1935–1941* (Cambridge: Cambridge University Press, 1988). The movement was named after a coal miner, Aleksei Stakhanov, who set a record for hewing over one hundred tons of coal in one shift in August 1935.

23. Nik. Viktorov, "Zametki moskovskogo shofera," *Za rulem*, no. 1 (1937): 15. See also Nik. Viktorov, "Bliusti distsiplinu truda," *Za rulem* no. 3 (1937): 25.

24. A. G. Tumanian, *Avarii na avtotransporte* (Moscow: Zhur-ob"ed., 1936), 28. One driver complained in 1956 that he often heard the phrase "He swears like a driver" and confessed that drivers were to blame. See *Za rulem*, no. 3 (1956): 9. Much of this behavior corresponds to what Stephen Meyer calls "rough masculinity."

25. *Krasnyi Transportnik*, nos. 22–23 (1932): 5; *Za rulem*, no. 1 (1934): 31; no. 3 (1934): 24–25, 31; no. 6 (1934): 19.

26. Tumanian, *Avarii*, 22–27; *Za rulem*, no. 3 (1934): 24–25; no. 14 (1935): 12–13.

27. David Priestland, *Stalinism and the Politics of Mobilization: Ideas, Power, and Terror in Inter-war Russia* (Oxford: Oxford University Press, 2007), 37–57, 324–28.

28. Ar. Tumanian, "Dlia chego proizvoditsia obmen shoferskikh knizhek," *Za rulem*, no. 6 (1935): 10–11.

29. *Pravda*, June 6, 1935, 1; *Za rulem*, no. 7 (1935): 6–8; no. 13 (1935): 2, 11.

30. Anatolii Rybakov, "Voditeli," *Oktiabr'*, no. 1 (1950): 27.

31. Stenographic report of sessions of First All-Union Congress of Union of Workers of Auto Transport, October 17–19, 1947, GARF, f. 7314, op. 2, d. 75, ll. 130–33.

32. Minister of Internal Affairs reports on technical condition of autos, April 24, 1947, GARF, f. 9401, op. 2, d. 169, l. 101. Paved roads, which totaled only 7,100 kilometers in 1940 (5 percent of all roads), made up 87,100 kilometers in 1961 (30 percent of the total). B. P. Orlov, *Razvitie transporta SSSR, 1917–1962* (Moscow: Izd. Akademii nauk SSSR, 1963), 347–49. Between 1940 and 1960 automotive freight traffic increased from 8,896 million to 98,520 million kilometer-tons or more than eleven times. See Goskomstat, *Transport i sviaz SSS: Statisticheskii sbornik* (Moscow: Finansy i statistika, 1990), 42.

33. Orlov, *Razvitie transporta SSSR*, 364.

34. *Za rulem*, no. 12 (1960): 10–11, 16. The base pay of truck drivers ranged from 580 to 1,100 rubles per month, depending on the carrying capacity of the vehicle. This compares with 580–680 for car chauffeurs and 925–1,175 for bus drivers.

35. Andrey Shlyakhter, "Trade Routes: Reflections of a Soviet Truck Driver" (unpublished paper, 2003, cited with permission of the author), 10.

36. R. Danilovich and P. Koval'chuk, "Doroga—Rabochee mesto shofera," *Za rulem*, no. 4 (1959): 30. For membership figures see Statistical returns on professional membership, GARF, f. 7314, op. 2, d. 1118, ll. 1–2.

37. On auto tourism see Siegelbaum, *Cars for Comrades*, 205–6, 227–29.

38. *Za rulem*, no. 1 (1982): 22–23; no. 6 (1982): 18; no. 11 (1982): 17. The editors report having received hundreds of letters.

39. For the case of Mariia Chudnova, who complained to the union in August 1944 that her assignment as dispatcher violated the law, see Materials associated with protocols of sessions of the union's presidium for 1944, GARF, f. 7314, op. 1, d. 96, ll. 54–55. On percentages of women drivers, see GARF, f. 9401, op. 2, d. 169, l. 243.

40. *Za rulem*, no. 3 (1979): 28.

41. Rybakov, "Voditeli," 83.

42. Anatolii Rybakov, *Fear* (Boston: Little, Brown, 1992), 457. Rybakov modeled Pankratov on his own experience. For details, see Anatolii Rybakov, *Roman-vospominanie* (Moscow: Vagrius, 1997), 55–56.

43. Ferenc Hammer, "A Gasoline Scented Sinbad: The Truck Driver as a Popular Hero in Socialist Hungary," *Cultural Studies* 16, no. 1 (2002): 84; Victor Turner, *The Ritual Process: Structure and Anti-Structure* (Chicago: Aldine, 1969), 95.

44. For words to both songs see http://songkino.ru/songs/ocher_reis.html (accessed October 20, 2008). Translations are mine.

45. Parthé, "Shukshin at Large," x.

46. Denisenko, *Sirenevyi tuman*, 362–63.

47. Evgenii Evtushenko, "Stantsiia Zima (poema)," in *Pervoe sobranie sochinenii v vos'mi tomakh* (Moscow: Neva, 1996), 1:309.

48. "One More Mile," *Dave Dudley Trucker Classics*, Sun Record Company, 1996, compact disc, track 9; "Two Six Packs Away," *20th Century Masters. The Millennium Collection: Best of Dave Dudley*, Mercury Nashville, 2002, compact disc, track 5.

49. Lawrence Ouellet, *Pedal to the Metal: The Work Lives of Truckers* (Philadelphia: Temple University Press, 1994), 105. See also James H. Thomas, *The Long Haul: Truckers, Truck Stops, and Trucking* (Memphis: Memphis State University Press, 1979), 5–7. For fascinating pictorial evocations of U.S. truckers' big rigs, see Bette S. Graber's books, especially her *Big Rigs: On the Road with the World's Best Semi Trucks* (St. Paul: Crestline, 2004).

50. GARF, f. 7314, op. 2, d. 75, l. 133.

51. Plot summaries are available at http://www.videoguide.ru/ (accessed November 12, 2008). For a story that refers to truck drivers who *intentionally* transport illegal goods, see the novel *Olenka* (1955) by Mikhail Zhestev as summarized in Ann Livschiz, "De-Stalinizing Soviet Childhood: The Quest for Moral Rebirth, 1953–58," in *The Dilemmas of De-Stalinization: Negotiating Cultural and Social Change in the Khrushchev Era*, ed. Polly Jones (Abingdon, UK: Routledge, 2006), 125–26.

52. Shlyakhter, "Reflections of a Soviet Truck Driver," 1–11. Shlyakhter conducted three interviews with his relative, Grisha Goldshteyn, in Chicago in November 2003. All quotations are taken from Shlyakhter's account, in which Grisha does "most of the speaking." Grisha is now deceased.

53. Michael V. Alexeev, "Underground Market for Gasoline in the USSR" (Occasional Paper No. 9, Berkeley-Duke Occasional Papers on the Second Economy in the USSR, Department of Economics, Duke University, Durham, NC, 1987), 1–25.

54. Hammer, "A Gasoline Scented Sinbad," 86. Stewardesses on Malév, Hungary's national airline, enjoyed the same privilege.

55. Shlyakhter, "Reflections of a Soviet Truck Driver," 10–11.

56. Elena Osokina, *Ierarkhiia potrebleniia: O zhizni liudei v usloviiakh stalinskogo snabzheniia, 1928–1935 gg.* (Moscow: MGU, 1993). Osokina refers to the period of rationing and formally defined quotas, but as others have argued, differential access to goods by virtue of one's occupation and the connections it afforded continued for decades thereafter.

57. This point is made by Shlyakhter, "Reflections of a Soviet Truck Driver," 11, citing Alena V. Ledeneva, *Russia's Economy of Favors: Blat, Networking, and Informal Exchange* (Cambridge: Cambridge University Press, 1998), 130.

58. Shlyakhter, "Reflections of a Soviet Truck Driver," 5; Elena Bakhanova, "Dal'noboishchiki," *Ogonek*, no. 40 (October 2, 2006): 34–37.

11 Women and Cars in Soviet and Russian Society

1. Lewis H. Siegelbaum, *Cars for Comrades: The Life of the Soviet Automobile* (Ithaca: Cornell University Press, 2008).

2. Rostislav Kononenko, "Sovetskaia zhenshchina za rulem: Gosudarstvennaia politika i kul'turnye kody gendernogo ravenstva," in *Sovetskaia sotsial'naia politika. Tseny i deistvuiushchie litsa, 1940–1985*, ed. Elena Iarskaia-Smirnova and Pavel Romanov (Moscow: Variant, 2008) 358–371.

3. Lewis H. Siegelbaum, "On the Side: Soviet Car Culture, 1960s–1980s," *Technology and Culture* 50, no. 1 (2009): 1–23. There are studies that apply to other countries: Sean O'Connell, *The Car and British Society: Class, Gender and Motoring 1896–1939* (Manchester, UK: Manchester University Press, 1998); Merritt Polk, "Gendered Mobility: A Study of Women's and Men's Relations to Automobility in Sweden" (PhD diss., University of Gothenburg, 1998); Deborah Clark, *Driving Women: Fiction and Automobile Culture in Twentieth-Century America* (Baltimore: Johns Hopkins University Press, 2007).

4. On the social role of women in the Soviet Union see Mary Buckley, *Women and Ideology in the Soviet Union* (Ann Arbor: University of Michigan Press, 1989); Anna Köbberling, *Das Klischee der Sowjetfrau. Stereotyp und Selbstverständnis Moskauer Frauen zwischen Stalinära und Perestroika* (Frankfurt am Main: Campus Verlag, 1993); Monika Rosenbaum, *Frauenarbeit und Frauenalltag in der Sowjetunion* (Münster: Verlag Westfälisches Dampfboot, 1991); Kristine v. Soden, ed., *Lust und Last: Sowjetische Frauen von Alexandra Kollontai bis heute* (Berlin: Elefanten Presse, 1990); Lynne Attwood, *The New Soviet Man–Woman–Sex Role Socialization in the USSR* (Bloomington: Indiana University Press, 1990).

5. Martina Ritter, ed., *Zivilgesellschaft und Gender-Politik in Russland* (Frankfurt am Main: Campus Verlag, 2001); Elena Mecherkina, "Frauen auf dem Arbeitsmarkt in Russland," *Feministische Studien* 17, no. 1 (1999): 49–60; Olga Lipovskaja, "Der Mythos der Frau in der heutigen sowjetischen Kultur," *Feministische Studien* 10, no. 2 (1992): 64–74; Vitalina Koval, *Women in Contemporary Russia* (Providence: Berghahn, 1995); Mary Buckley, *Perestroika and Soviet Women* (New York: Cambridge University Press, 1992).

6. There are journalistic pieces, such as Barbara Kerneck, *Die starke Seite Russlands. Frauenportraits aus einem Land im Aufbruch* (Munich: Heyne, 1994).

7. Various projects and publications have come from the St. Petersburg Center for Independent Sociological Research. In 2004–7 the center conducted a project on the transformation of daily life: "Novyi byt. Forma semeinoi organizatsii i izmenenie domashnego prostranstva." On gender relations and ideal roles: "Muzh'ia i zheny: Razpredelenie semeinykh obiazannostei," both at http://bd.fom.ru/report/cat/home_fam/famil/d070922 (accessed March 1, 2008). On the change in consumption habits, see B. S. Gladarev and Zh. M. Tsinman, "Potrebitel'skie stili peterburgskogo srednego klassa: Iz ekonomiki defitsita k novomu bytu," *Ekonomicheskaia sotsiologiia* 8, no. 3 (2007): 61–81; Olga Shevchenko, "In Case of Fire Emergency. Consumption, Security and the Meaning of Durables in a Transforming Society," *Journal of Consumer Culture* 2 (2002): 147–70; Margit Keller and Triin Vihalemm, "Coping with Consumer Culture: Elderly Urban Consumers in Post-Soviet Estonia," *TRAMES* 1, 9, 59/54 (2005): 69–91.

8. See http://www.womantaxi.ru/ and the related men's discussion, http://www.lacetti-club.ru/vb_forum/printthread.php?s=5f61a80ac339eeaf45b8eb5aab7b5f9e&t=8373 (accessed October 24, 2008).

9. The less active club in Togliatti, http://www.lada-auto.ru/cgi-bin/press-search.pl?id_article=19127&prev=3&startdate=01&enddate=31&month=03&year=2005 (accessed May 22, 2008), and a very active one in Vladivostok, http://www.women25rus.ru/club.htm (accessed October 22, 2008).

10. Driving classes for women by BMW Moscow, http://www.bmw.ru/russian/services/training/default.asp?cont=course_basic_women.asp (accessed October 22, 2008).

11. The column "Zhenskii klub" ran from 1997 until 2002. In 2004 the journal tried to establish a column called "Zhenskii vzgliad," ("Women's View"), but it lasted for only a few issues.

12. The interviews were all conducted in Moscow. They were based on a list of questions, all of which were raised during the course of a narrative interview. Follow-up questions were used to complement the accounts of the persons interviewed.

13. From 1956 until the end of the Soviet period, *Za rulem* was published by DOSAAF, the paramilitary Voluntary Society of Assistance to the Army, the Air Force, and the Navy.

14. For example, *Za rulem*, no. 3 (1970): 6, 19; no. 8 (1970): 2; no. 3 (1971): 11; no. 3 (1972): 6; no. 3 (1984): 8. There are, however, no portraits of "woman truckers"—those who might transport goods across the entire Soviet Union in large trucks.

15. Cf., e.g., *Za rulem*, no. 3 (1971): 11; no. 3 (1972): 6.

16. It is hardly a coincidence that a satiric piece about the growing problems in road traffic since women started to drive, dated 1970, is a translation from the Polish. Cf. *Za rulem*, no. 3 (1970): 29.

17. Interview with Elena Nikolaevna Iartseva, July 4, 2008.

18. Michael Voslensky, *Nomenklatura. Die herrschende Klasse der Sowjetunion* (Munich: Moewig Taschenbuch, 1984) 293–361.

19. On the difficulty of buying a car see Siegelbaum, *Cars for Comrades*, 239–51, and Luminita Gatejel in chapter 8 of this book.

20. Interviews with Nadezhda Ia. Sharigina, June 5 and 12, 2008. The photographs are from her family archive.

21. Sometimes cars were also used as campers. This was particularly true of the Volga, in which the seat backs could fold down to form a continuous resting surface. Interview with Anna Vasilevna Artsechovskaia, January 11, 2009. The advantage of these seat benches was also praised in a compendium to the popular culture of the Soviet Union, Leonid Parfenov, ed., *Namedni Nasha era. 1961–1970* (Moscow: Kolibri, 2009), 65.

22. See, for example, Irina Latycheva, "Bud'te nezavisimy," *Za rulem*, no. 5 (1998), http://www.zr.ru/print/articles/?id=37872 (accessed January 16, 2008); Irina Kisolgubova, "Mify i real'nosti," *Za rulem*, no. 8 (2005), http://www.zr.ru/print/articles/?id=44640 (accessed January 16, 2008); "Zhenshchiny ruliat!" *Zhenshchina za rulem*, no. 8 (2007): 24; "Oni i my," *Zhenshchina za rulem*, no. 3 (2008): 32.

23. Lewis H. Siegelbaum, "Cars, Cars, and More Cars: The Faustian Bargain of the Brezhnev Era," in *Borders of Socialism: Private Spheres of Soviet Russia*, ed. Lewis H. Siegelbaum (New York: Palgrave, 2006) 83–106.

24. Cf., for example, the interview with an actress who inherited her father's Zhiguli at the age of seventeen. Tat'iana Drubich, "Vozhu mashinu luchshe mnogikh muzhchin," *Za rulem*, no. 7 (1997), http://www.zr.ru/print/articles/?id=38940 (accessed January 16, 2008).

25. Conversation with Vera Evgeneva Kazakova, May 14, 2008.

26. An old Russian town, fifty kilometers northwest of Moscow, it was one of the popular places where members of the nomenklatura had dachas.

27. A comparable attitude can be found in the interview with a woman worker at the auto shop GAZ who also has been driving for more than twenty years. See Leonid Sapozhnikov, "Est' na GAZe zhenshchina...," *Za rulem*, no. 10 (2002), http://www.zr.ru/print/articles/?id=41072 (accessed January 16, 2008); Drubich, "Vozhu mashinu."

28. Interview with Nina Petrovna Valvenkovo, October 28, 2008.

29. Interview with Nadezhda Iur'evna Kanishcheva, November 13, 2008.

30. Interview with Vera Evgeneva Kazakova, May 14, 2008.

31. According to official statistics, there were 218,322 accidents in 2008, in which 29,936 people died and 270,883 were injured. Cf. http://www.gibdd.ru/news/main/?20090113_report. For traffic in Moscow see Robert Argenbright, "Moscow's Third Transport Ring: Making Space for the New Middle Class," *Osteuropa* 53, nos. 9–10 (2003): 1386–99; Viktorija Bitjukova and Ekaterina Sokolova, "Vor dem Kollaps. Moskaus verkehrter Verkehr," *Osteuropa* 58, nos. 4–5 (2008): 351–58.

32. On kul'turnost' cf. Catriona Kelly, *Refining Russia: Advice Literature, Polite Culture, and Gender from Catherine to Yeltsin* (Oxford: Oxford University Press, 2001) 321–93.

33. *Za rulem*, no. 1 (1984): 1; no. 7 (1984): 19; and no. 10 (1984): 5.

34. All the aspects of this debate came to light at the turn of the year 2008–9, when drivers took to the streets nationwide to protest the introduction of higher customs duties on foreign cars. Cf., for example, http://www.gazeta.ru/politics/2009/01/23_a_2929098.shtml (accessed January 24, 2009).

35. Valvenkovo and Kanishcheva interviews.

36. According to the official statistics of the Russian Federation:

The number of private passenger cars in the Russian Federation for every 1,000 residents

Year	1970	1980	1990	1995	2000	2001	2002	2003	2004	2005	2006
Number of cars	5.5	30.2	58.5	92.3	130.5	137.2	145.8	153.2	159.3	169	177.8

Source: http://www.gks.ru/scripts/db_inet/dbinet.cgi (accessed October 22, 2008).

Number of cars in Moscow from 2000 to 2007 according to the official website of the city of Moscow, http://www.mos.ru:

2000/2001	2,022,100	2004/2005	2,460,700
2001/2002	2,128,400	2005/2006	2,556,200
2002/2003	2,301,500	2006/2007	2,714,700
2003/2004	2,393,500		

A recent survey about the owners of cars and their attitude toward cars is found at http://bd.fom.ru/report/cat/business/ec_trans/avto/d082223/printable/ (accessed October 24, 2008).

37. In 2005, 19 percent of the total population drove a car, about 33 percent of men and 6 percent of women. In Moscow approximately one-third of the population was motorized, in other large cities about one quarter. See "Russlandanalysen 67/05," http://www.laender-analysen.de/russland/ (accessed October 24, 2008).

38. See "Srednyi klass po russkii," http://www.statistika.ru/uroven/2007/11/16/uroven_9307.html (accessed October 22, 2008).

39. *Zhenshchina za rulem*, no. 8 (2007): 16. In view of the slump caused by the worldwide financial and economic crisis, which also hit the Russian car market beginning in the fourth quarter of 2008, the Russian government established a special credit program for cars of this price range (up to 350,000 rubles) that were produced in Russia in order to drive the sales figures back up and to support the Russian automobile industry. http://www.gazeta.ru/auto/2009/01/13_a_2923662.shtml (accessed January 15, 2009); http://www.gazeta.ru/auto/2009/01/12_a_2923244.shtml (accessed January 15, 2009).

40. See Leonid Sapozhnikov, "Blin so stola revoliutsii," *Za rulem*, no. 5 (2003), http://www.zr.ru/print/articles/?id=38304 (accessed January 16, 2008). According to him, the number of women drivers in the Soviet period was a maximum of 5 percent of the total, but by 2003 this number had grown to 40 percent.

41. Conversations with Nina Ivanovna Mikhailovna, January 23, 2008, and Olga Petrova Nekrassova, February 2, 2008.

42. Or, as the actress Tat'iana Drubich puts it, "A free person is a person at the wheel." Drubich, "Vozhu mashinu."

43. See note 4.

44. In an article from 1997 one woman driver even states the hypothesis that men now only behave as expected in traffic. Natal'ia Maysheva, "Est' chemu pouchit'sia u muzhchin," *Za rulem*, no. 2 (1997), http://www.zr.ru/print/articles/?id=36011 (accessed January 16, 2008). The magazine *Zhenshchina za rulem*, no. 6 (2008): 28 posed a question regarding the helpfulness of men in traffic and reported on a corresponding test. A woman whose car had apparently been damaged stood at the side of the road and waited to see who would stop. Success was limited. The result is not important here; rather, the point is that this "modern" magazine for women who drive transmits the corresponding traditional roles to its readers.

45. Valvenkovo interview.

46. For example, see Anna Stavrova, "Damskaia agressiia," *Za rulem*, no. 4 (2004), http://www.zr.ru/print/articles/?id=42634 (accessed January 16, 2008).

47. Drubich, "Vozhu mashinu."

NOTES ON CONTRIBUTORS

ELKE BEYER teaches at the Institute for History and Theory of Architecture at the Swiss Institute of Technology (ETH Zürich), where she is currently writing her dissertation on the planning of city centers in the Soviet Union in the 1960s.

VALENTINA FAVA, PhD, is a researcher at the Helsinki Collegium for Advanced Studies and teaches at the Department of Social Science History of the University of Helsinki. She is the author of *Storia di una fabbrica socialista. Saperi, lavoro, tecnologia e potere alla Skoda Auto (1918–1968)* (2010) and has published articles on the history of the Italian and Czechoslovak automobile industry.

LUMINITA GATEJEL is a Max Weber Fellow at the European University Institute, Florence (Italy). She wrote her PhD dissertation on cars and consumerism in the Soviet Union, East Germany, and Romania for the Free University of Berlin.

MARIUSZ JASTRZĄB is an assistant professor of economic and social history at Kozminski University, Warsaw, Poland. Book publications include *Puste półki. Problem zaopatrzenia ludności w artykuły powszechnego użytku w latach 1949–1956* [Empty shelves: Supply of basic consumer goods in Poland 1949–1956] (2005).

CORINNA KUHR-KOROLEV, PhD in history, is a senior researcher at the Department for East European History at the University of Bochum, Germany. Research interests include the social history of the Soviet Union. Her current project is "Justice and Power in the Perestroika Years." Publications include *Gezähmte Helden— Die Formierung der Sowjetjugend* (2005).

BRIGITTE LE NORMAND is an assistant professor of history at Indiana University Southeast. She was the recipient of a doctoral fellowship from the Social

Sciences and Humanities Research Council of Canada, which helped finance the research for her chapter, as well as a Max Weber fellowship from the European University Institute.

ESTHER MEIER is a research fellow at the University of the Federal Armed Forces in Hamburg. Her doctoral dissertation is entitled "Mass Mobilization in the Brezhnev Era? The Large-Scale Project Naberezhnye Chelny/KamAZ." She is the author of *A Theory for "Developing Countries": Soviet Agitation and Afghanistan, 1978–1982* (2001).

KURT MÖSER, Dr. phil. habil., teaches Contemporary History at the Karlsruhe Institute of Technology. He is on leave from the Technoseum in Mannheim, where he is curator for mobility history. He has published extensively on mobility and cultural history. His recent book is *Fahren und Fliegen in Frieden und Krieg— Kulturen individueller Mobilitätsmaschinen 1880 bis 1930* (2009).

GYÖRGY PÉTERI is a professor of Contemporary European History at the Norwegian University of Science and Technology, Trondheim. He is the author of several books, most recently *Global Monetary Regime and National Central Banking: The Case of Hungary, 1921–1929* (2002), and the editor of *Imagining the West in Eastern Europe and the Soviet Union* (2010).

ELI RUBIN is an associate professor of history at Western Michigan University. He is the author of *Synthetic Socialism: Plastics and Dictatorship in the German Democratic Republic* (2008) and is currently working on a book about Plattenbau and material memory in Marzahn, as well as a book on material destruction and the end of World War II in Germany.

LEWIS H. SIEGELBAUM is a professor of history at Michigan State University. He has published widely in Russian/Soviet history. He is coauthor of the award-winning website http://www.soviethistory.org and most recently author of *Cars for Comrades: The Life of the Soviet Automobile* (2008).

INDEX

Albania, 1
Aleshkov, Nikolai, 109
Alexanderplatz. *See* Berlin
AMO, 172–73, 174–75
architects and town planners. *See* urban planners and planning
Argenbright, Robert, 9
Athens Charter (1943), 7, 93, 94, 96, 114
Auto, 17, 18, 21
Auto:Jugoslavenska revija za automobilizam, 99
Autobasteln. *See* car tinkering
auto mechanics, 156, 174
automobilism, 5, 49, 159–61
automobility: and car culture, 92; and congestion, 101; costs of, 61, 65; definitions of, 9–10, 88, 159, 170; dissemination of, 226n8; in the Eastern Bloc, 10–13, 163, 169; failure of, 121–23; individual, 61, 79; planning for, 88; in post-Soviet Russia, 203; private, 67; and social distinction, 147, 159, 169; socialist, 103, 144, 155, 169; stages of, 159; and trucks, 171, 185; Western, 10, 158, 163
automobilization, 9, 174
auto rallies, 99
auto tourism and tourists, 11, 180
Avtodor, 177
avtoprobegy, 174–75
AvtoVAZ. *See* VAZ
AZNP (Automobilové Závody, Národní Podnik), 7, 8, 20, 24, 26–27

Behind the Wheel (*Za rulem*), 177, 179, 180, 188, 189, 196–97, 208n40, 233n13

Belgrade, 7; first master plan (1950) for, 93, 95; second master plan (1972) for, 93, 101–3. *See also* New Belgrade
Berggolts, Ol'ga, 176
Berlin (East): Alexanderplatz in, 72, 80–83; Allee der Kosmonauten in, 135–36, 139; Frankfurter Tor/Karl-Marx-Allee in, 80–82; housing in, 132, 134; reconstruction of, 80, 82, 84; resettlement of population of, 134, 138, 225n24
Berlin-Marzahn. *See* Marzahn
Bewegungssystem (movement system), 124–25, 136
Brezhnev, Leonid, 106, 146

camping, 167–68, 190
car culture, 92, 144; American, 161; do-it-yourself, 158, 168; in the Eastern Bloc, 13, 143, 163; middle class, 93, 98–99; socialist, 143, 147, 151, 155–56, 161, 169; Soviet, 198; Western, 145, 151, 155, 163, 169; youth, 99
car hierarchies and preferences, 35–36, 40–41, 44, 147–49, 169
car maintenance and repair, 129–30, 153, 158–59, 194. *See also* car tinkering
car rental and sharing, 47, 57–61, 145
car safety, 161
car tinkering, 10, 129, 159–64, 167
Ceaucescu, Nicolae, 148
Chaika, 147, 154
chauffeurs, 52, 216n23
Chevrolet, 7, 153, 154
China, People's Republic of, 205n2
Chuiskii Highway, 172

239

INDEX

cities, 126; centers of, 79, 83–84; Communist ideal of, 71–72, 80, 84–85; as functional system, 74, 220n38; linear model of, 112–15, 122; post-Stalinist, 105–6, 118–19; satellite, 87, 125; socialist, 122, 220n38; Stalinist, 73, 75, 106, 118–19; and tiered system of centers, 86–88. *See also* Gosstroi; New Towns; public transportation

COMECON, 8, 26, 146, 207n25

Congrès Internationaux d'Architecture Moderne (CIAM), 94, 114, 122, 220n38

consumption: capitalist, 149; rational, 31; socialist model of, 3, 5, 48–49, 104, 144, 147

Cooke, Catherine, 3

Crvena Zastava, 97

Cuba, 205n2

Czechoslovakia, 7; automobile industry in, 18–20, 29; automobiles in, 18, 21; automobility in, 18, 21; car density in, 9, 24; car production in, 24, 211n42; export of cars from, 25–26; industrial tradition in, 17, 21, 22; marketing of cars in, 27–28; mass motorization in, 21–23, 25; Ministry for General Mechanics (Ministerstvo Veobecného Strojírenství—MVS), 22; Ministry of Transport and Farm Machines (Ministerstvo Automobilového Průmyslu a Zemědělských Strojů), 24; people's car in, 17–18, 20, 24, 210n27; and Soviet system of industrial administration, 22; technicians in, 20, 22, 25, 27. *See also* AZNP

Dacia, 2, 146, 147, 148, 149–50, 152

David-Fox, Michael, 6

drinking, 178, 179, 183

Drivers (Voditeli, 1950), 179, 181

drivers and driving, 158, 164, 166, 174–76, 177, 191–95; professional drivers, 179, 180. *See also* chauffeurs; motorists; truckers

"Driver's Song, The" (*Shoferskaia pesnia*), 182

East Germany. *See* German Democratic Republic

Edensor, Tim, 10, 21

Eigen-Sinn, 11, 130

Fadeev, Aleksandr, 176

Fiat Company, 8, 32, 35

Fića, 97, 99

Finland, 12

Ford, Henry, 29

Fordism, 5, 6, 12

Ford Motor Company, 6, 20, 172

Frankfurter Tor/Karl-Marx-Allee. *See* Berlin

FSO (Fabryka Samochodów Osobowych), 34–35

gasoline, 184, 201

GAZ (Gor'kovskii Avtomobil'nyi Zavod), 172, 176

General Motors, 6, 20

German Democratic Republic (GDR), 4, 143–44; car culture in, 158, 167; car density in, 9; car maintenance in, 10; car production in, 128–29, 147, 160; city centers of, 71; demand for cars in, 160; General Principles of Planning and Design of Socialist City Centers (1960) of, 72; housing in, 131–32; industry of, 127–28; New Towns in, 88; Seven-Year-Plan (1959) of, 72; Socialist Unity Party (SED) in, 164; technical education in, 10, 166

Gierek, Edward, 30, 36

Goldshteyn, Gershon (Grisha), 183–85

Gomułka, Władysław, 30, 35, 214n24

Gosstroi, 79, 106

Halle-Neustadt, 72, 88, 89–90, 133

Hammer, Ferenc, 181, 184

Honecker, Erich, 72, 130–1

Hungary, 4, 181; motorization in, 65, 68; private cars in, 48, 56; public (collective) transport in, 60; "sneaking privatization" of cars in, 5, 49, 52–54, 58; taxi system in, 57–58; waybills in, 5, 52–53

Hungarian Socialist Workers' Party (HSWP), 49; apparatus class of, 51, 54, 57, 61–62; cars belonging to, 54, 59, 65; Central Committee of Revision of, 50, 60, 64; Central Control Committee of, 50; and chauffeurless driving, 62–63; Department of Party-Economic and Administrative Management (PGO) of, 49–50, 52–53, 57–59, 62–63, 66; expenditure on cars of, 54, 66; and ownership and use of private cars by apparatus class for official business, 63–66; personal use of cars by apparatus members of, 50, 52, 54–55, 216n28; and resistance of apparatus to using public transport, 60, 67; and resolution of July 7, 1972, 56, 58, 61–62, 64–65

Inber, Vera, 176

Jeep, 201–2

Kádár, János, 50

KamAZ, 105, 106–9, 118, 120, 222n8, 224n36

Kamm, Henry, 1

Khrushchev, Nikita, 47, 77, 87, 145

Kol'ka-Raika legend, 172–73

Korea, Democratic Republic of, 1

INDEX

Kosygin, Aleksei, 146
Kott, Aleksandr, 172, 173
Kucherenko, V. A., 74, 84
kul'turnost', 195, 197, 203

Laczkó, Pálné, 50–51
Lada, 2, 13, 109, 147, 190, 199, 203, 208n40; outside the Soviet Union, 11–12, 40–41, 44, 45, 105, 147–48, 162, 163, 169
Lavrov, V. A., 73, 77–79
Le Corbusier, 7, 94–96, 122, 132–33, 138
"Leningrad Poem" (1942), 176
Lüdtke, Alf, 130, 138

Marzahn, 7, 72, 125, 131, 132–33, 135–39
mass production of cars, 17, 128, 208n1
Mercedes-Benz, 1, 152
Miliutin, Nikolai, 114, 119
Mladá Boleslav. *See* AZNP
mobility, 218n12; car-driver, 10; collectivist, 68; everyday and leisure, 73; individual, 47, 49, 68, 71; modern, 48; planning for, 71; private, 13, 57, 67; socialist urban, 80, 84
modernity: capitalist, 48; entangled, 6; socialist, 6, 48, 80, 128
Mom, Gijs, 5, 6
Moscow: All-Union Conference on Urban Planning (1960) in, 71, 74; cars in, 234n36, 235n37; driving in, 198; General Plan for, 71, 86, 87, 220n40; Prospekt Kalinina in, 72, 82–83, 84; reconstruction of, 85
Moskvich, 147, 190
Motokov, 25, 26, 27–28, 210n24
motorcycles, 21, 34, 158, 190, 203
motorists, amateur (liubitel'skie), 171; as private persons (*chastniki*)180
motorization: and car owners, 149–50; capitalist, 76; "from above," 146; individual, 75–76; mass, 105, 143, 144, 147, 149–50, 155, 189, 196; private, 23, 143–44, 146, 155; socialist form of, 48
Motor Jahr, 160
Mototechna, 27, 28, 210n24
movies about cars: *Accident, The* (Accident, 1976), 152; *Driver's Ballad, The* (Shoferskaia Ballada, 1986), 172; *Kopeck* (Kopeika, 2002), 13; *Miscellaneous Brigade in the Mountains and at Sea* (Brigada Diverse la munte și la mare, 1971), 152; *Ordinary Trip, An* (Ocherednoi reis, 1958), 181, 183; *Rumiantsev Affair, The* (Delo Rumiantseva, 1955), 183; *Smokey and the Bandit* (1977), 182; *There Lives This Guy* (Zhivet takoi paren', 1964), 172; *Two Drivers* (Ekhali dva shofera, 2001), 172; *Uncle Martin, the Billionaire* (Nea Marin Miliaradar, 1979), 152; *White Line Fever* (1975), 182; *Young and Healthy as a Rose* (Mlad i zdrav kao ruža, 1971), 99–100

Naberezhnye Chelny, 7; alcoholism in, 121; cars in, 110, 120–1; center of, 123; child-care centers in, 115, 118; functional zones in, 111, 122; as linear city, 111–12, 117, 119; microdistricts (*microraiony*) in, 115–16; minibuses in, 119; mobility in, 119–20; as modern city, 110–11; and Orlovka, 107–9; population of, 106; residential districts of, 116–17; streetcar system in, 117, 120; streets of, 105, 107, 117, 121
New Belgrade, 94, 100
New Towns, 71, 73, 88–89, 220n42
New York Times, 1

"Ol'shanskii Highway, The" (*Ol'shanskii trakt*), 172
Oullet, Lawrence, 182–83

pedestrians, 75, 78, 95
Peters, Günter, 132–35
Poland: coupons (*talony*) in, 5, 37–38; car ownership in, 31, 35–36; car prices in, 34, 35, 37; car production in, 34–35, 45, 214n24; distribution of cars in, 31, 46; mass motorization of, 36; Office of the Council of Ministers (URM) in, 38–39; patron-client relations in, 31, 46; petitions and petitioners for cars in, 38–45; prepayments for cars in, 37; trade union activists in, 44, 46
Polonez, 37, 40, 44
Polski Fiat 125p, 12, 35, 36, 40–41, 45
Polski Fiat 126p, 36, 40–41, 43, 45, 147, 148
Posokhin, Mikhail, 87, 218n13
Practic, 160
privatization, 49, 52–54, 58
Prospekt Kalinina. *See* Moscow
public transportation, 60–61, 75, 84, 89, 93, 96, 102–3, 122
PZInż, 32

Reid, Susan E., 4, 144
Renault, 144, 146
"road of life" (Lake Ladoga), 176
"Road, The, the Road" (*Doroga, doroga*), 181
Romania, 8, 143–44, 146, 151–52
Rubanenko, Boris, 106
Russia (post-Soviet), 171, 186–88, 197–99, 202–3, 234n36, 235n37

Rüthers, Monica, 110, 119
Rybakov, Anatolii, 179, 181

shopping, 77, 103–4
Shukshin, Vasilii, 172, 182
Škoda Auto. *See* AZNP
Škoda (cars), 11–12, 26, 41, 97–98
Sloanism, 6, 149, 159, 228n4
socialism: acquisitive, 4; *bigos*, 30–31; consumer, 4; meanings of, 2, 48; and modern mobility, 47; "real existing," 5, 130–31
Soría y Mata, Arturo, 112, 119
Soviet Union, 107, 143, 222n7; automobility in, 171, 186; in the Brezhnev era, 106, 109, 111; car ownership in, 8–9, 122, 180, 189–91, 196; car production in, 144, 146, 170; city centers of, 71, 77; consumption in, 3–4, 8, 196, 198; Fordism in, 6; gender relations and roles in, 11, 180, 187, 188–89, 191–93, 195, 200; motorization in, 146, 197; New Towns in, 77, 88; roads in, 231n32; truckers and trucks in, 11, 171–85; veterans and cars in, 150; women in, 186–87, 191
spare parts, 11, 129, 148, 152, 165
Stakhanovites, 176, 178, 231n22
Svět Motorů, 17, 21, 23
Syrena, 34

Taub, Alexander, 18, 20
taxis, 47, 57–58, 60, 199–200
Taylorism, 5–6
technology, 2, 6–7, 12, 23, 41, 151, 157, 164, 166
Tirana, 1
Tito, Josip Broz, 4, 97
Togliatti, 71, 88, 105, 106, 146, 220n44
Trabant, 2, 13, 138, 140, 148, 168; demand for, 41, 129; export of, 11; maintenance and repair of, 160, 162, 167; P50 model, 128; P601 model, 128–29; plastic body of, 128–30; pollution by, 128; as symbol, 5, 124, 145; as system, 124–25, 138–39; two-stroke engine of, 6, 129–30, 138
traffic behavior, 194–97, 199, 201, 203, 235n44
traffic planning, 71, 75, 76, 80, 82, 117, 119, 219n31
truckers, 171; American songs about, 182; and freedom, 181–83; as heroes, 173, 175; Hungarian, 181, 184; liminality of, 181; as loners, 181; pay system of, 177, 179, 321n34; as professionals, 177, 179–80; subculture of, 182–83; trade unions of, 173, 179; as wheeler-dealers, 183; as workers, 185
Truckers (Dal'noboishchiki), 171–72

trucks, 170; and automobility, 11, 185; Soviet-made, 11, 172; and Soviet state, 174; as symbols, 109; use of for private purposes, 50, 183
two-stroke engine, 126–28, 140

Ulbricht, Walter, 72
Union of Auto Transport Workers, 179, 183
Union of Transport Workers, 174
United States of America, 5, 28, 126, 182
urban planners and planning, 73–74, 77, 79–80, 84–85, 89, 92–93, 96, 101–4, 125, 221n3
Urry, John, 9, 12, 144, 226n8

Vashurov, Andrei, 108–9
VAZ (Volga Automobile Factory), 12, 29, 105, 106
Volga, 147, 198, 203, 234n21
Volkswagen, 145

Warszawa, 34
Wartburg, 40–41, 44, 45, 126, 129, 148, 162
West and western cars, 5–6, 8, 10, 122, 144, 148–49, 151–52, 163–66, 168, 203
Wieczorek, Janusz, 38–40, 45
women: and anti-emancipation, 201–2; "auto"-biographies of, 188, 202–3; as car owners, 11, 190, 196; as drivers, 176, 186, 188–89, 191–96, 199–202, 233n16, 235n40; emancipation of, 188, 195; independence of, 186, 200–1; as passengers, 11, 188–89; photographs of, 191, 198; in post-Soviet Russia, 198–99; technical education of, 166; and trucks, 172–73, 180
Women behind the Wheel (Zhenshchina za rulem), 188, 202

Yugoslavia: automobility in, 92; car ownership in, 100; market socialism in, 92, 93, 99–100, 103; middle class in, 98, 100; motorization in, 98, 102; public transportation in, 93, 102–3; as socialist state, 96; urban planning in, 93, 96, 100–102
Yurchak, Alexei, 151

Zaporozhets, 40–41, 147
Za rulem. *See Behind the Wheel*
Zastava, 40–41, 147
Zelenograd, 87
Zhenshchina za rulem. *See Women behind the Wheel*
Zhiguli. *See* Lada
ZIL (Zavod im. Likhacheva), 147
ZIS (Zavod im. Stalina), 172, 176
Zwickau factory, 126–27